RED BLOOD, BLACK SAND

RED BLOOD, BLACK SAND

FIGHTING ALONGSIDE JOHN BASILONE
FROM BOOT CAMP TO IWO JIMA

CHUCK TATUM

BERKLEY CALIBER, NEW YORK

THE BERKLEY PUBLISHING GROUP
Published by the Penguin Group
Penguin Group (USA) Inc.
375 Hudson Street, New York, New York 10014, USA
Penguin Group (Canada), 90 Eglinton Avenue East, Suite 700, Toronto, Ontario M4P 2Y3, Canada
(a division of Pearson Penguin Canada Inc.) • Penguin Books Ltd., 80 Strand, London WC2R 0RL,
England • Penguin Group Ireland, 25 St. Stephen's Green, Dublin 2, Ireland (a division of Penguin
Books Ltd.) • Penguin Group (Australia), 250 Camberwell Road, Camberwell, Victoria 3124, Australia
(a division of Pearson Australia Group Pty. Ltd.) • Penguin Books India Pvt. Ltd., 11 Community
Centre, Panchsheel Park, New Delhi—110 017, India • Penguin Group (NZ), 67 Apollo Drive,
Rosedale, Auckland 0632, New Zealand (a division of Pearson New Zealand Ltd.) • Penguin Books
(South Africa) (Pty.) Ltd., 24 Sturdee Avenue, Rosebank, Johannesburg 2196, South Africa

Penguin Books Ltd., Registered Offices: 80 Strand, London WC2R 0RL, England

This book is an original publication of the Berkley Publishing Group.

The publisher does not have any control over and does not assume any responsibility for author
or third-party websites or their content.

FIRST EDITION: May 2012

Library of Congress Cataloging-in-Publication Data

Tatum, Charles W. (Charles William)
Red blood, black sand / Chuck Tatum. — 1st ed.
p. cm.
ISBN 978-0-425-24740-2
1. Tatum, Charles W. (Charles William). 2. Iwo Jima, Battle of, Japan, 1945—Personal narratives,
American. 3. Basilone, John, 1916–1945. 4. Marines—United States—Biography. 5. United
States. Marine Corps. Marines, 27th. Battalion, 1st—Biography. 6. World War, 1939–1945—Personal
narratives, American. I. Title.
D767.99.I9T382 2011
940.54'2528—dc23
2011038476

PRINTED IN THE UNITED STATES OF AMERICA

10 9 8 7 6 5 4 3 2 1

Penguin is committed to publishing works of quality and integrity.
In that spirit, we are proud to offer this book to our readers;
however the story, the experiences and the words are the author's alone.

This book is dedicated to my brothers, the Marines who fought the Japanese Army on one of the darkest islands on earth—Iwo Jima. On our voyage to Iwo, we had dreams and plans for our futures. We were young and buoyant. Our hearts were filled with love for our families, our buddies, and our country. We wanted to survive, to come home together. Then we felt the flames of that Pacific inferno.

To my Marines brothers who fell on that rock, I owe every day of the life I've led, to you. *Semper Fi.*

ACKNOWLEDGMENTS

So many hands touched this book to make it a reality.

I'm thankful for the support and encouragement of my family: my wife and inspiration, Evelyn, and my loving kids, Nanci, Tracy, and Blake.

I'm thankful to my editor, Natalee Rosenstein, who saw this story's potential and took a leap of faith to share it with the world. Thanks to my agent, Greg Johnson, for bringing the book to her desk.

I'm thankful to Tom Hanks, who endorsed this book, lending the weight of his reputation. My thanks to Tom's right-hand lady, Sooki Raphael, for making the endorsement possible.

I'm thankful to Gary Goetzman, Tom Hanks, Steven Spielberg, and the people at HBO for investing their time and talents to make *The Pacific*, a story that needed to be told and to which only they could do justice.

I'm thankful to my friend and budding movie star Ben Esler, who played me on screen and cared immensely to get to know the old man he was portraying.

I'm thankful to my old friend Frank Taylor for his writing guidance and my Marine buddies, their children, and widows like Lena Basilone, the wife of my hero, John, for sharing their memories and photos.

I'm thankful to the Makos family of Valor Studios, who resurrected this manuscript from my dusty bookshelf to give it a second life. Thanks to Adam Makos for reworking the story with fresh eyes and to Bryan Makos for designing a powerful cover. Thanks to their parents, Bob and Karen, and sister, Erica, for keeping the boys in line.

No doubt I've forgotten some people who deserve credit and I'll probably remember you as soon as it's too late. Please know that you all are very special to me.

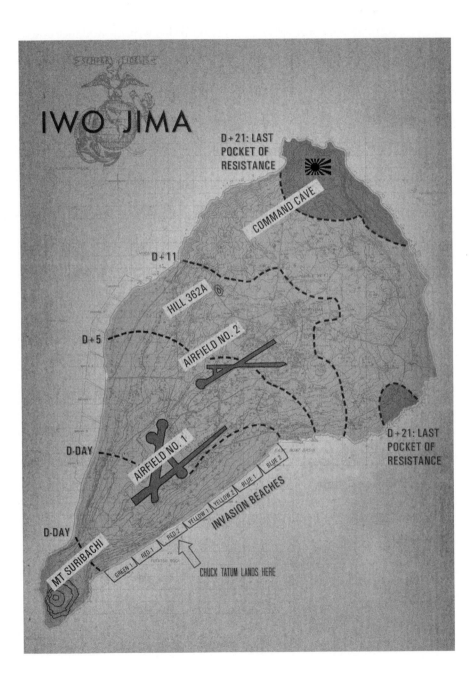

The Pacific Apocalypse

It was February 19, 1945. The amphibious assault on Iwo Jima was beginning and I was eighteen years old. I found myself gripping—white-knuckled—a .50-caliber machine gun aboard a steel amtrac churning toward Iwo's beaches. Ahead of me lay an island that God forgot and left to the devil.

Behind and below me, in the 'trac's belly, huddled my buddies, the Marines of Baker Company's machine-gun platoon. We belonged to the 1st Battalion, 27th Marines, of the soon-to-be-legendary 5th Marine Division.

A wave of amtracs ahead of us didn't carry troops but supplied direct fire support from their cannons. My comrades and I would be the first wave of assault troops who would hit the beaches and kick open the door to the conquest of Iwo Jima.

This was the first of the Japanese home islands to be invaded by American troops and the largest single amphibious assault of the Pacific war to date, involving three Marine divisions (roughly sixty thousand men) and a good portion of the U.S. Pacific Fleet.

Iwo Jima, of the Volcano Islands Group, was chosen because of its position between Saipan, Guam, and Tinian and the mainland of Japan. Enemy fighters from the island had been seriously disrupting America's B-29 long-range bomber program.

The United States wanted to intensify the air war over Japan and it was imperative to capture the strategic island. Control of Iwo would give the United States a "pit stop" for B-29s, and it provided a base for fighter escorts.

As a private first class in the ranks, I didn't focus on the overall strategy, but what little of it I did understand led me to believe somehow that this would be the main event of my short life. Iwo Jima was a major event of World War II and one of the toughest, bloodiest battles in the history of the United States Marine Corps.

What was of most immediate concern to me that February morning was the knowledge that I would soon be in violent combat. My year and a half of training and exercises was over.

Previously we had studied the island's terrain, and during briefing we had been told that five thousand "Sons of Nippon" were waiting for us. Unknown even to our generals was the price in blood, agony, terror, and physical torment that assaulting troops would encounter in this effort to seize eight square miles of island fortress.

My journey to this moment in history began much earlier, when I persuaded my mother, Opal Sheaffer, to let me join the Marines. She couldn't understand my ardent desire to join the Marine Corps when I turned seventeen. She wanted me to wait until I was eighteen to see if I would be drafted. Now, with Iwo Jima just a mile away, smoking under the bombardment our Navy was laying on it, I wondered if my mother hadn't been right after all.

When the USS *New York* fired a full salvo from its sixteen-inch battery and I could see where the shells impacted Iwo Jima's rockbound hide, I knew it was too late to turn back. A great battle had begun.

This is my recollection of that assault and the ensuing fight for

Iwo Jima. The computer has made it possible for me to record events that I witnessed from the ranks of the 1st Battalion, 27th Marines, 5th Marine Division fifty years ago.

I have felt a need to tell of the heroism of the men with whom I went to war. To write about the death of good friends and comrades-in-arms is extremely painful. At times I have written with tears in my eyes. For that I do not apologize. I want today's generations to know of the heroism that was required to win the devil's rock pile, Iwo Jima. Survivors like me have a responsibility to pass on to the next generation an account of what is required to defeat our enemies until the days when war is no more.

It is difficult and painful to dredge up old memories, but I am proud to remember the men of valor I was privileged to serve with. The Marine Corps was my high school, my college, and my graduate school in manhood. The lessons and values I learned as a Marine have stood me in good stead throughout my life.

I have never shot or owned a gun of any kind in the past forty-eight years. I never intend to, but I have no quarrel with people who do own guns. Iwo Jima gave me my fill of guns forever.

I also made myself a promise on Iwo Jima that if I got off that rock alive, I would never sleep on the ground or go hunting or cook over a campfire again. I have violated that promise once. My eldest son's Boy Scout group was short one father to go on a camping trip. As a good ex-Marine, I saw this as a clear call to duty. So I volunteered—but just that once.

CHARLES "CHUCK" TATUM
Stockton, California

CHAPTER ONE

Journey to War

I could easily visualize myself on the deck of that same battleship in full dress blues. I also assumed they would be a magnet for girls.

DECEMBER 7, 1941

Our plan to go rabbit hunting was all set. I stayed up late Saturday night talking it out with my pal Bob Ross, who was to meet me early Sunday morning so I could help on his paper route. Bob sold the Sunday *San Francisco Examiner* door-to-door to earn spending money. I was envious of Bob and his paper route; he sometimes made one dollar and fifty cents! He had to beat on the back door to wake me; I wasn't used to getting up at five-thirty in the morning to do *anything*.

This was my first hunting trip and I was looking forward to firing a .22 single-shot rifle, with all its awesome firepower compared to my Daisy BB gun. Embarrassed to have overslept, I quickly washed the sleep from my eyes and brushed my teeth while Bob urged me, "Hurry up, Tatum!"

It was still dark when we left on our bicycles to meet the *San Francisco Examiner* route manager for east Stockton. If we were late, Ross would miss his papers.

After paying twenty cents per paper—in advance—Bob and I rolled and snapped a couple of rubber bands around each one. The *Examiner* used all the space in our canvas saddlebags. Their weight made our bikes hard to control. An *Examiner* carrier needed good balance!

I was anxious to help him sell papers so we could get to our main plan, rabbit hunting.

By 9:30 a.m., we had covered his regular customers, then went to Merrill's grocery store and hawked papers there until we were sold out. Ross tallied up the take. He had made the princely sum of $1.55 for *our* morning's work.

Our next stop was to pick up J. R. Wyatt. Now the three of us went to Ross's house, where he got two .22 rifles. One was his; the other was his dad's. He had "borrowed" his father's weapon for me to use.

J.R. was using an oily rag to clean some of the rust off his single-barrel shotgun. Ross handed me a box of fifty .22-caliber long rifle shells to carry. I appreciated his confidence in letting me handle this assignment.

Wyatt's mongrel dog sensed something was happening and followed us as we left the yard. We rode our bikes to the Stockton Diverting Canal, which we had selected for its remote location.

A large field of stubble seemed a good place to start our rabbit hunt. We spread out fifty yards apart and started a sweep from the field's western edge.

I figured our hunt was doomed when J.R.'s crazy mutt went wild, running and jumping over the field, barking at bugs and any other creature that moved, alerting every rabbit within ten miles that we were on the prowl.

A squirrel took a quick look at us and, seeming to feel no immediate danger from our skills as outdoorsmen, scurried to safety.

A loud yelp from our volunteer hunting dog indicated that he had routed a large jackrabbit and was in close pursuit. J.R. got off the first shot with his ten-gauge shotgun. He missed! Ross was quicker than I was and got off the next bullet. *He missed!*

The rabbit's speed and agility made getting a shot at it difficult, but I had him in my sights. Excited, I pulled the trigger—and missed!

Our hunting dog faltered in the stretch. Mr. Rabbit dove from sight, safe from the onslaught of three novice hunters.

Disgusted at our feeble shooting, we spent the rest of the morning blowing holes in tin cans and smashing glass bottles we found in a dump.

When we rode into our yard, my younger brother, John, ran out of the house shouting: "Japan has bombed Pearl Harbor!"

"Where's Pearl Harbor?"

"Honolulu, in the Hawaiian Islands! Mom says this means war!"

It was 1:45 p.m., December 7, 1941.

We all dashed for the Philco console radio. Mom warned us to be quiet while she listened for more news. After a while Ross and Wyatt went home and I wandered into the kitchen looking for something to eat.

I went to sleep that night wondering what the future would bring.

OFF TO WAR

When war broke out with the empire of Japan, December 7, 1941, I was fifteen years old and was swept up in the same patriotic fever that was engulfing other American males. The villainous sneak attack of the Japs at Pearl Harbor *had* to be avenged!

Immediately after the military debacle, outraged men, young and old alike, swamped the nation's recruiting stations, answering the national call to arms. Nearly every man able to walk into a recruiting place wanted to enlist.

I had tried to talk my mother into allowing me to join the Marine Corps when I was sixteen, but she was emphatic: "No way. You just wait until you are eighteen and *have* to sign up for the draft."

All my pestering didn't help. No mother wants her son going off to fight in a war—no matter how patriotic!

I never gave joining the Army or Navy any consideration at all.

My one and only choice stayed with the Marines. It may have been the movies about them, but probably it was the recruiting poster in front of our main post office. A Marine in dress blues, standing on the deck of a battleship, with an American flag whipping in the wind, stopped me in my tracks every time I mailed a letter.

I could easily visualize myself on the deck of that same battleship in full dress blues. I also assumed they would be a magnet for girls.

In my opinion then, the two best uniforms in the world were the U.S. Marines' formal uniform and the Royal Canadian Mounted Police's scarlet tunic with dark blue trousers and pointed campaign hat.

I followed the headlines every day, listened to war news on my mother's radio, and, at the weekly movies, watched riveting newsreel footage of the Marines' bloody defense of Guadalcanal. Perhaps newsreels finally clinched it for me. Whatever the impetus was, I remained steadfast in my desire to become a United States Marine!

SIGNING UP

The waiting as I approached my seventeenth birthday was almost unbearable. I constantly harassed my mother for a year and a half. *"Please! Let me enlist."* Shortly after my birthday on July 23, 1943, she gave up the fight and agreed to sign the papers for me, saying, "If you truly want to go off to war and the Marine Corps will take you, I'll sign the papers."

I had the green light!

Only in retrospect, and when I had sons of my own, did I appreciate my mother's courage and personal sacrifice.

At thirty-seven, she was still a young woman who had suffered the tragic loss of *two* husbands. The first one, Clayton Young, an Oklahoma state trooper, was shot to death in an ambush near Tulsa because of a family feud.

My father, John Willie Tatum, was eighteen when he joined the Army in 1917. After training at Fort Dix, New Jersey, he served in France as a corporal in the field artillery. Seeing pictures of him in his uniform on the walls of our home inspired my earliest military dreams.

In December 1943, while on a business trip, my father caught a cold, which turned into pneumonia, and all efforts to save him failed. He died ten days before Christmas, with my mother at his side holding his hands. Small wonder Mother didn't want her oldest son running off to *this* war.

My mother and I went to the Marine recruiter together, and there she signed the papers on August 31, 1943. I was going to be a Marine!

The Corps took prompt action. My first orders told me to "report to San Francisco for a physical." I passed.

After that hurdle, the waiting was hard to take. When would I be called to active duty? Time crawled by.

Finally, in early October 1943, my good news arrived. I was to "report to the Marine Recruit Training Depot San Diego, California. Leaving Stockton on 27 October 1943: transportation by train, meals included."

Everybody I knew came to see me off. The two-story brick depot building teemed with activity. Uniformed men and women seemed to be everywhere, coming and going. Wartime had increased the tempo of activity to a new high. Not at all like the prewar train trips I had made.

Now that my decision was irrevocable, I confessed to myself a few doubts about my choice of early enlistment.

My bon voyage party featured my mother, Opal; stepfather, Orvil; and my eight brothers and sisters. Audrey the oldest, Bertha Lee a stepsister, brothers John and Dale, sisters Joan and Mary, and stepbrothers Bert and Billy. Bob Ross and Lory Lucchesi, childhood pals, also came to make sure I really left. I had my own cheering section.

The whistle blew. Looking through the window, I saw a platform full of people waving good-bye. My great adventure was officially under way!

CHAPTER TWO

Boot Camp

First they dehumanize us, reduce us to zero, undermine our self-respect, and then start over to make Marines out of us.

When the train arrived in San Diego, we were picked up by a Marine sergeant and led to waiting buses for transfer to the recruit depot.

I discovered that the Marine Corps regarded inductees as raw material, human clay to mold and form to a new standard of their choosing and specifications. Humans are easier to work when "softened up." To build a Marine it was necessary to tear down old attitudes and behaviors. The softening up for us started the moment we entered the recruit depot.

Immediately after our brief "swearing-in-swearing-at" ceremony, we were yelled at and cursed at, and rude references were made to the circumstances of our births, in a continuous harangue.

The Corps wanted to be sure the raw material they received was in good condition, so Navy doctors and corpsmen peered and probed into *every* orifice of the body. Immunization shots were given with needles stuck in both arms at once! This idea must have come from Detroit's assembly-line techniques.

Notes were made on copious medical forms listing scars, tattoos, or deformities. Height was measured and weight recorded while we stood in long lines stark naked. We were formed up by height, tall guys in the front, in our newly created platoon, and told: "You are not a group, an assembly, or herd, you are now a *recruit training platoon*."

HIGH FINANCES

Our trip to the finance officer proved to be interesting! We were offered an "opportunity" to purchase a $10,000 life insurance policy for a measly $6.40 per month, the premium to be deducted automatically from future pay.

Opportunity is the wrong word. This was our first introduction to the term *mandatory option*. It wasn't an *option*, it was *mandatory*.

Next, an old staff sergeant said gruffly, "You will be given a mandatory option to sign up for a war bond, *only* six dollars and twenty-five cents per month."

Until then I didn't know that in addition to *fighting* a war, we were going to be asked to *finance* it. With $12.65 per month in deductions, our private's basic pay of $49 was going fast. Married men went to another station and signed up for a dependent's deduction. If the Corps continued taking deductions, crap! I would soon have to pay them to fight!

The first step in dehumanizing us was to remove all vestiges of civilian life. Haircuts started the process of stripping the patina of our former selves. At the base barbershop, we lined up like sheep, waiting to be sheared. Four at a time, we were cut from the flock and sent for shearing.

I know the man cutting my hair must have worked on a sheep ranch. He didn't have a comb; he used his fingers to hold my hair up as he ran electric clippers smelling like hot oil over my head like a runaway lawn mower.

Getting out of the barber chair, I looked in a mirror; what I saw offered a preview of what I would look like if I became bald. *Like a peeled onion!*

Also, I didn't know I had such a misshapen head!

Back in the line waiting for the rest of the platoon to be sheared, I saw a *lot* of other people with ugly heads. I also had another lesson in Marine Corps funding. Haircuts were *not* free; they cost twenty-five cents—to be deducted from our first paycheck!

Next we were double-timed to the quartermaster's warehouse, lined up in single file, and sent station to station. At the first one, we received a seabag. A seabag isn't an ugly sailor's wife; it's a heavy-duty canvas bag, thirty-six inches long, with drawstrings to close it. Barely large enough to hold all of the possessions we would be allowed in the Corps.

You couldn't have anything that wouldn't fit in the bag. It was the only means we had of carrying possessions when we moved. There was a prescribed method of packing it to prevent wrinkling—but it didn't work.

Next we received skivvies (Marine-speak for "underwear"), four sets of boxer shorts, including high-neck T-shirts, in any color as long as it was white. (During the Guadalcanal campaign it was realized that white T-shirts made perfect targets. As an emergency measure, dye was used. Later all underwear issued was green.)

At stop three, we were tossed shirts and trousers. Our officer said, "Remember! Marines wear *trousers, women* wear pants."

Our vocabulary was constantly changing as we underwent our first day's indoctrination. New words like *boondockers* for shoes, *chow* for food, and phrases like *you people* (Marine-speak for recruits as a group) became part of our vernacular. "You people" was followed by "Pay attention!" and additional instructions.

At other stations we received all the clothing we would need in boot camp (Marine-speak for the six-week training course all Marines receive).

The quartermaster clerks didn't measure anyone to see what fit.

When they were dispensing, they just grabbed a size from the shelf and tossed it your way—and you had better catch it! Part of our training was not to let our clothes touch the deck (Marine-speak for "floor").

One wiseacre remarked, "The Marines have only two sizes: too big and too small!"

I didn't see any Marine dress blue uniforms on the shelves, so I thought we would receive them when we graduated from recruit training.

Oh yes! We received some other very important items: a metal bucket; a stiff-bristled, wooden-handled brush; and a large brick of laundry soap. These would play an important part in our lives as Marines. Their cost was also deducted on our first payday. The bucket went in our seabag when we moved.

With the order "Fall in! Forward, march!" we proceeded to an area filled with rows and rows of Quonset huts (Marine-speak for huts that were developed during World War II as fast, efficient, housing, office, and storage structures).

NEW QUARTERS

We halted in front of the building that was to be our new home. A Quonset hut looked like a very large pipe cut in half and placed on a wooden foundation. The walls were constructed of corrugated tin, wrapped around a steel framework. It had doors at each end and windows along the side. With double-decker beds, ours would sleep a training platoon of sixty men.

We were ordered to "Fall out!" and then "Fall in!" inside.

The interior was called the "squad room"—not a room, a *squad room*.

The DI (Marine-speak for "drill instructor") conducted a school on how to make up a bunk (Marine-speak for "bed"). I had made up my bed at home, but boy, did I have a *lot* to learn! Folding sheets and tucking them in approached geometrical precision. The proper amount of turndown was as important as the placement of the pillow.

Our DI put the top blanket in place and stretched it taut. He tested the surface by bouncing a quarter on it. The material didn't sag, and yours better not either!

Self-imposed rules became a habit. Example: You *never* sat on another man's bunk unless you were invited. Most of our sitting was done on our footlockers (Marine-speak for "wooden suitcase") to *avoid* having to remake a bunk.

Bed-making class was followed by a short break that allowed time to try on our new duds. In general, the fit was good, which surprised us, but some of us traded back and forth to adjust for size and comfort.

A marker was provided for printing names and serial numbers on all our gear (Marine-speak for "possessions"). By now, the squad room smelled like mothballs, a smell that lingered for days.

TABLE MANNERS

At 11:45 a.m. we were instructed to "Fall in!" then "Forward march!"— which we did, to the mess hall for our first Marine chow.

The simple pleasure of eating required a new set of rules, and Marine table manners were a subject quickly learned. We discovered that personal space at the mess table consisted of the eighteen-inch width of our metal trays.

It was an unforgivable sin to "shortstop" anyone (Marine-speak for taking something from a platter before passing it on). If you took the last piece of bread or *anything* from a platter, duty compelled you to hold the empty platter above your head until it was "surveyed" (taken away) by a mess man.

If you requested a dish be passed, it was taken at once; *never* did you let someone hold it while taking something. Any delay and you would find it *in* your tray.

The food was good, wholesome, and there was plenty of it, although it was on the starchy side (lots of potatoes and gravy). It put meat on our young bones. For some of us, it was the best food we had ever enjoyed.

After eating, we went to a large auditorium where a captain from the adjunct's office read us "the Rocks and Shoals." An explanation was made of military law and how it applied to each of us. We were warned, military justice paralleled Napoleonic law, under which the accused are guilty until proved innocent.

When we returned to our barracks, the assistant drill instructor, a private first class, taught a class on how to fold our new gear and place each item correctly in our footlockers. Each one was large enough to hold all our new belongings, including the seabag, but not the bucket and brush! Those went under the edge of our bunks.

"A place for everything, and *everything* in its place," our instructor informed us. Heavy gear went on the bottom, blouse, trousers, and then shirts; next the skivvies, folded neatly in a prescribed square, socks folded, one end tucked around the other. Each item of clothing we owned was folded and placed in a specific Marine Corps manner.

Footlockers had a lift-out drawer that was used to store lighter gear. Everything placed here was arranged in a precise manner dictated by the *Guidebook for Marines*. We all received a copy and it would be the "Bible" for the rest of our enlistment.

A large trash can was in the middle of our squad room, and we were "invited" to dispose of all extra toiletries. We could keep a razor, toothbrush, toothpaste, and shaving cream. Everything else we owned went into the trash can.

Next we packed our civvies (Marine-speak for "civilian clothes") and tagged them for shipment home.

After evening chow, we were allowed a brief time to get acquainted with our fellow inductees. Bedtime was 10 p.m. when taps were played on the public address system followed by "Lights out!"

We had survived our first day as Marines.

FIRST REVEILLE

We were rudely awakened from a sound sleep at 6 a.m. by an irritating bugle bellowing reveille. We made our beds and dressed quickly in our new dungarees. Next was a two-mile run around the main parade ground by platoon. Stragglers were still coming in fifteen minutes after the main group returned. Some had to be revived by corpsmen.

Our DI allowed thirty minutes for showers and shaving. During this process we discovered that modesty wasn't a virtue in the Marine Corps!

Next on our tight schedule was cleaning our quarters. This task was called "GI-ing" (Marine-speak for cleaning anything). At 7:15 a.m., we marched to breakfast chow. While in line at the mess hall, we were warned: "Be back at the area and ready to fall out at eight-thirty a.m."

We double-timed to the armory and stood in *another* line, as one by one we received our rifles and bayonets. The venerable 1903 Springfield would be our training weapon. It had seen service on Guadalcanal. By 1943, it was considered outmoded, with the introduction of the M1 Garand, but we trained with it anyway; there weren't enough of the new rifles to go around yet.

We were informed that our Springfield was a *rifle,* not a *gun,* and instructed to remember its serial number and be prepared to recite it anytime our instructor asked. We were also expected to remember *our* serial number.

Later, one of the recruits made the mistake of calling his rifle a gun. To help him remember the difference, the drill instructor had him recite some doggerel while standing in front of the platoon holding his *rifle* in one hand and "privates" in the other:

"*This is my rifle, this is my gun, this is for shooting, this is for fun!*"

He was instantly cured of his mistake, and fifty-nine others took note!

With our Springfields, we returned to the Quonset hut and received instruction in disassembling and assembling, plus the care and cleaning of our piece (Marine-speak for rifle or pistol).

We were taught to *always* treat our weapon as if our life depended on it. In battle, a weapon failure could be fatal!

GI-ING

The second day was going *fast.*

After attending more intensive instruction in the afternoon, we learned the purpose of our metal bucket, brush, and lye soap. We were told to change our uniforms and put our dirty clothes in the bucket. We were marched to the laundry area, where there were rows of wooden racks with a water faucet for each man. The racks were constructed on a V-slant to collect runoff water.

The base had a commercial laundry service, but it wasn't for recruits. We would be our own laundry service. We were informed that *every day* while in Boot Camp, we would, *without fail,* wash a complete set of clothing, and make *sure* we got them clean, as there would be an inspection later. We were also told by our corporal: "Snap to it! You have thirty minutes to finish!"

The platoon was all "assholes and elbows" as we vigorously attacked the washing of our clothes, paying particular attention to our white skivvies.

After washing, we hung our wet gear on clotheslines with wooden clothespins supplied in our buckets. In true military fashion, each platoon had its own assigned clothesline facility so we knew exactly where to find our finished laundry.

Back in our area, we had a short break before evening chow; some recruits wrote home, others fiddled with their Springfields.

Later, another school was held in our hut on military protocol, insignia, and rank. We were taught the correct way to salute and to always use the words *yes sir!, no sir!,* and *no excuse, sir!* when replying to questions from superior officers.

We were informed that an officer's *wish* was a *command.* You never saluted without your cover (Marine-speak for a hat of any kind) on. You never wore your cover inside a building. So it wasn't necessary to salute when indoors.

If any officer came upon a group of men, it wasn't required for all present to salute. The person in charge called "Attention!" and saluted for the entire party.

When walking in the same direction and about to overtake an officer, you were to salute and say, "By your leave, sir."

In response, he would return the salute and reply, "Granted!" or "Carry on!"

In order for "boots" (Marine-speak for recruits in boot camp) to identify their superiors and for them to recognize one another, the Marine Corps, like most military organizations since the Roman legions, have employed a chevron and insignia system.

The Corps system consisted of chevrons or stripes (Marine-speak for *V* and inverted *V*) for enlisted personnel. The officer system used insignias, based on bars, gold and silver acorns, gold and silver winged eagles, and stars in silver. Privates didn't wear insignia. No markings at all told everyone how *low* a boot was on the military totem pole.

The number of stripes told the rank of enlisted personnel above us. From the *Guidebook for Marines* we learned all about rank. It went like this:

Private: no stripe
Private First Class: one stripe
Corporal: two stripes
Sergeant: three stripes
Platoon Sergeant: three stripes up and one down
Gunnery Sergeant: three stripes up and two down
Master Sergeant: three stripes up and three down
First Sergeant: three stripes up and three down
The Corps has an in-between rank—warrant officers—whose rank
    was granted by a warrant rather than by receiving a commission.
    Warrant officers outrank all sergeants, but are below a second
    lieutenant.

INSIGNIA FOR OFFICERS:

Second Lieutenant: one gold bar
First Lieutenant: one silver bar
Captain: two silver bars
Major: one gold oak leaf
Lieutenant Colonel: silver oak leaf
Colonel: silver eagle
Brigadier General: one silver star
Major General: two silver stars
Lieutenant General: three silver stars
General: four stars

The Corps, unlike the Army or Navy, has no five-star-rank generals to correspond with the rank of general of the Armies or fleet
admiral.

A corporal has two stripes, yet his commands carry the same
weight as any other officer. His commands come down to him from
superiors and he issues them as a link in the chain of command. A

private first class didn't ordinarily issue orders, but a private-first-class DI's instructions rated full compliance.

Later at Camp Pendleton, I learned that a corporal was in charge of a squad of eight men; a sergeant, a section that is composed of two squads of seventeen men; a gunnery sergeant is second in command to a lieutenant, who commands a platoon.

A machine-gun platoon is composed of 58 men including an ammunition corporal. Rifle platoons have a similar makeup, except a platoon sergeant is second in command. A company of 250 men is commanded by a lieutenant or a captain.

From our *Guidebook for Marines* we learned that rank had its privileges, but all ranks carried heavy responsibilities, including life-and-death decisions in battle.

I was happy to learn ranks and whom to salute, because one day, in my ignorance, I had saluted a private first class. He was startled, quickly returned my salute, and said with a smirk, "Carry on, Mac!"

School ended at 9 p.m. or 2100 hours. No more "a.m." or "p.m."; the Corps had a different way of telling time. From now on, we would use military time. For instance, 0100 is the first hour of a day. Midnight is 2400, the end of twenty-four hours. This disposed of the civilian time system and worked well to avoid the confusion between a.m. and p.m.

GET IN STEP

On my third day in boot camp, I wanted to *QUIT*! I decided this after I received my first ass chewing from the "prick" Pfc. DI.

While practicing close-order drill, I kept screwing up the formation by falling out of step. The DI said *twice*: "Tatum, get in step." The *third* time I fell out, he screamed: "Halt! Tatum, front and center!"

I stepped forward. With his face so close to mine I could smell his aftershave lotion, he hollered: "Tatum, you are one real screwup!

Do you have two left feet? My God, Tatum, you don't even have the grace of a *hog on ice*! You better shape up, or I will ship you out of this man's Marine Corps."

I was shocked and humiliated; I had never been talked to like that before! The worst dressing-down I had ever experienced was a severe scolding by my *mother*. I hated that assistant DI! *Fine!* If he didn't want me in the Marines, I *would* go home! To HELL with him and the Corps! *I QUIT!*

After chow, my spirits improved and I decided to stay. To HELL with him! He wasn't shipping me out. Later I found out he had no combat experience, and wondered if his harshness was his way of compensating for this.

Our days and nights until 2100 were filled with activity. Evenings were spent on maintenance of our piece, bayonet, gear, and few personal possessions.

The hour between 2100 and 2200 was free! This allowed us to goof off. Our drill instructor, however, *suggested* we write home instead. He didn't want parents or wives writing the base commander asking: "How's my boy?"

That evening I was sitting on my bunk feeling sorry for myself, when the recruit next to me said, "Don't let him get you down. You were not all that bad. He wanted to make an example of someone, and today it was you."

My new friend had some Reserve Officer Training Corps experience in college and had keen insight into military training methods.

He said, "First they dehumanize us, reduce us to zero, undermine our self-respect, and then start over to make Marines out of us. Everything they tell us or have us do will have a purpose. Military training is as much psychological as it is physical. You watch, tomorrow he will make an example out of someone else."

The next day a baby-faced Marine got the ass chewing. At morning inspection, the prick DI called to his newest victim: "Front and center! Boy, did you shave today?"

"No sir!"

"Why not?" the asshole DI asked.

"I don't ever shave, *sir,* I have no beard, sir."

"Now you hear me loud and clear, boy. From this day forward, you *will* shave every day you are in the Marine Corps, and don't you forget it. Be at my quarters after evening chow and I will school you in how to shave the Marine Corps way!" roared the DI.

When our baby-faced Marine returned to the hut, he was clean-shaven but bleeding from a couple of nicks. Someone asked, "What happened?"

"Well, I had to shave dry, with no shaving soap. The worst part was doing it lying *under* his bunk."

No one had to repeat the "dry shave lesson" in *our* training platoon.

Our conditioning was physical as well as mental. The first time we ran the obstacle course, we found who was in good condition and who needed improvement. The trial demanded all-out physical endurance and agility. The barriers increased in severity and in height, until we reached the twenty-foot vertical wall. It was scaled by using ropes, and doing this took its toll. Some had to pass around it; others made it after a couple of tries. The water barrier was traversed by swinging across on a rope. One heavyset recruit didn't make it and fell backward into the three-foot-deep water. He made a *big* muddy splash and everyone had a good laugh. When the Marine Corps got rid of his "baby fat," he was still big, but a trim fighting machine!

GOOD DI, BAD DI

My platoon had lost some of its "boot raggedness" and at times we surprised the DIs with our precision footwork in close order drill and executing their orders. I was feeling so elated I *almost* liked the assistant (prick) DI—a *little* bit, bulldog face and all!

I realized he had a vital job converting civilians into Marines, and people like me, with two left feet, didn't make his life or task easier.

I liked my corporal DI a lot better because of his kinder approach. Sometimes he treated us like we were human! It was almost like the good cop, bad cop routine, only we had a good-DI-and-a-bad-DI gig going on. Whatever the routine was, it was working.

On the sixth day of boot camp, I learned how the Marine Corps utilized peer pressure to control our actions and behavior. We had finished washing our clothing when the Pfc. DI called for an inspection of our clothes.

For an inspection, the drill was to display wet clothing draped across our arms. Skivvies on top of dungaree jacket, left arm; socks on top of dungaree trousers, right arm.

The DI carried a riding crop at all times, striking it across his hand to make emphatic points. Trooping the line, inspecting our labors, he would use his crop to lift items for inspection.

When he reached a Marine next to me, he paused. Eyeing him top to bottom, he lifted his skivvies with the riding crop, carefully inspecting the crotch. "Oh, what do we have here?" he snarled sarcastically. "Nicotine stains?"

"Sir, I don't know, sir," was the nervous response.

"What do you *mean* you *don't know*! Boy!" Holding the offending skivvies under his nose, he said, "If it isn't nicotine, then it must be *shit*! You didn't get your skivvies clean, *did you, boy*?"

"Sir, I don't know, sir."

"Well I do! It's pure shit! ATTENTION!"

We had to drop our clean clothes on the deck.

"Right face! Forward march!"

We walked over our wet clothing, grinding it into the dirt. When we had gone forty feet, the DI called, "About-face!"

We marched over our laundry again. This process was repeated over and over.

Calling a halt, the DI said, "You have fifteen minutes to get your clothes *clean* or you will miss evening chow."

Boy! We were pissed at the offending recruit for causing the trouble. Next day at wash time we inspected one another's labors, *especially* checking skivvies for "nicotine stains." *Their plan was working.*

NICOTINE BLUES

We learned not to light a cigarette unless "the smoking lamp was lit" (Marine-speak for permission to smoke). As usual, there was also a Marine way to dispose of your butts. The prescribed procedure was to stub out your butt, break it in half, scatter the tobacco to the wind, roll the paper into a tiny ball, then dispose of it by putting it in your pocket; or, if the DI wasn't looking, kick a hole in the sand and bury it.

One Marine momentarily forgot the rules in a nicotine fog and threw his butt on the deck. Unfortunately, the prick DI saw him. The punishment meted out was to collect *one hundred butts* on a *string* and present them to the DI.

This was how the recruit now spent all of his time off, looking everywhere for cigarette butts. They proved hard to find, because now *no one* threw their butts on the deck. He was a sad sight looking and searching for old butts. In desperation, he resorted to following smokers around, begging them to help. "Please! Give *me* your butts!" he pleaded.

Even this expedient didn't solve the problem, so he bought three packs of "smokes" and broke them in half. By smoking the stubs as quickly as possible, the string of butts gradually accumulated for the presentation. Because of the humiliating ordeal, the guy was lucky not to die of lung cancer at an early age.

The butt incident shows that behavior modification and training never let up on us for a moment.

"Cleanliness is next to godliness" in the Corps. We were warned,

"Bathe as often as possible." The *Guidebook for Marines* recommended "at least two times per week. An unclean body could be the cause of disease." We were to pay particular attention to armpits, parts between the legs, feet, and under the foreskin.

Our senior DI insisted we bathe every day, and always wash our hands before eating and after using the toilet. Films cautioned us to inspect for body and crab lice. "*Never* wear wet shoes or clothing! Change as quickly as possible to prevent catching cold or serious illness."

Our *Guidebook* gave instructions for the "Marine way" to brush your teeth. We were told to brush on the inside and the outside, away from the gums and toward the cutting surfaces of the teeth. Food particles remaining were to be promptly removed, but care was to be taken not to injure the gums. Required brushing was to be done twice a day, once at dawn and again just before taps.

LESSONS TO LIVE BY

Among the Corps' recommendations for daily life were:

1. Get into the habit of having your bowels move regularly once each day.
2. Drink plenty of water at intervals during the day, but do not drink a large amount at one time.
3. Drink only from your own glass or cup, never use a cup that has been used by others. Do not exchange or use pipes, cigars or musical instruments played by mouth; handkerchiefs, towels or shaving outfits, for the reason they might be infested with germs or disease.
4. Always use your mosquito net when mosquitoes are present. Make sure it is well tucked in and has no holes in it.
5. Flies and cockroaches carry disease germs and leave them on food. Get rid of flies. Whenever you see a fly in the barracks, kill it.

The *Guidebook* contained the following information relating to hygiene and sanitation:

> Keep your barracks and squad bay clean. If you encounter bed-bugs, in bed, or in the barracks, this fact is to be reported to the company commander. Keep your hair cut and fingernails clean. This is especially important if you are a baker or handle food in any manner.

SOCIAL INTERCOURSE

Venereal diseases received special attention in the Marine Corps. A film we saw and the *Guidebook for Marines* warned us about catching social diseases, explaining that they were caught "by sexual inter-course with an infected woman." It wouldn't do any good to tell a Navy doctor that you caught the "clap" from a toilet seat. "If you should feel you have caught a venereal disease, report to the medical officer at once and do exactly as he tells you. Failure to report for treatment of venereal disease is a court-martial offense."

We were warned, "Report for prophylactic treatment within two hours after the encounter." Compliance with this regulation might have caused many females to be left suddenly alone. Our *Guidebook* continued, "Any venereal disease can be cured more quickly if proper treatment is begun early. Above all do not try to treat yourself, or go to an advertising 'quack doctor.' Either way you may permanently damage your body." Abuse of government property (i.e., us) was not going to be tolerated.

In the case of gonorrhea, which might take several months to cure, all pay ceased until medical clearance was received. The warning seemed to work by shocking the hell out of us. Although no Marine I knew embraced a celibacy oath, we *were* worried. The attraction of young women, however, neutralized most of the message.

Sometimes rude references were made to the quality of the girls who were seen with friends on liberty and we often made jokes about this, saying things like "I hope that girl you were out with last night doesn't rot your cock off!"

Venereal diseases were serious subjects, but continued to be the butt of jokes and humor. One day on "sick call" I heard a salty Navy first pharmacist mate tell another one, "Marines will screw anything from a stovepipe to a horse collar."

Maybe he was jealous of the Marines' reputation. I personally wasn't concerned about all this; I didn't know any "floozy" women.

CHAPTER THREE

Gung Ho!

*Many of us had arrived as boys; we would all march
out of the gates of boot camp as men.*

Several weeks into boot camp, I decided I really *liked* becoming a Marine. We were a group of strangers who were forming loose friendships based on new associations and rigorous training. Shared experiences were the cement of comradeship and esprit de corps.

The Marines had been at their business for a long time and had the drill down pat. That's how they were able to accomplish such a remarkable transformation in eight weeks. I was an eager recruit who thrived on my training. In fact, I now believe being in the Marine Corps was the best thing to happen to a kid like me.

I weighed 155 pounds when I enlisted. Arduous training and Marine Corps chow brought me up to a fighting weight of 175 pounds. I had new pride in myself and felt I was becoming a *man* as well as a Marine. We were *all* becoming Marines.

Then I suffered a terrible setback. I was well past the halfway mark of boot camp when I contracted a form of pneumonia called "cat fever," and spent two weeks in the base hospital.

After recovering, I found my original platoon had graduated and shipped out to Marine units throughout the Pacific. Most were ordered to report to the 4th Division and saw their first combat on Saipan and Tinian.

My rabbit-hunting buddies, Bob Ross, and Lory Lucchesi, after seeing me off on the train, followed my example and joined the Marines. Because of my unfortunate sickness, they entered boot camp *after,* and left it *before,* I did!

The Corps didn't have a platoon to put me in at the same level of training I was at when I got sick. To my consternation, I was put in one that was formed the day I got out of the hospital!

Now I had to do boot camp all over again! The only thing I didn't have to repeat was getting a haircut and drawing clothing. I was sent to the transit storage to retrieve my original gear before reporting to my new platoon.

My hair was already regulation length and I enjoyed watching the shearing and discomfort of the new men. I was an amused and detached observer at the process of induction and a "spare tire" trailing along from place to place.

This whole process was becoming redundant!

THE SHARPEST DI

The drill instructor of my new recruit platoon was Corporal Daniel Leary. He was a veteran of Guadalcanal and had been handpicked to train recruits. Leary was six feet tall, slim as a rail, and the sharpest DI I had ever seen.

He would control and direct our every waking moment for the next eight weeks. Not one to brag, he never spoke of his combat experiences on the 'Canal, and only wore his Purple Heart at parades. Our corporal's experience in combat made his excessive demands credible. We felt he knew what the Corps expected of recruits, and fully recovered, I was ready to do all of it again.

Squad and close order drill conditioned us to respond to orders and take pride in our eventual success, but my lack of grace while marching irritated and confounded Corporal Leary. My inability to follow cadence was a source of great consternation to me—and to the men in front of me, whom I kept tripping.

Corporal Leary shouted at me one day, "Where did you learn to march, Tatum? In the Girl Scouts?"

His question was a prelude to my enrollment in Leary's "awkward squad," an activity that ate up my free time. My stride was measured, and it was determined that it was four inches too long. Every third step I gained a foot, which compelled me to perform the famed "Tatum-skip-step-shuffle"—a maneuver that allowed me to get back in step momentarily, prior to screwing up the platoon again. I was tired of listening to Leary shout, "Tatum! Get in step," and tried hard to get marching in formation right.

My trials helped others avoid my mistakes, if not my feet!

CORPS LORE

The Marine Corps also insisted we learn its history and traditions. Our own Corps heroes were given special attention in official publications and magazines like *Leatherneck,* which were consumed avidly. Two new heroes we eagerly read about were Sergeant John Basilone and Platoon Sergeant Mitchell Paige, who had both received the Medal of Honor for actions on Guadalcanal. They joined the new pantheon of legends emerging from the humiliating catastrophe of Pearl Harbor in 1941.

Our platoon hero was Corporal Leary, who never mentioned his frontline actions on Guadalcanal to us. Secretly I longed to know. I believed if he and I were sent into combat together, I would follow him

To ward off boredom we also resorted to our *Guidebook,* which overflowed with facts like the four-looped, embroidered swirls on top of an officer's hat. Called the quatrefoil or French love knot, it dated back to the era of John Paul Jones, when Marines fought from the rigging of sailing ships. The peculiar design of the knot made the men recognizable as Marines, not members of enemy boarding parties, to sharpshooters fighting up above in the rigging.

COLD STEEL

Bayonet training was a new experience none of us would forget. It was tough, rugged, and required perfect physical conditioning. After we read the bayonet chapter in our *Guidebook*, Corporal Leary marched us to the training range along the shore of San Diego Bay to learn this lethal art of war.

I remember one paragraph in the bayonet chapter that got my attention:

> The rifle and bayonet in the hands of a Marine become a deadly combination of spear, sword, club and shield. At night this combination weapon can kill silently and with surprise. In hand-to-hand fighting when the rifle cannot be reloaded and the use of grenades would be impractical, it is the decisive weapon. At these times the aggressive bayonet fighter will win.

Leary quietly explained, "An assault is the critical moment of any combat and a *bayonet assault*, executed by determined Marines, can turn the tide. Men eager to engage an enemy with cold steel will strike terror in their ranks."

He emphasized four points:

1. *Get the blade into the enemy.* It's the blade that kills.

2. *Be ruthless, vicious, and fast in your attack.* Never pause in your attack until you have won. There is only one winner in a bayonet fight. Make sure it's *you!*

3. *Seek vital areas, but don't wait for an opening; make one.* The best "killing zones" are the throat and belly. A solid rifle butt stroke in the groin will open your enemy's guard. Deliver it hard and then go for the kill.

4. *Protect yourself.* Your rifle and bayonet make a good shield; use their protection by dodging and parrying, but remember, the best defense is to attack first, strike the first blow, and follow through.

Corporal Leary demonstrated the key movements for bayonet fighting, saying, "It is like being a prizefighter; that is, all moves should be natural." Our first stance was the guard position, like fighters squaring off in a ring. Attack maneuvers consisted of eight basic movements. The first six are used to *kill* the enemy. They are: slash, jab, vertical butt stroke, horizontal butt stroke, horizontal slash, and smash. The last two positions are protective: parry left and parry right.

Leary paired us off and we began practicing the basic movements, then he stopped us and said, "Your practice is being conducted with the skill of a fouled-up Chinese fire drill. Luckily, no one has been stabbed." He offered more pointers to help us.

Next was the running-in-practice bayonet course, which was the length of a football field, with ten stations or "straw men" to attack. Some stations had targets, swinging straight arms, or posts. We were to parry right or left and then stab or slash them as needed. Some we stabbed, then withdrew the bayonet and went on to the next target. Others got the butt stroke. We were encouraged to run at full speed, shouting and hollering like wild Indians on the warpath.

Corporal Leary, during the rest break, said, "In actual combat, if you stab an enemy in the chest, you may have a difficult time extracting your bayonet. It might be necessary to discharge your rifle to extract it."

On the second day of bayonet drill we improved to the point where we were timed, like running a hundred-yard dash. Everyone was anxious to improve his time by exerting maximum effort.

Late in the afternoon, when Corporal Leary was demonstrating right and left parrying, his recruit opponent accidentally stabbed him in the right forearm with his bayonet point. Frightened, the man stopped in his tracks, but Leary insisted he continue the practice until our lesson was over. Our instructor assured the Marine, "It wasn't your fault. Don't worry about it. It's part of the training."

Corporal Leary took his handkerchief, made a compress bandage, and tied it on the wound with one hand. Calling "Attention! Forward march!" he returned us to our area before going for treatment.

I decided then that Corporal Daniel Leary was a *real* Marine and the best drill instructor in the Marine Corps!

No facet of training was left to chance. In the final weeks we studied: common military terms, interior guard duties, packs and equipment, first aid, drill for foot troops, combat formations and signals, and protective measures.

PROTECTIVE MEASURES

"Protective measures" didn't pertain to venereal disease but to entrenchments, like digging in a one- or two-man foxhole or individual prone shelters. Connecting trenches was also on the agenda. Later, on Iwo Jima, I was glad I paid attention to the training in protective measures at boot camp.

One full day was spent instructing us about chemical warfare and how to protect ourselves against its possible use with a gas mask, creams, and special clothing. Practical demonstrations were given by sending us through a room filled with tear gas with our masks on. In the last half of the test, we removed the mask and ran to the door without it.

This exercise was deemed very important because of the widespread use of mustard gas in World War I. (Neither side used chemical warfare in World War II.)

OUR "NEW" WEAPON!

Qualifying with the rifle was the most important event of boot camp. I missed going to the rifle range with my first platoon, so I was looking forward to our move to a tent city at Camp Matthews.

Here, we were issued M1 Garand rifles (U.S. rifle, caliber .30 M1) to use at the range. The first night at Matthews, Corporal Leary "held school" on our new weapon. We learned the M1 weighed 9.5 pounds and was 43.6 inches long without bayonet. Its average rate of fire when well aimed was ten to twelve rounds per minute. Clip capacity was eight rounds and with an M2 cartridge; the Garand's effective range was 440 yards. A *very* impressive weapon and standard issue for all Marine infantry units.

The M1 was a gas-operated, clip-fed, air-cooled, semiautomatic shoulder weapon. Its main tactical advantage was rapid mechanical operation, allowing an individual rifleman or a group to deliver a large volume of accurate fire on a given target.

At Camp Matthews, "Jungle Jim"–style pith helmets were issued to us. This cover was ideal for use at the rifle range. Its wide brim protected against long days in the scorching sun and allowed good head ventilation.

An entire week was dedicated to firing positions: prone, sitting, kneeling, plus standing. We learned how important sling and sight adjustments were to accuracy and spent hours "dry-firing," an exercise Marines called snapping in.

Fear of not qualifying haunted many. I was one of them. Not being previously around guns—oops, I mean *rifles*—increased the pressure.

Our instructor told us how important it was to take a deep breath, let some air out, then hold your breath while squeezing the trigger gently—*so gently* you didn't know when your weapon would fire. Failure to master this technique proved to be a real problem for me later, when we fired "for the record."

GRAB ASSING

Extra stress and worry about our scores led to horseplay and "grab ass." One example occurred one evening while we were waiting in line for chow. A recruit, in a playful mood, took his pith helmet and struck the man in front of him on the head, driving his cover over his ears. Our DI spotted the "grab assing" and called the two participants to "Front and center!"

"You think that was fun, don't you?" he asked.

"Sir, no sir!" the men responded in unison.

"Oh yes you *do*! Since it's so *much* fun, let's give your buddy a chance to repay all that fun," he told them. "Face each other, arm's length apart!"

He directed the second man to hit his opponent with his cover. The first smack was a little on the soft side. "Apply a harder blow! Inflict more *fun*!"

The second smash was a real "hit," driving the helmet down over the ears—so we couldn't see the man's eyes. "That was better," our DI proclaimed sarcastically. "Now it's *your* turn," he told the first recruit.

Mad about the power of the second blow, *he* retaliated with a two-handed, overhead smash that sent the cover past the second recruit's ears. Now in full swing literally, they traded hits, smacks, blows, and whacks, until their pith helmets were smashed to a cardboard pulp. The sideshow was witnessed by hundreds of cheering troops, waiting for chow. Calling "Attention!," our DI shouted, "That *wasn't* funny, you feather merchants!"

One time, the DI noticed a member of my platoon who always

wore a smile as his standard expression, and thought he was snickering. Calling the smiling Marine to "Front and center!" he demanded, "Did you think that was funny, son?"

"Sir, no sir!"

"Then why in the hell are you smiling, boy?"

"Sir, I'm not smiling, sir! I *always* look this way, sir."

"You listen to me, *boy*! As soon as this formation is over, get your butt in front of a mirror—and practice looking different."

FLINCHING

Back on the range after our snapping in, we were ready to fire live ammunition. My initial shots were scattered all over the target, along with a couple of "Maggie's drawers" (Marine-speak for a red flag waved after a completely missed target).

Observing my lack of progress and waste of government resources, my instructor came to my assistance by explaining that I was flinching, anticipating the recoil, not squeezing the trigger properly, *and* closing my eyes when I fired. I couldn't believe I was flinching.

The instructor took my rifle and secretly put in an empty shell casing, telling me to assume the prone position, repeating his earlier admonition: "Take a deep breath, exhale some, then hold it." Then he said, "*Gently* squeeze the trigger."

I did as instructed. When the trigger "clicked" on a dead chamber, I pushed my shoulder forward, which upset my aim.

"See, Tatum! What you are doing is *anticipating* the recoil and screwing up your shots."

He pulled me out of the firing line and had me snapping in for the next four hours! After this boring practice session, I mastered the "squeeze" and did much better in the afternoon. At least there were no Maggie's drawers on my firing record.

The day we spent "firing for the record" I passed, but barely. I shot "marksman," the lowest rating. Shooting "expert" paid an extra five dollars per month, nearly a 10 percent increase in a private's pay! "Sharpshooter" was an intermediate ranking, but probably didn't pay extra.

The second day on the range, our platoon had the duty of "pulling targets" for those on the firing line. It was hard but interesting work. While so engaged, we *never* looked over the parapet to see what was going on!

Large, thick paper targets were attached to a metal frame that could be raised and lowered to check the scores. After a rifleman fired, we lowered the target and marked his score. To do this, we used a round wooden disk with a peg in its center that indicated where the shots had impacted. We raised the disk so the results could be checked.

BACK TO DIEGO

After two weeks at Camp Matthews, we returned to Diego. (As we recruits got "saltier," we skipped the "San" part of San Diego.)

Training with my second platoon was nearing its end! Only two weeks to go! Time went fast, and we still had a lot of training to accomplish before graduation, but I could see a marked difference in the platoon. We were executing commands with a high degree of precision and polish.

Our appearance took on a new luster, our dress was sharper, and our military demeanor improved. Our dungarees, through repeated washings, had a softer texture and lost their "boot" look and (thankfully) their mothball smell.

When we marched by new boot platoons now, we gave them a preview of what they would look like at the end of eight weeks!

PERIL FROM THE SKY

The recruit depot and Lindberg Field were separated by a wide road with a high chain-link fence on each side. Our section of the base was under the main flight path of new B-24 bombers when they made their maiden flights from the factory.

Giant bombers roared over us day and night, so close we could see the blue-and-white exhaust flames and feel vibrations from their thundering motors and straining props. If we hadn't been so tired, the frequent flights of the bombers would have made sleeping so close to an airport difficult.

Our Sunday afternoons were free time. We wrote home, cleaned gear, or waited in the Coca-Cola line. Cokes were a nickel, so even a Marine recruit could afford one or two. I calculated that there was probably one Coke machine per five hundred thirsty "boots." Such overdemand and undersupply created very long lines.

After an hour of a boring wait, I had almost forgotten what I had come for. I stuck in my nickels for two Cokes and went back to the Quonset to drink them. Finishing my drinks, I lay down on my "sack" (Marine-speak for "bed" or "cot") to rest, when I heard the sound of an airplane in trouble, its engines screaming and straining to high heaven, followed by what sounded like a bomber crashing.

We all jumped up and ran outside to see what was happening. A B-24 bomber failing on takeoff had torn down two chain-link fences and used six Quonset huts for brakes.

We rushed to the crash to see if we could help. The huge ship had crushed the buildings so thoroughly, we believed anyone in those barracks was killed or injured. Luckily, the Corps had recognized the danger of having personnel billets in a flight path and didn't house any troops there. Once we realized that the huts were vacant, our concern was for the crew.

The pilot, a captain, climbed out of the cockpit and stood on the nose section of the battered ship. Taking off his "fifty-mission" cap

(Marine-speak for any Army Air Corps pilot's cover with a worn, comfortable look), he reached into his hip pocket, pulled out a comb, and proceeded to nonchalantly adjust his curly blond locks.

No one was injured, but the government had to write off six huts and one B-24.

The crash was our main topic of conversation for days. From then on, I always listened intently every time a B-24 took off on a test flight!

HAPPY BIRTHDAY

November 10, 1943, was a special day in the whole Marine Corps. That year we celebrated the Corps' 168th birthday.

From my *Guidebook for Marines* I learned: "An organization of Marines, as a regular branch of the country's service, was formed by an Act of the Continental Congress, passed on November 10, 1775."

Well, I knew the Corps had been in business for a long time, but I didn't know there was a Marine Corps *before* there was a United States!

Traditions said an early meeting place for the Marines was Tun Tavern in Philadelphia. I wondered if that was why, ever since, Marines have spent a lot of time hanging around saloons and bars. Are they just observing time-honored traditions?

We didn't get the day off, but we did enjoy a special menu at the mess hall that included a slice of birthday cake.

GRADUATION DAY!

The "big day" finally came: *graduation from boot camp.*

The previous day was spent in meticulous preparations for the final inspection and graduation parade. Corporal Leary told us, "I want this platoon to be the sharpest one out there. Uniform of the day *will* be dress greens [dark green wool uniforms], full packs, *and* weapons."

Our dress greens had only one rear pocket, on the left side. I guessed this was a wartime economy measure.

We broke out two electric irons and boards, and as sixty anxious boots clamored for them, the tension built up in the crowded squad room.

To achieve a sharp crease in the legs of our trousers, we used our yellow soap on the *inside* of the crease. When pressed, the trousers maintained a razor edge—for a while.

The squad bay smelled like mothballs, starch, and scorched wool, commingled with the odor of brass polish and sweat.

We starched our khaki field scarves (Marine-speak for "necktie") along with our dress khaki shirts, then ironed the creases so sharp you could cut yourself on the edges!

Each item of clothing gear and insignia had to be personally inspected by Corporal Leary. Part of our preparations included efforts to "antique" our image by giving our uniforms and insignias a "saltier" appearance. All of us wanted to look as sharp as Corporal Leary.

The big day dawned warm and humid.

At 1000, we were ordered, "Fall out of the huts! Fall in, outside!" Corporal Leary trooped the line, checking us individually. After passing his thorough inspection, we marched to the main parade ground in the center of the base. We waited in the hot morning sun while other training platoons assembled.

From far away, we could faintly hear the Marine Corps band. As their formation approached we heard it playing the "Semper Fidelis" march written by one of the Corps most famous Marines, John Philip Sousa.

As the musicians entered the main parade ground, Sousa's "Washington Post" march floated on a light breeze while they took positions so our parade could start.

Leary shouted, "Attention! Left face! Forward march!"

We marched to the end of the parade ground, where Leary called out, "To your right. March!" This command brought us to the center of the field.

"To your right. March!" We were now standing in the middle of the parade ground. From there we moved three hundred yards forward, where Leary ordered, "Halt!"

We were the third formation in line; behind us were three other platoons.

A "full bird" (Marine-speak for highest rank of colonel, signified by silver eagles) colonel inspected us and made a speech, congratulating all of us on our achievement of becoming Marines. "You have joined the finest fighting force in the world," he declared.

Next we marched in review. As our platoon passed the reviewing stand, Corporal Leary called, "Eyes left!" and saluted for the platoon. Farther back in formation, the Marine band played the "Marines' Hymn."

The hairs stood up on the back of my neck; I was choked with emotion and ecstatic to be a Marine *and* an American! When the band played "The Star-Spangled Banner," I had to fight back tears of pride. I have never been so proud of myself and my country, before or since.

We were no longer *boots;* we were authentic *United States Marines.*

Back at our hut, Corporal Leary called, "Dismissed!"

We broke ranks, slapping one another on the back and shoulder, shaking hands, jumping up and down with joy and relief. At last our training ordeal was over.

Many of us had arrived as boys; we would all march out of the gates of boot camp as *men.*

Leary called us to "Attention!" for the last time. Facing us in ranks, he said, "You are the best platoon I have ever had the privilege to train. I'm proud of you. Make me and the Marine Corps proud in the days to come."

Ramrod straight, he shook hands with each Marine and passed out our duty assignments. As he looked into my eyes, I felt an extra pressure of goodwill in his handshake as he wished me, "Good luck."

Corporal Daniel Leary and I never crossed paths again.

CHAPTER FOUR

Home in the Corps

From across America, thousands of determined men wearing the Marine Corps green were concentrating at Camp Pendleton, California. I felt privileged that my first billet was to be the new Fifth Marine Division.

I graduated in early January of 1944 and hoped to get a short leave to go home. After all my training, I could have used a break. Besides, I was a little homesick. Instead of time off, I got my shipping-out orders:

```
Pvt. Charles William Tatum USMCR 522829 is
    to report to, no delay en route.
Co. B 1st Bn.
27th Marines
Fifth Division
Camp Pendleton
Oceanside, California
Assignment: Advance Cadre Machine Gun
    Platoon
```

The Marine Corps offered three choices of duty stations recorded on a request chit.

My choices were:

1. Seagoing
2. Tanks
3. Machine guns

I believed the "options chit" was a little ploy designed to make me feel good about their choice of assignment for me. I couldn't complain, I guess. I got my third choice, machine guns. Not knowing anything about the weapon, I picked what I thought would be a glamorous job.

Since I had only fired a marksman level, it was probably a good idea that the Marines put me behind a machine gun. The Japs wouldn't have been in much danger from my marksmanship with an M1 rifle!

My platoon's duty instructions were varied, like the Fleet Marine Force (FMF), aviation, and radio school. Most of us, however, were sent to the newly forming 5th Division at Camp Pendleton, up the coast from Diego, "no delay en route."

FALSE ADVERTISING

I had always wanted seagoing duty after seeing the recruiting poster in front of my hometown post office. I innocently believed that if I was seagoing, I would wear the famed Marine Corps dress blue uniform.

Come to think of it, I had been in the Marines for *four months* and hadn't seen a Marine dressed in the formal attire that had lured me into the Corps at Stockton, California! I now started to believe that this state of affairs was an early form of "bait and switch" advertising!

I planned to sue the Marine Corps for false advertising with seductive Marine recruiting posters in front of U.S. post offices. Particularly the one with a Marine in dress blues aboard a *battleship,* with an *American flag* whipping in the wind behind him. They *had* been clever. That scene really sucked me in! Hell! I didn't even know that the Marines *had* an army! Now, my green uniform told me otherwise, that I would be a ground-pounder, not a fighter on the high seas!

Suddenly, I was wishing I had seen a Royal Canadian Mounties' poster first and given *them* my business. The scenery in Canada is beautiful.

FORMING THE 5TH DIVISION

To prosecute war in the Pacific, America developed an "island-hopping" strategy for the defeat of Japan. To feed the voracious appetite of this plan, an amphibious war machine was needed in the Pacific. Our nation needed thousands of new "soldiers of the sea" for amphibious attack troops. The Corps expanded rapidly, filling orders, cut by the chiefs of staff, to grind out "gyrenes" as fast as men and women could be recruited and trained. They used assembly-line operations and precision training techniques, and Marine recruits, like myself, were the final product. We were "green troops," now eager to undergo advanced military training to avenge the national disgrace of Pearl Harbor.

In December 1941, the United States possessed two active Marine divisions—the 1st at Camp Lejeune, North Carolina, and the 2nd in Southern California. Men of the 1st Division, with attached raider and paratroop battalions, were ordered into combat in August 1942 at Guadalcanal. Elements of the 2nd Division, whose scattered regiments were assembled at Wellington, New Zealand, were trained for the assault on Tarawa, and participated in the battle of Guadalcanal. Both divisions were led by veteran officers and NCOs, with decades of faithful service in the "old" Corps. These "old hands," some with experience in World War I, formed the tight nucleus of our "new" Corps.

By 1943, eighty thousand men, enough for four Marine divisions, were under arms, either in Pacific combat or undergoing training to join their frontline comrades.

However, for the Corps to accomplish its ever-expanding offensive mission, another new division was required. The 3rd and 4th Divisions were created after Pearl Harbor and quickly added luster to the fighting legend of the "leathernecks." In the island-hopping strategy of the Navy brass, there would be an island for each division. Organized from scratch, our new 5th Marine Division was the beneficiary of veterans from bitter Pacific battles who were blended with new recruits to produce a division fully prepared for the terrible mission assigned to it that would come on February 19, 1945.

From scattered battlefields, bases, and hospitals came veterans for the 5th Division. From San Diego and Parris Island, South Carolina, came recruits; from Officer Candidate School, Quantico, Virginia, came eager young officers. From across America, thousands of determined men wearing the Marine Corps green were collecting at Camp Pendleton, California. I felt privileged that my first billet was to be the new 5th Marine Division.

I was assigned to the machine-gun platoon of Baker Company, 1st Battalion, 27th Marines, 5th Marine Division. Our division consisted of three infantry regiments (the 26th, 27th, and 28th Marines) and an artillery regiment, the 13th Marines. As a rule of thumb, a reinforced division is 20,000 men, regiments are 3,000 men, a battalion 1,000, a company 250, and a platoon 58. There are three battalions to a regiment. Tables of organization called for three infantry companies, plus a headquarters and weapons company for each battalion. An infantry company is composed of three rifle platoons, a machine-gun platoon, a mortar section, and a demolition squad.

Major General Keller E. Rockey would be our first commanding general. He had fought with gallantry in World War I, but the 5th Division would be his first combat command of this war. A few months after the battalion was formed, we received a new battalion commander, Lieutenant Colonel John Butler. Butler was an Annapolis graduate, class of 1934. As a young officer, he was assigned to the Marine detachment of the USS *Trenton*, one of several vessels on permanent station in the Caribbean. In 1940, Captain Butler was assigned as Naval attaché to the Dominican Republic. He could easily have remained safely there throughout the war, but the Marines were on Pacific battlefields and the colonel wanted to be with them. His frequent requests for a combat assignment were finally granted and he was ordered to the 5th Marine Division, even without combat experience. Colonel Butler was a seasoned Marine officer and qualified for the task given him.

For me, the similarity between Colonel Butler and my late father was striking. My dad had been a doughboy in World War I, and his picture was always displayed proudly in our home. Both were built the same—lean and rugged, over six feet and 180 pounds. The colonel had coal-black hair and a swarthy complexion like my dad. Each man had an extremely dark beard, the kind that might require shaving twice a day. My father's family was from New Orleans, as was the colonel's. Their dark penetrating eyes often seemed to look right through me. Maybe I wanted to see more in Colonel Butler than there was. Because of the close resemblance to my father, I became a secret Colonel Butler watcher. In my young mind, he personified my idea of a Marine officer. The colonel and I had conversations on occasion, not "chitchat," but straight military talk.

During an inspection one day, he yanked my carbine out of my hands so fast I thought I would lose both arms. After approvingly peering down the barrel of my piece, he asked, "Tatum, are those regulation boots you're wearing?"

"No sir!"

"Where did you get those boots, Tatum?"

"From California, sir!"

"Will you wear regulation shoes at the next inspection?"

"Aye, aye, sir!"

I never dreamed anyone would notice my deviation in footwear. Having these boots was a result of envy. I always wanted paratrooper footwear instead of regulation boondockers. The higher tops were functional and kept stickers out of my socks—and even fake jump boots made me feel accepted. The closest I could come to paratrooper footwear was to buy a pair of shipyard worker's boots with steel top protectors. Little if anything went on in the 1st Battalion that Colonel Butler was not aware of—including my unconventional choice of boots!

Because the effectiveness of a military unit in combat is largely dependent on its leadership and the quality of the training it has received, the officers of 27th Marines underwent the same training as the men under their command. The purpose of our combined training was to create an invincible fighting team, and the 27th Marines were lucky to have both leaders and troops with the mettle needed to get a tough job done.

My company, Baker Company, got off to a rocky start, leadership-wise. Our first commander was Captain Wilfred LeFrancois, a seasoned combat veteran. LeFrancois, as a second lieutenant in the 2nd Raider Battalion, led a platoon on the August 1942 Makin Island raid. During a hot firefight in the early morning, LeFrancois's platoon wiped out a sizable enemy force. In the same battle, Lieutenant LeFrancois was wounded by machine-gun fire, taking five bullets in his right shoulder and upper arm. For this action, he was awarded the Navy Cross, America's second-highest decoration. One weekend, Captain LeFrancois went to Diego on liberty and never came back to the company. Replacing him was a former professional football player with the New York Giants, First Lieutenant Benjamin "Big Ben" Sohn. Sohn hailed from San Diego and had been an outstanding college football player at the University of Southern California before turning professional. After completing basics, Lieutenant Sohn was a training officer at the Officer Candidate School. At six feet four inches and 235 pounds, he easily fit my image of a company commander.

Second in command to Lieutenant Sohn was his executive officer, First Lieutenant James Mayenschein. Affectionately called "Lieutenant Jimmy" by his men, he was a former enlisted man who received a battlefield commission on Guadalcanal, where he demonstrated leadership ability under combat condition. He was the only officer in B Company with combat experience. "Lieutenant Jimmy" was also a paratrooper. Despite his height of only five feet six or seven inches, he was all man and *all* Marine. He had a certain something about him that everyone liked. He was confident to a fault, and some thought him to be cocky. "Lieutenant Jimmy" got the job done. His blond good looks and ready smile gave him a winning personality, which was why he was probably B Company's favorite officer.

The organization of a Marine company of 250 men is as follows: There are four platoons in each company—three rifle platoons (1st Platoon, 2nd Platoon, and 3rd Platoon), one machine-gun platoon (4th Platoon), and a mortar section. A machine-gun platoon has three sections of 17 men each. In maneuvers or combat, a "section" of machine guns is attached to a rifle platoon. I was assigned to the second section of the machine-gun platoon with 16 fellow Marines who would become closer than brothers to me.

Second Lieutenant John Dreger, from Philadelphia, commanded our machine-gun platoon. Dreger was very tall, probably six feet four inches. He had intended to be a pilot, but was too tall for a fighter cockpit. Besides, he once told me jokingly, his mother didn't want him doing anything "dangerous," like flying. Instead, he became a Marine ground officer! Lieutenant Dreger was our commanding officer and he was a likable one. Luckily, we had him to balance off Gunnery Sergeant Stanley "Blackie" Kavato of Pottstown, Pennsylvania, who was his second in command. Kavato and I would have a rocky relationship, to put it kindly.

The rest of our company ranks came from all points of the compass, it seemed. Raw recruits like me joined others with no combat experience, drill instructors, embassy guards, and clerk typists. Some were veterans just recovered from wounds. Others were Paramarines; the swashbuckling, cocky attitude of the raiders and paratroopers exerted a strong influence on the makeup of the 5th Division, but most of all, their combat experience was an invaluable training aid.

With its combination of recruits, stateside Marines, and veterans, our outfit would be allowed ample time to train and organize itself at Camp Pendleton, California, the largest of all Marine bases and named for Marine general "Uncle Joe" Pendleton. Its vast acreage of hills, valleys, cliffs, and deep, ragged ravines was ten miles from the Pacific Ocean. The 5th Division's amphibious exercises would be conducted at Oceanside and California's offshore islands. These and other physical factors seemed perfectly suited to the future missions of the 5th Marine Division, which would include large-scale amphibious attacks on Pacific real estate that was "owned" by the Japanese.

A contest was held to design a new "patch" or logo for our division. Lieutenant Fergus Young was the winner, with a drawing depicting a scarlet shield and gold Roman numeral V, with a blue spear point superimposed inside a pointed border. Perhaps this was the inspiration for calling our new outfit "Spearhead Division."

CHAPTER FIVE

First in Baker Company

Looking straight at us, a smile crossing his lips, the new arrival said quietly and with authority, "At ease, men. How's everything going? I'm Platoon Sergeant John Basilone."

A low coastal fog masked the landscape as I arrived at Camp Pendleton. We were greeted by sharp-looking sentries in dress greens who waved our vehicle to a stop, took a quick glance at the driver, and passed us through.

The trip from the front gate to B Company barracks was ten miles. During the ride, I saw tent cities and a busy staging area for DC-3s. And I was continually impressed with the vast warehouses and long lines of parked tanks, trucks, trailers, half-tracks, and the multiplicity of other military vehicles. Division and regimental administration buildings punctuated the roadside. At all intersections were signs that directed traffic to specific regimental areas.

In one valley was a sprawling bivouac area. Word had it that the 26th Marine Regiment, three thousand men, lived in this canvas billet because of a lack of barracks space. I learned later how fortunate the 27th Regiment was to be in a permanent structure with amenities, as opposed to the makeshift tent quarters of other regiments.

The austere military appearance of the base was muted by nature's beauty, which added a scenic backdrop. Peeking through the clouds were the mountains that formed California's coast range.

My new home seemed to be an ideal place to train the twenty thousand men who would compose our new division. I was pleased to see the vast material might our nation had mobilized in the short time since Pearl Harbor.

Stepping down from the back of the GMC 6x6 truck, I thought the driver had made a big mistake. The barracks building exhibited no sign of human occupation. A low, clinging ground fog added to the vacancy of the lonely scene. A chill in the air made me shiver, a quick reminder I hadn't worn enough warm clothes from Diego.

Concerned, I asked, "Is this the right place?"

"Bet on it, Mac," the driver hollered from the cab. "Welcome to the Fifth Division! You're the first one here."

Well, I said to myself, *my orders* did *say "advance cadre."*

Confused by the lack of a welcoming committee, I hesitated before picking up my gear and venturing inside. The wooden building had a rough, hastily constructed, wartime look. It was two stories high, forty feet wide, and about a hundred feet long, and had been painted a dull, flat, creamy yellow; like everything else I had seen so far, the barracks were desolate. No attempt had been made at landscaping.

Inside I saw rows of bunk beds whose steel skeletons resembled a kid's giant Erector Set. There were no mattresses. Built to a standard Corps design, it could accommodate a Marine company of 260 men, including noncommissioned officers, who had their own quarters. These were four to a room, with single beds. Commissioned officers' quarters were about a mile away from us. Scuttlebutt had it that *their* billets were two to a room and each officer had a private desk.

As I entered the barracks, all I heard were my echoing footsteps. I was surprised to see I was not alone! Crapped out on a bunk was a sleeping form, with a GI blanket covering it. Dumped on the floor was a seabag.

The faint smell of whiskey hung in the damp, cold, air.

I shook the lump, which responded, "Knock it off, Mac! Leave me alone! Can't a guy get a little shut-eye in this man's Marine Corps?"

A man's head appeared from under the blanket, saying, "Don't forget to wake me up for noon chow. I missed breakfast and I'm starved to death." He sounded to me like he really needed sack time to sleep off a liberty hangover. Secretly, I nicknamed my bunkmate "Lump." We were Baker Company for the time being.

The next two days were spent waiting for more personnel to arrive. We were at loose ends, with no officer to tell us what to do. Bored, I read everything in sight, including faded orders on the squad room bulletin board.

On my third day at Pendleton, I was sitting on my bunk when I heard footsteps echoing through the empty barracks. I looked up, and through the hallway came a cheerful-looking Marine in dress greens. On his arm were the chevrons of a platoon sergeant, a hash mark adorned one sleeve, and combat ribbons decorated his left chest. The "Lump" and I jumped to immediate attention after spotting the sergeant's stripes on his sleeve. Looking straight at us, a smile crossing his lips, the new arrival said quietly and with authority, "At ease, men. How's everything going? I'm Platoon Sergeant John Basilone." He was husky, with genial handsome looks, and his uniform had a comfortable, traveled look. I noticed strands of jet-black, curly hair peeking under his garrison cap, which was set at a cocky angle. While I responded to his greeting, it hit me!

This was some Marine!

As we shook hands and he asked our names and rank, I was awestruck. At seventeen, I was in the presence of a Marine Corps legend. I didn't know what to do or say. Stories and photos had appeared in *Life* and *Collier's* magazines about "Manila John." In the barracks, we flipped through publications with shots of him with beautiful movie stars on both arms and actors like John Garfield crowding around him.

"MANILA JOHN"

"Manila John" Basilone was the first Marine enlisted man to receive the Medal of Honor in World War II, for actions on Guadalcanal. We had heard about *him* in boot camp! This was like meeting a movie star, or a president of the United States!

I noticed my knees were trembling from excitement. I hoped he didn't. My bunkmate revealed later that he had experienced feelings similar to mine.

Our new sergeant asked casually, "How long have you two been here?"

We answered in unison, "Three days."

Noting that we were the only men present, he commented, "Don't worry, other Marines will be arriving in a few days. We're forming the Fifth Division, best one in the Corps."

A living *legend* was going to be in our company. I hoped I was going to be in *his* machine-gun platoon.

As excited as I was, I had the feeling he had other things on his mind. Selecting a sergeant's billet, he disappeared. Left alone in the cavernous squad room, I asked the other Marine, "What do you think of him?"

Like everybody else in the Corps, the "Lump" had heard of John Basilone, but he didn't seem as impressed as I was. He lay on his sack and went to sleep without further comment.

I wondered to myself, *How do you talk to a legend?*

After pondering the question, I reached a conclusion. If you are seventeen and in awe of heroes like Sergeant Basilone, you waited until *they* spoke to you. I never had the courage to ask Basilone directly why he had received the Medal of Honor on the 'Canal. I didn't have to ask. I already knew. All America knew. His story was required reading in every red-blooded household.

John Basilone had been a "dog face" for almost four years before joining what he called "a real man's outfit." He was quoted as once telling his mother, "I'm joining the Marines because the Army isn't tough enough." But in 1936, Basilone figured his best chance for a good start in life was to join the Army, which offered three meals a day, a place to sleep, free clothing, and the princely sum of nineteen-dollars-a-month pay, plus thirty days paid leave! Army recruiting posters promised "adventure, travel to foreign lands, and a chance for advancement." It seemed a good way to escape the confines and limited horizons of a small New Jersey town.

With his mother's blessing he enlisted in the U.S. Army on February 5, 1936, and was sent to basic training. After basic, John was assigned to Company D, 16th Infantry Regiment. He was discharged on May 10, 1937, after serving fifteen months. The reason? "Convenience of the government," a catchphrase for termination of a short-term enlistment. The next day at Fort Jay, New York, he reenlisted in the Army for a three-year hitch. John was elated with this first overseas assignment, the Philippine Islands! Manila, "Pearl of the Orient," was the capital, and peacetime duty in the archipelago was considered "the best duty in the Army."

Garrisoning with Company D, 31st Infantry (Post of Manila), was considered light duty. Stationed in a hospitable country where nearly everyone spoke English, John discovered the ratio of desirable women to men was unequaled by any other duty station. Best of all, in the limited vision of all soldiers Basilone's age, there was no obvious threat of war on the Pacific horizon, and his PFC's salary of twenty-one dollars per month was the equivalent of half a year's pay to native workers. Any soldier with a pocketful of money would make a prize catch with local women. Basilone's coal-black hair, swarthy complexion, and movie-star good looks didn't hurt him a bit either! Added to this combination was his cheerful, boyish charm. He was a remarkable young man.

To enliven the dullness of peacetime Army life, troops played baseball and football and teams competed in intercompany rivalry.

Boxing attracted Basilone. His strong muscular frame and quick hands made him a man to reckon with in the ring. He needed a better name, though. A fighter couldn't box with a plain "vanilla" name like John. "Real boxers need a real slugger's name," his buddies told him. Before his first fight, his coach wrote on the card, " 'Manila John' Basilone." The moniker stuck. Hollywood couldn't have dreamed up a better name. The win–loss record of "Manila John" is forgotten, but from what I'd learned from personal observation, I wouldn't have wanted to meet him as an opponent in the ring or on the battlefield!

When his enlistment ended on September 7, 1938, Basilone took another crack at civilian life. During his hitch, the job market hadn't improved in his hometown of Raritan, so he found work in Reistertown, Maryland, as an installation man for the Philgas company. It was grunt work, but hard times were a way of life across America in 1939.

Anyone reading the newspapers that year knew that war was almost inevitable. Young, experienced soldiers were being courted by the military and there was an impending draft threat. To avoid another tour of duty in the Army, Basilone resigned from the Reserves and joined the Marine Corps in July 1940 at Baltimore, Maryland. With four years of Army time under his belt, John didn't go through a regular Marine boot camp. The Corps recognized his seasoned abilities and sent him to his first billet promptly.

His orders read:

```
Private John Basilone, USMC 287506
Report at once: "No delay in route."
D Company, 1st Battalion, 7th Marine Regi-
    ment, 1st Marine Division
Assigned: Weapons Platoon
Duty: Machine Gunner
```

The 1st Battalion was under the command of Major Lewis B. Puller, and it was Puller who signed Basilone's promotion to sergeant on January 23, 1942, while they were stationed at New River, North Carolina. Both Basilone and "Chesty" Puller would win recognition nine months later defending Henderson Field, Guadalcanal.

How well Basilone and other sergeants taught their men was evidenced by the 3,500 Japanese they killed in the battle of Henderson Field/Lunga Point in the early morning hours of October 25, 1942. Sergeant John Basilone's Medal of Honor citation read: "While the enemy was hammering at the Marines' defensive positions, Sergeant Basilone, in charge of two sections of heavy machine guns, fought valiantly to check the savage and determined assault."

President Franklin Delano Roosevelt, Basilone's commander in chief, personally signed his citation. Witnesses who investigated the results of the night's action during daylight remarked on the gruesome evidence of wholesale slaughter of Japanese soldiers. In front of Basilone's position they counted thirty-eight riddled and mangled enemy bodies and credited the kills to the "fighting sergeant using a .45 and his faithful machine guns." This remarkable feat was accomplished during a night when Basilone was at the same time changing spent machine-gun barrels, clearing jams, and running barefoot for ammo to keep his section's guns spitting death.

At the time of Basilone's heroics, Americans were hungry for heroes after our shattering naval losses at Pearl Harbor and the humiliating loss of seventy thousand men on Bataan and Corregidor in the Philippines. Also, added to the string of depressing defeats by the Japanese, was the loss of our strategic island possessions, Guam and Wake Island. On the home front, our national politicians figured the populace would buy more war bonds if they were urged to do so by celebrities and heroes. When bond sales lagged, clarion calls rang out for fresh heroes, and Sergeant John Basilone was our newest living legend.

In August 1943, Basilone was ordered back to the States from a deserved R&R in Australia to star in a war bond drive. He reluctantly followed orders and tried to fulfill his new assignment. War bond tours were easy duty, but they weren't his favorite kind of activity, no matter how important or patriotic they were. He was a Marine, trained for war, a man used to the discipline and comradeship of the Corps. He *especially* didn't like making speeches begging for money, even in the cause of selling war bonds. But like everyone else in uniform, heroes follow orders in the Marine Corps. He was no exception. At last, though, tired of the high-style living and anxious to get back with the troops, Basilone went to his CO and said, "Sir, I want the fleet." Understanding his sentiments, his CO sped up the cadence of paperwork and "Manila John" was on his way to the new 5th Marine Division and, though he didn't know it yet, an ugly island named Iwo Jima. Happy to be back soldiering, he set to work training us eager young Marines as machine gunners.

GETTING SQUARED AWAY

The next morning, Sergeant Basilone took charge, marching the Lump and me to the battalion mess hall a quarter mile away, three times a day. Because the squad bay was in such sad shape, he also started a cleaning detail.

Little dust balls lay in corners and what looked like the remnants of spiderwebs streaked windowpanes. The whole building was permeated with a damp, musty odor. Pouring liberal amounts of pine oil in mop water, we swabbed the wood deck of our empty barracks.

After approving our initial efforts, Sergeant Basilone told us, "I want this whole place squared away when I get back."

I remember thinking that this drill was a lot like boot camp. "Clean, clean, clean!"

Two full days of "GI-ing" by the Lump and me saw the barracks shipshape enough to satisfy our hero's demands. The Lump eventually discovered he was in the wrong unit, and after all the cleaning we had done together, he was *pissed*! He had GI'd the wrong barracks. I bet he hoped his new quarters were already clean!

For a period of several months, Sergeant Basilone was assigned to B Company's machine-gun platoon as its leader and instructor. We would always claim him afterward as "ours," even after his transfer to C Company, a block away. But that would come later.

The first troops to arrive were from a Paramarine training battalion at Camp Gillespie, the Marine training center for parachute troops.

As I watched them leap off their trucks, their mirror-finished jump boots hit the ground with a solid *thud*. It was apparent to me that they felt they were hot stuff. Paramarines wore their trousers "bloused" and tucked into jump boots that laced above the ankle.

Uncomplimentary comments were made about their new assignment as "regular" Marines. I heard them bitching to one another: "The brass must have their head up their butt to disband *our outfit*."

From their conversation, I could tell they were pissed. Paramarines figured they were an elite outfit and didn't like being thrown in with ordinary Marines. Maybe they thought we would contaminate them with our mediocrity.

The Pacific war had rendered Paramarine forces obsolete because they couldn't jump into the dense jungles. The changing nature of the war required men trained for amphibious assaults. For this kind of fighting, *all* Marines had to be qualified.

A Paramarine named Pfc. George Van Conkelberg bunked next to me. Immediately I nicknamed him "Van." A fellow Californian from Taft, he was quiet for a Marine. Of Dutch ancestry, he was six feet two inches with blond hair worn in a close crew cut. To me he looked like the All-American Marine. There was one physical blemish in his otherwise perfect physique. The back of his head was flat, probably from not being turned often enough as a baby, or was he just a "square head"? He also gambled almost every minute of his off-duty time. For an *ex-paratrooper*, I thought Van was okay.

I met another paratrooper, the man who was to be our section leader, who would later lead us through the gates of hell on Iwo. He was Sergeant Raymond Windle, a redheaded freckle face from Snyder, Oklahoma, and a fellow Okie. (I was born in Tulsa, but raised in California.) Sergeant Windle was serious-minded and a little gruff at times, but he liked me okay. Windle was twenty-four years old, about five feet ten inches tall, almost skinny, and he was always hungry. Some swore that the sergeant had a tapeworm. His demeanor and carriage said "career Marine." The sergeant carried a single red slash trimmed in green on his right sleeve signifying four years in the Marine Corps. What that hash mark meant to me was that we were being led by one of the best, as Windle was already a veteran of the war in the Pacific. He had joined the Corps before 1941 and had seen action with the 2nd Paratrooper Battalion, which made raids on Vella Lavella and Choiseul. He would prove to be an outstanding and dedicated leader of Marines.

As the kid of our outfit, I was in awe of these "older" Marines. Many others, like me, were fresh out of boot camp but were quickly assimilated and absorbed within the ranks of the hardened veterans and elite Paramarines. Strong friendships were forged during the intensive training and daily living together in the months ahead. Some have lasted a lifetime.

LESSONS FROM "THE OLD BREED"

Machine-gun orientation was the first order on our training schedule. We were under the guidance of two of the Corps' best instructors, men with real, practical, on-the-job training: Platoon Sergeant John Basilone and Sergeant Rheal "Biz" Bissonnette. Bissonnette was a gunnery expert and armorer for Baker Company. Also a paratrooper with ten "free falls," he was a bit of an extrovert who was fond of doing one-arm handstands on the rail of the ninety-foot jump tower.

Basilone had earned *his* Ph.D. in machine guns on the 'Canal. Good as "Biz" was, "Manila John" could have taught him a lot about

the Browning machine gun, caliber .30, M1919A4. Among Bissonnette's other talents was his ability to instruct us in the art of jujitsu
and gymnastics. "Biz" taught us how to escape a half-nelson headlock
by relaxing, holding our arms straight, and letting our body go limp.
Once out of the hold, we could reach back and pull the legs out from
underneath our attacker. *Then* by pulling a KA-BAR knife, "Biz"
showed us how to dispatch our assailant.

From Sergeant Bissonnette, we learned the M1919A4 machine
gun was recoil operated, assisted with expanding powder gas; its cyclic
rate of fire, 400 to 550 per minute. (In combat, its usable rate was close
to 150 rounds per minute.) Basilone told us that in a flat trajectory
mode, the rounds would not rise above the height of a man for six
hundred yards, which made it an exceptionally deadly, antipersonnel
weapon. He explained the tripod weighed 14.75 pounds; the weapon
alone weighed 31 pounds. I know the last was true. As an assistant
gunner, I had the "opportunity" to carry my deadly hunk of metal
halfway around the world.

I was totally responsible for the weapon. Sometimes I felt like I
was its mother. I had to carry my regular gear plus the gun wherever
I went. The assistant gunner wore special shoulder pads, which served
to protect his body from bruising and incapacitating injuries. Hours
of marching increased the damned gun's weight almost double—at
least it felt like it!

Other members of the squad would help the assistant gunner for
spells, or he would have had a permanently bent back. Imagine a
twenty-mile hike, in the heat or cold, packing thirty-plus pounds of
solid steel on aching shoulders! You *had* to be tough to be the assistant
gunner. But I was young and strong, and this kind of heavy training
whipped my muscles into what felt like strands of steel. In time, I
could hold my machine gun stiff-armed at right angles to my body
for very short periods of time. Training to be a combat Marine was a
great adventure for me. Still seventeen years old, I was being instructed

by veterans I admired and almost worshipped. I knew I was in exceptionally good company!

Marines came in increasing numbers. Fresh training schedules were posted in the barracks every week, and as we reached our assigned strength, we began unit exercises. One day I ran into a friend from Stockton at the mess hall. Pfc. Tom Piper had driven a delivery truck for Maxwell's Auto Supply, and he often came to the Army supply depot where I worked before joining the Marines. While still a deliveryman he told me, "You won't be seeing me anymore. I've joined the Marines!" Hearing that made waiting for my seventeenth birthday that much harder. Tom was in C Company, 1st Battalion, 27th Marines. In fact, his company barracks were just up the hill from ours! He had been in a paratrooper replacement battalion at Camp Gillespie. It was good to see a friendly face from my hometown. Now I didn't feel so alone, and Tom and I planned to go on liberty together. We would spend two leaves together in Stockton before shipping out. We were destined to go to Iwo together.

By now, the barracks were almost full, and paratroopers were everywhere. The Marine Corps had moved entire battalions into the 5th Division, and we were becoming a serious fighting force.

MY SECTION'S CAST OF CHARACTERS

The ranks of my machine-gun section, like the entire Marine Corps, included a diverse array of individuals from Sergeant Windle on down. There was Corporal Angelos Tremulis, a really streetwise guy with time in the Corps. He was an authentic seagoing Marine who learned the art of open-ocean swimming the hard way—by jumping from the burning deck of the USS *Yorktown*, torpedoed in the Battle of Midway in 1942. Before rescue, he paddled eight hours in the Pacific. Surviving the *Yorktown*, he joined the Paramarines. He was a squad leader, and we felt lucky to have the benefit of his calm, deliberate, and professional leadership; when Tremulis talked of combat perils we listened. Tremulis was of Greek parentage, but no one dared call him "Greek." His hometown was Rockford, Illinois, where his parents operated a flower shop. His sister owned another one in Chicago, and in his reflective moods, he often spoke of going back to the family business after the war. Everyone in Rockford knew about their hero from the *Yorktown* who had manned the 20mm "ack-ack" guns below the flight deck.

Pfc. Bruno "Spike" Mierczwa, of Polish extraction, was from Springfield, Massachusetts. His real name was John Bruno, but we affectionately called him "Spike." I guess that if my name had been Bruno, I would have found myself a nickname, too! Even Spike. A Paramarine, he was particularly pissed that his beloved outfit had been disbanded. The elite status that went with being a paratrooper suited Spike to a tee. He was all of five feet seven inches, but from the way he walked, you might think he was six feet tall. Spike was a perfect physical specimen and he knew it. So did everyone else, because he went without his shirt at every opportunity. His close-cut, curly blond hair and muscular physique gave him the look of a chiseled Greek warrior—even though he was Polish.

Spike's sidekick was Pfc. Loyal Leman, from Cleveland, assistant gunner for the 1st Machine Gun in the second section. "Loyal" was appropriately named; he worshipped the ground Spike walked on and followed him around like an adoring puppy. Loyal was *really* chunky and weighed 175 pounds. At five feet eight inches, he was tough as nails, though, and the ideal assistant gunner.

Pfc. Billy Joe Cawthorn had a baby face and looked like he couldn't be a day over fifteen. Cawthorn came to the Marine Corps from Temple, Texas, and was the first ammo carrier in Tremulis's squad. It was said he still had the original razor blade he had been issued. He stood five feet seven inches and weighed 155 pounds in full uniform—when it was wringing wet. If our "grizzled" Sergeant Windle had a favorite in the platoon, it was Cawthorn. Windle was comparatively "old" at age twenty-four, so I think he felt someone had to look out for our company's baby-faced Marine. As youthful as he appeared, Billy Joe always pulled his share of duty.

Nicknames were sometimes cruel, but everyone in our outfit had one, just like a belly button! Sergeant Windle was "Willkie" or "Windle Willkie," after the Republican presidential candidate Wendell Willkie, who lost to FDR in the 1940 campaign. Pfc. John "Gopher Gus" Henderson was an ammo carrier in Tremulis's squad. He got his handle because of a curious overbite problem. His jaws just didn't match. And, he was a little more portly than the rest of us wiry guys.

There were six of us in my gun squad, all dedicated to the maintenance and operation of one machine gun. Our squad leader was an ex-paratrooper, Corporal William Whaley, from Tennessee. I liked this soft-spoken man right away. Whaley was twenty years old and had been in the Corps for two years.

Another squad mate soon became my best friend, Pfc. Clifford "Steve" Evanson, from Spokane, Washington. For whatever reason, he chose to call himself "Steve." A little over six feet tall, he was blond, good-looking, and as strong as an ox. He said he was seventeen, the same age as me. Steve was an "ammo humper" (Marine-speak for "ammunition carrier").

Pfc. Carl "Tex" Thompson, from Omaha, Nebraska, was the second ammo carrier in my squad. Don't ask me where he got that nickname. Maybe he thought girls would like a Marine named "Tex" instead of "Carl." Maybe it should have been "Cornhusker." Tex was another good-looking Marine and wore a pencil-thin moustache after the fashion of Clark Gable.

Another ammo humper, Pfc. Charles "Pops" Whitcomb, was from Chattanooga, Tennessee. At age twenty-eight, he was old for an enlisted man. "Pops" was a nickname attached to any guy over twenty-five. He wore his wavy blond hair in a marcel-wave style, like a thick comb-over. I knew I *had* to like him because our first and middle names were the same! The difference in our ages, though, prevented us from being close buddies. Pops barely tolerated me because he thought I was a screwup. "You'll be in, lookin' out of, Leavenworth if you keep screwing around," he warned me. I think he had it in for me. We were both PFCs, but the ten-year difference in our ages and my two months' seniority in the Corps irked him. Seniority, though, worked both ways. When Van was assigned as the first machine gunner in my squad, I was assigned as his assistant gunner, partly because he outranked me and had more time in the Corps even though he was younger than me.

When the company assignments were posted, the roster of the second section, machine-gun platoon, read:

Sergeant Raymond R. Windle: .... section leader

1ST SQUAD

Corporal Angelo Tremulis: .... squad leader
Pfc. Bruno "Spike" Mierczwa: .... first gunner
Pfc. Loyal Leman: .... assistant gunner
Pfc. Billy Joe Cawthorn: .... first ammo carrier
Pfc. John "Gopher Gus" Henderson: .... second ammo carrier

2ND SQUAD

Corporal William Whaley: .... squad leader
Pfc. George Van Conkelberg: .... first gunner
Pfc. Chuck Tatum: .... assistant gunner
Pfc. Clifford "Steve" Evanson: .... first ammo carrier
Pfc. Carl "Tex" Thompson: .... second ammo carrier
Pfc. Charles "Pops" Whitcomb: .... third ammo carrier

We still needed men to fill out our section, the rest of the machine-gun platoon, and the company overall. As I came to know others in my platoon, I realized we had quite a cast of characters there as well.

Pfc. John Luman was the *cleanest* man in the platoon. He was also a paratrooper; as such, his jump boots didn't just shine, they *glistened*, and his dungarees were tailored to fit like a glove. He kept his hair combed at all times and spent extra time on his physical upkeep in the "head" (Marine-speak for "toilet"). Given the chance, he might take three showers a day. He was the original Mr. Clean. My nickname for Luman was "Slick." He didn't know it; it was my secret. Tidy and clean as he was, Mother Nature played a dirty trick on Luman. He had a rather large nose and was sometimes called "Durante" (behind his back, of course!) after the famous comedian Jimmy Durante. We filled out a form called "My Outfit," and most of us put down a nickname. Luman wrote "Le Nose" after his name.

Pfc. Edward J. Tucker from the Motor City—Detroit, Michigan—was the most likeable paratrooper in the platoon. He had a natural friendliness and sincerity and we became good friends. Tucker was twenty-one but acted older. We shared confidences. He was serious-minded and once told me quietly, "I won't make it back if we go into battle." Startled, I said, "Bullshit, Tucker! Don't talk like that." Smiling, he replied. "Wait and see, Tatum, wait and see." Tucker had a sixth sense.

Another ammo humper, Pfc. Theron W. Oriel, from Wilkes-Barre, Pennsylvania, had really light blond hair, almost albino white, which he wore in a crew cut. His hair stood out like toothpicks. It was rumored that Oriel still had the first cake of soap received at boot camp because he did not shower very often. He was always getting into trouble with me, and our company's gunnery sergeant, Stanley Kavato, kept a sharp eye on both of us. Kavato didn't like Oriel . . . or me . . . and for what he felt were good reasons! Kavato had two nicknames: "Blackie" and "Old Black Joe." He was Italian and had a very dark complexion. His training in the National Guard might have been a factor in making him a gunnery sergeant without combat experience. Kavato was a weapons expert and a "chickenshit DI" transferred to us from Parris Island.

Sergeant George Lutchkus was like Sergeant Windle, a section leader and ex-paratrooper. He fought the Japanese in the Solomons and on the 'Canal. A soft-spoken man, he carried himself with a confidence only combat experience brings to a soldier. Never one to raise his voice, he commanded respect with phrases like "Hey, Sonny! Listen up! This advice might save your life!" When *he* spoke we listened, and listened good. As a professional soldier, he never discussed the Silver Star he had been awarded during the Solomons campaign. I knew he had one because one day I saw his blouse lying on the bunk when he was getting ready for liberty. There were two rows of ribbons pinned above his upper left-hand pocket. One was red, white, and blue—the Silver Star. I never had the courage to ask him directly how he had received it. However, I finally got the chance to find out. One day, when a "take-five" break message came down the line on a training exercise, I slipped off my pack and, sitting next to Sergeant Windle, asked how Lutchkus won his Silver Star.

When Windle started his explanation, a group quickly formed. He related to us that Lutchkus, then a corporal, was a member of Headquarters Company, 1st Parachute Battalion, and was attached to the 1st Marine Division at Guadalcanal. During the fighting against the Japs' best troops on the 'Canal, on September 13, 1942, he helped kick the crap out of the enemy during a prolonged firefight. Corporal Lutchkus returned fire with great devastation, but accurate Jap gunners' bullets thinned the ranks of his squad. In the absence of a corpsman, the wounded were untended. Though under heavy hostile fire, Lutchkus repeatedly removed wounded men from the battle area, returning each time with ammo, which enabled his squad to continue the firefight.

When an assault by 1,200 screaming Japanese troops seemed to turn the tide of battle against the weary Marines, Lutchkus rallied his men with shouts of encouragement. His conduct was an inspiration to the exhausted troops, and his squad prevailed against the human-wave tactics used by the Sons of Nippon. The action extended through the night because of a second attack. Corporal Lutchkus continued to lead his men until he was wounded and evacuated. Sergeant Windle told us Lutchkus's actions had "saved the bacon." I had always respected Sergeant Lutchkus, but now I added him to my private list of 'Canal heroes in Baker Company.

Having never been in combat before, our platoon leader, Lieutenant Dreger, was thankful for veteran NCOs like Windle and Lutchkus. Someone said Dreger had barely made it out of Officer Candidate School in Quantico. The word was he was a "hot-shot" college basketball player. He was also a champion swimmer. Tall, almost skinny, he had a sharp-looking face with a large Roman nose and eyes that could look right through you. Now that I was in a "line company," I started to see lieutenants in a fresh light. In boot camp, I'd been awed by their exalted, demigod status, so I didn't know what to expect from Dreger. I didn't know why they needed second lieutenants in the first place; sergeants ran everything in the Marine Corps. But he seemed to be an all right kind of guy.

One day in the barracks, Dreger was holding school on machine guns. Thinking I wasn't paying attention, he snapped, "Tatum! Explain flat trajectory fire!"

Standing at attention, I answered from the book: "Flat trajectory fire is where the bullets of a machine gun won't rise above the height of a man for six hundred yards, sir!"

"Okay! Sit down, Tatum!"

SNAPPING IN

The training at Camp Pendleton was on a full-time, around-the-clock schedule. The war had continued to spread all over the globe, and there was no doubt we were being prepared for mortal combat in the near future.

Our preparation included a full spectrum of military snapping in as we polished our individual and collective skills of war. As the Corps fought an unrestricted war, hard lessons had been learned. Guadalcanal, Bougainville, and Tarawa had been "textbooks" on the art of amphibious attacks and the annihilation of enemy forces.

Our training employed new tactics, which ensured that old mistakes wouldn't be repeated and built on the successes our leaders had achieved. Our training had many facets. Since we were an amphibious fighting force, we had to prove we could swim by passing a rigorous test in the regimental pool and underwent "abandon ship" drills.

We were bound to pass.

All we did was jump from a twenty-five-foot wall simulating the hull of a ship while observing the following instructions:

1. Hold your nose with one hand.
2. Hold your testicles with the other.
3. Don't worry! Gravity will take care of the descent.

One man was overwhelmed by acrophobia and refused all instructions and inducements to jump, until Colonel Butler mounted the platform.

Now it was only the reluctant Marine and the colonel of the 1st Battalion on the tower platform. All eyes of B Company were focused on the pair. Too far away to hear their conversation, 250 anxious men watched the pair leap into space.

Enthusiastic applause broke out when they emerged from the

foaming water. I don't know the others' reactions, but I personally respected our colonel's "leading by example" style of leadership.

FATAL FLAWS AND DELAYED PLANS

In February 1944, as our brand-new 5th Division accelerated its combat-ready development, a minuscule island named Iwo Jima, seven hundred miles from the Japanese mainland, suddenly loomed large on maps of Hideki Tojo's wartime planners.

The American island-hopping strategy, adopted in 1942, was paying big dividends for our troops. We had conquered and recaptured vast tracts of previously held Japanese strongholds in the Pacific.

Islands like Rabaul and Truk were ignored as Americans leapfrogged onto the other, more important targets. The policy of isolating and cutting off from resupply whole garrisons with thousands of enemy troops saved lives and allowed the United States to bring larger forces to bear against islands selected for assault.

As 1944 dawned, our forces at times seemed to be racing across the Pacific toward Tokyo. As part of the grand strategy approved by President Franklin Delano Roosevelt and the Joint Chiefs of Staff (JCS) on October 3, 1944, General Douglas MacArthur and Admiral Chester Nimitz were ordered to begin preliminary planning to occupy one or more islands in the Bonin and Volcano Islands Group.

Target date: January 20, 1945.

Attempting to stall the steady advance of U.S. forces and deny American access to the Bonins, Japan began extensive military construction and deep subterranean fortifications on Iwo Jima.

For the first time in the war, the strategic importance of the Volcano Islands, and especially of Iwo Jima, became apparent to both sides. However, it seems to have been less obvious to the JCS in Washington than to the strategic planners in Tokyo.

As of September 1944, the JCS were still debating, "What island or islands are next?" Indecision in not targeting Iwo Jima sooner was a tragic flaw, which would cost thousands of American lives in February–March 1945, when the island was finally invaded *thirty days* behind the original JCS timetable.

Base theaters were used for entertainment and instruction in the arts of warfare. On one occasion, to our surprise, we watched a film about a mysterious Japanese island with a funny name, "Iwo Jima." No one attached any importance to this film, or to Iwo Jima as a potential invasion target for the 5th Division, and both were soon forgotten.

Had Iwo been assaulted shortly after the capture of the Marianas in August 1944, when fewer than five thousand Japanese troops were garrisoned there, it might have been the three-day campaign we were promised in our final training sessions aboard ship in January–February 1945.

OUR DIVISION RECEIVES ITS COLORS

A new division's inauguration is a major military event. Presentation of the regimental colors to each of the three regiments, the 26th, 27th, and 28th, was the highlight of our local social season.

Receiving the regimental flag is a one-time-only event in the history of a regiment, and ours proved to be a *big* one. It was a symbolic object, and the embodiment of the spirit and dedication of the men who served under it.

Its preservation from capture and peril was considered a sacred duty by all members of a regiment. This attitude was also true of our enemies. On Iwo Jima, when faced with certain annihilation, Japanese regimental officers would burn their colors rather than let them be soiled by capture.

The first announcement of our impending ceremony was made

on the squad room bulletin board: "Regimental Colors Ceremony will be held on the main parade ground. Uniform of the day will be khakis, field scarves, cartridge belts, helmets, and personal weapons." *All* the big brass we knew about would be there.

Major General Rockey, commanding general, 5th Marine Division, headed up the reviewing stand with the 27th Marine Regiment's officers' cadre in the second echelon of brass.

As we approached the field, we heard the stirring "shipping-over" music Marine bands are famous for echoing across the assembly area.

In battalion formation, we marched past in review then stood at attention while the presentation ceremony took place. We listened to speeches before the new colors were unfurled. I was proud to be a Marine and a member of the 27th Regiment. My pride swelled even more when I saw our new regimental colors beside the star-spangled banner of the United States drifting in a light breeze that was sweeping across the tarmac. It was a great day to be an American.

RKO Pictures in Hollywood sent two of their stars, Pat O'Brien and Ann Blyth. Miss Blyth was voted mascot of the 27th Marines and posed for pictures with the generals, which were widely published.

The best part of the whole affair for those in the ranks was "holiday routine," which meant only essential duties were performed for the rest of the afternoon. To further honor the event, our cooks came up with a special printed menu and fancy chow.

Officially, we were now an authentic regiment!

CHAPTER SIX

Our Social Calendar

Females, young and attractive, or unattractive, were a rare sight in Oceanside. Wise parents sent their eligible daughters off to distant schools, to live with maiden aunts, or kept them under tight lock and key.

All work and no play would make us dull Marines, and the Corps knew this, so to alleviate boredom, there were organized sporting activities—baseball, football, and basketball all received due attention.

Camp Pendleton had several movie theaters, a PX (Marine-speak for the nonprofit post exchange), laundry, and dry cleaners. The cleaners were important to us. Not doing our own laundry by hand left us more time for recreation. A hand-ironed and starched shirt was as low as ten cents at the PX.

The post United Service Organization (USO) was a hugely popular place, even though it was no "stage-door canteen" with eager movie starlets to dance with—and no mom's hot apple pie. With twenty-five thousand "gyrenes," on base it was a tough ticket. There was no admission charge, but it seemed like every time we had an opportunity to go, we couldn't force our way in.

It was our suspicion that post troops (Marine speak for "permanent personnel") spent a lot of time there looking for girls and they got to monopolize what few volunteer female hostesses were at the USO. Our chances to dance with one? Slim to none!

SMOKES

The post exchange was a godsend to cash-starved Marines like me. Brand-name cigarettes, Tailor-Mades, were five cents a pack. At prices like this, money wasn't a deterrent to chain smoking.

But some cheapskates still tried bumming smokes instead of buying their own. Impatient for a smoke, I once tried to bum one myself and was informed, "I'm not your mother, and don't intend to support your smoking habits. I don't care if you die of a nicotine fit! Semper Fi, Mac!"*

In the early forties, we were encouraged to engage in the nasty habit by radio stars, magazines, newspapers, and film actors like Ronald Reagan.

There were no warning labels, and only a few guys suggested that smoking might be bad or even dangerous. It was completely socially acceptable. I started smoking when I was eighteen, in the Marines.

Sometimes people would say to me, "Give me a smoke." When I replied, "I don't smoke," guys would be shocked. "You don't smoke?" was usually the incredulous response. Seeking social acceptance, I was soon puffing away with the best of them.

In the Marine Corps, it was an accepted fact that most men would light one up at any opportunity. In the barracks, we could smoke whenever an officer said, "Smoking lamp is lit."

They were still called "coffin nails," but no one took this seriously. Cardsharps!

---

* Semper Fi had a variety of meanings. It might mean, "okay," one time or, used sarcastically, it had numerous applications. In my case, it meant, "I've got mine, you get yours!"

With no TV, little radio, crowded movie theaters, a jammed USO, and no library, we had few ways to entertain ourselves; but when left alone, Marines can provide their own amusements. The main boredom killer was gambling, which created its own excitement. There was no such thing as a dull poker game when a semipro, like my bunkmate Van, was involved. The Marine Corps didn't condone gambling, but our officers knew bored soldiers would do it every chance they got, so savvy leaders looked the other way when cards or dice were broken out. I never saw officers stop a card game. I guess they figured gambling was good for their men's morale!

One of the most colorful Marines I met at Camp Pendleton was Corporal Guy Brookshire of Lufkin, Texas. Brookshire led a squad (3rd) like Whaley (2nd) and Tremulis (1st). Brookshire also operated what I called the "First National Bank of Brookshire." He lent money with interest rates exceeding the usury laws of any state. He would lend two dollars and get three back on payday. Chicago loan sharks offered better deals.

Brookshire always said, "Don't borrow if you don't want to pay it back." His collection rate was 100 percent. No one defaulted on the banker from Lufkin, Texas. On payday he stood at the head of the line with his little black book and his hand out. As he checked each man's name off the list, he would declare him eligible to borrow again.

Brookshire was considered an "old salt," a man with time in the Corps. He had a hash mark on the left sleeve of his blouse, indicating that he had served four years in the Marines. Our "banker" had seen combat with the 2nd Paramarines in the Solomon Islands, at Vella Lavella, and at Choiseul. Brookshire loved to gamble, and would bet on *anything*. His steely stare bluffed many opponents out of a winning pot.

Corporal Brookshire and Van were bosom companions, linked together by their lust for gambling. They spent many free hours in the barracks beating unlucky and conned Marines out of their money. When people were broke, matchsticks were used. A win at poker meant extra liberty money; on the other hand, a loss usually resulted in forgoing liberty to stay in the barracks and read or wash clothes. The games of choice were dice and poker. As soon as we got paid, Van would shuffle cards and ask if anyone wanted to play. I didn't know the fine skills of poker, and what I did know I had learned on a "pay-as-you-lose" basis.

Feeling lucky after payday, I decided to join one of Van's well-advertised games, to be played on my lower bunk, Corporal Brookshire presiding. Producing a deck of cards missing the queen of hearts, our corporal looked for another deck without success. For a moment it looked like the game would be canceled. But Van was not to be denied and came up with the idea of using the six of spades as a substitute. A hastily organized rules committee agreed that the six of spades would be used as normal in straights, pairs, and flushes, or we could substitute it for the queen of hearts, but only when it would improve a hand.

The game was seven-card stud. As it got under way, the winnings went back and forth. Soon I began to lose and was down to five dollars. Brookshire was dealing, and everyone playing acted as if they had a good hand. I had two queens in the hole and a six of spades showing as my first three cards. Van showed a jack of hearts. Our betting accelerated and the pot grew rapidly with each fresh raise. Every player thought he had something good. I drew a seven of spades and Van followed with another jack. With my liquid funds totaling less than five bucks, I knew I would definitely not be going on liberty if I lost this hand. On the next round I drew an eight of clubs and Van showed a third jack. Van bet again, and everyone dropped out except me. Brookshire continued to deal. Van couldn't believe I was still in the game, since my last draw was a five of diamonds. Van was dealt a fourth jack.

At that moment I realized he had forgotten that the six of spades was a substitute for the queen of hearts. He was figuring the best I had was a small straight.

He showed four jacks, as Brookshire dealt my last card, facedown.

Payday! It was the third queen!

Nevertheless, Van reached for the pot.

"Wait a minute, Van," I said. "Hold it right there!"

"Screw you, Tatum! The pot's mine! You don't know shit about playing poker. I have four jacks. You have three queens and need five cards to make a straight."

In a calm voice, Brookshire replied, "No, Van, Tatum is right. He has four queens. Remember, the six of spades doubles for the queen of hearts."

Van was stunned. He realized Brookshire was right.

When I reached across the bunk for the big stack of money, Van flipped out. He had just lost his entire month's pay! Throwing his cards down, he grabbed mine and ripped them to shreds, then took the rest of the deck and threw it all over the squad bay.

As he angrily departed, his final over-the-shoulder comment was, "Stupid amateurs shouldn't be allowed to play poker!"

On all other matters, Van and I maintained a good relationship; however, he *never* invited me to join another card game.

L.A. LIBERTY

Liberty was a valued commodity for Marines of the 5th Division. It was freedom measured in hours, days, or, in some cases, an entire weekend. With my poker winnings of forty-one dollars from Van and Brookshire, I had something to look forward to besides sightseeing and killing time off base.

I stayed in Friday night, with the idea of getting an early start Saturday. I didn't have to be back until roll call on Monday. So with forty-one bucks burning a hole in my pocket and no clear idea of where to spend it, I boarded a truck with other Marines going to

Oceanside. There wasn't much to do in town, but it was close by, and held a slight promise of entertainment.

I had become a creature of habit, and despite my new wealth, I didn't know what in the hell I was going to do. Just as I was climbing onto the truck, Corporal Frank Pospical, one of the Paramarines who had been with us from the start, called out, "Tatum, hold up a minute!" I turned, gave him a hand, and asked where he was headed.

"L.A., Tatum. Pershing Square in L.A. It's the place to go; why don't you go with me? We'll catch a ride from town."

It was obvious that Oceanside was already jam-packed with Marines, so I was open to suggestions.

We walked to Highway 101 and found wall-to-wall Marines also trying to hitch a ride. The line extended for two blocks. "It's going to be hell catching a ride here, Tatum. Follow me," Pospical said.

We strode past the line of Marines stretching north toward L.A. As soon as we had hiked past the end of the column and were well out of town, Pospical stopped and started thumbing. "We'll catch a ride sure as hell, Tatum," he reassured me.

I was skeptical and said so, but he was not the least bit discouraged. Soon a 1940 Buick sedan passed and suddenly braked to a halt, its rear tires grabbing and skidding in the gravel.

We ran quickly to the car and noticed that an older man was the passenger, and a young, attractive teenage girl was the driver. She offered us a ride, saying they were going to L.A.

Once we were inside, the man introduced himself. "I'm Mr. Weiss and my daughter's name is Ruth Weiss."

Our benefactor was a Jewish man in the ladies' garment business and was making uniforms for WAVES (a division of women in the U.S. Navy). His car displayed a C-ration gasoline sticker, which indicated the owner was in vital war production. Mr. Weiss said they lived in Beverly Hills.

I engaged Ruth in conversation by asking questions like "Where do you go to school? Do you like school?" I sat behind her in the backseat and noticed her looking at me in the rearview mirror. The wind through the vent window carried the smell of her perfume back to me, mingled with the smell of the Buick's silky mohair upholstery.

By peering to one side of Ruth's shoulder, I could see we were going forty-five miles per hour, the wartime speed limit. She was handling the large car nicely and was obviously a skilled driver.

I asked, "Do you drive much?"

She replied, "I travel with Father a lot and do most of the driving." Then she asked, "Where are you staying?"

Pospical answered, "At the Pershing Hotel."

Mr. Weiss asked, "Do you have plans for Sunday?"

We didn't. He offered to pick us up for Sunday dinner. We both jumped at the offer. In 1944, having servicemen for dinner was considered patriotic, and Mr. Weiss was *very* patriotic.

Plans were made to pick us up at the Pershing Hotel on Sunday.

Pospical and I checked in to the hotel, which was across from Pershing Square, an easy-to-find place to meet buddies. The park had kind of a run-down look, with lots of old men who had taken up residence on park benches.

We immediately ran into a bunch of our fellow B Company Marines. They were looking for a room, so we offered to share ours. With five guys using the place, our whole bill would come to twenty-five dollars, not a bad deal for wartime L.A.!

The Pershing was a favorite Marine hangout. Girls who frequented the bar were considered to be of the highest quality, so it was with great expectations that we began a night of drinking.

I was under the legal drinking age, but no one asked for my identification and I ordered freely from the bar. The ladies, I noticed, seemed to be meeting guys by prearrangement. As the hours passed, it was apparent that Pospical and I were going to draw blanks for the night.

Before midnight, we decided to turn in.

Rising bright and early, we shined our shoes and generally attempted to sharpen our appearance for our Sunday dinner. Mr. Weiss arrived exactly as scheduled with Ruth, who had thoughtfully brought a girlfriend named Marion.

Both girls were attractive. Ruth had coal-black hair and an ivory complexion; Marion was blond, tanned, and very well built. Both ladies had paid special attention to their grooming and we felt flattered. I thought Ruth was a little on the plump side, but she had a wonderful personality.

Pospical and I weren't shy, but we didn't know how to react to our new friends and their wonderful generosity, which made the drive to Beverly Hills a quiet one.

When we arrived at the Weiss home, Pospical and I were impressed. It was a mansion. We were greeted by a butler with an English accent who led us to a formal living room. He introduced us to the lady of the house, Mrs. Weiss, who offered a diamond-studded hand in greeting. The house was majestic, with a pool large enough to float one of our amtracs.

Mrs. Weiss, with Ruth and Marion following, led us into a game room, where we politely listened to classical music. When her mother left, Ruth produced several pop records that were perfect for dancing. Her taste in music and mine coincided perfectly.

The first record she played was Glenn Miller's "Juke Box Saturday Night," followed by other current hits: Glenn Miller's "Tuxedo Junction," "Take the A Train," and "Sunrise Serenade."

I was as awkward at dancing as I was at marching, but managed not to step on Ruth's toes, which I figured was the main danger in dancing. Pospical, however, was a real Fred Astaire, and kept Marion in motion as the records played on. We were informed by the butler that dinner was served long before we were through enjoying the music and one another.

The repast we enjoyed was a *real* change from Marine chow. The menu included consommé of asparagus and roast lamb. Pospical thought I was being too big a "chow hound" and let me know by kicking me under the table. However, I made a huge hit with Ruth's mother, despite the corporal's concerns.

I particularly made a big deal about the dessert, which she must have helped prepare. When asked if I wanted seconds, I said, "Yes!" It was a yummy chocolate mousse.

After dinner, we continued to engage in small talk with the family until Mr. Weiss announced that he was going to take us to the Museum of Natural History.

We piled into the family Buick again. Pospical was riding in front with our host while I climbed in the rear seat with the girls—a thorn between two roses!

This type of liberty certainly didn't fit the image of a fighting Marine ashore in L.A.! My vision of scoring with barroom belles at the Pershing Hotel evaporated in the close proximity of Ruth and Marion.

Ruth and I hung back when we reached the museum and talked teenage stuff. She wanted to know, "Do you have a girlfriend in Stockton?" (No.) "Do you enjoy being a Marine?" (Yes!) "Are you afraid of going into combat?" (No . . . Hell, YES!) "What was the last movie you saw?" (I couldn't tell her it was a Navy medical film on the perils of venereal disease, so I said it was "a Navy movie with doctors.")

Walking slowly, we held hands until we got near her father, then I let go. I was surprised when she took my hand back.

Ruth told me she was eighteen, so I lied and said I was almost twenty. The truth was, both of us were seventeen. I saw with satisfaction that Pospical and his girl were holding hands, too.

By two-thirty in the afternoon, we were all about as cozy as we could get. Perhaps noticing this, Mr. Weiss asked, "How will you get back to Oceanside?"

We answered in unison, "Hitchhike."

He wouldn't listen to our haphazard plan and insisted on driving us back.

On the way we would all take in a malt shop! The place selected was once fashionable, but now looked outdated. I ordered a chocolate malt, Pospical had a vanilla flavor, the girls asked for Cokes, and Mr. Weiss selected coffee.

Our drinks were served on a metal Coca-Cola tray by a girl in a white, smocklike outfit, wearing a hairnet.

In the tradition of American ice-cream parlors, there was a long mirror behind the counter. We sat on old-time, twisted wrought-iron chairs with matching tables painted white.

The drive back to Pendleton gave us time to enjoy the fresh perfumed smell of female company and the homey friendliness offered by our new friends.

Despite the wartime speed limit of only forty-five miles per hour, we were back at the Pendleton gate too soon. We thanked Ruth's father for his hospitality and shook hands at the car. Our dates asked to walk to the gate with us to say good-bye. Ruth gave me a long, warm kiss, followed by a peck on the cheek, and told me, "Be careful! Don't get hurt!" We promised to write each other.

From the corner of my eye, I could see Pospical and his girl going through the same routine. Our dates returned to the car and waved.

Back in the barracks, we kept our dates a secret, since they couldn't be compared to the wild tales of love and conquest told by our friends. I sure hoped the other guys used condoms, as recommended by the Navy medical films, with *their* girlfriends. Corporal Pospical and I still had ours tucked safely in our wallets.

OCEANSIDE, CALIFORNIA

In 1944, Oceanside, California, was a small town located along picturesque Highway 101, just outside the guarded and patrolled fences of Camp Pendleton. In the opinion of "seasoned" marines like myself, Oceanside was a second-rate liberty town, but it probably wasn't the town's fault. With a full Marine division and its training and support troops numbering more than thirty thousand next door, the little community had become a *Marine town*—like it or not!

Because of our wartime training, Oceanside's merchants experienced a *big* increase in their cash bank deposits; it was obvious that the Depression was rapidly fading in this part of California!

Two restaurants I knew of had Marines queued up for hours at peak times. To attend a movie theater, troops stood in lines to buy tickets, then stood in crowded aisles to see Hollywood's latest flicks. There were never enough seats—even for bad films. And in our opinion, there was no such thing as a bad movie.

Civilian "slop chutes" (Marine-speak for "beer joints") had Marines three deep at the bars ready to gulp down any alcoholic libation as fast as it could be mixed and poured. Beer, 3.2 percent alcohol rating, was top of the list with Marines, as its low cost matched the even lower wages we were paid.

However cheap the brew was, it was one "old boy" from Texas who said, "I've drank sody-pop with more steam than Marine beer!" We had to consume a lot of "suds" to get drunk and it still cost the same as real beer, even though they added more water!

It was hard to be a big spender on the thirty-seven bucks I had left each month. I often had the feeling most merchants wanted us to spend our money as fast as possible and get the hell back to the base!

The dry cleaners had a logjam of Marines standing in their skivvies, waiting to pay extra for a five-minute "press job" on their dress greens before hitting the road to the *main* liberty towns, Diego or Hollywood.

A personal favorite in Hollywood was Slapsy Maxie's, which featured racy burlesque skits that the audience viewed from tiny tables. These were used so more patrons could be jammed into the already overcrowded structure. With a cover charge of one dollar, Maxie's was "high-priced" entertainment for Marines like me!

I went with Pfc. Burnhart and Corporal Chergo, two Paramarines who had recently returned from the grueling Choiseul operation in the South Pacific. I will always hold them responsible for leading me astray! They were "older men," at twenty and twenty-one, respectively. I was seventeen, so my worldly companions gave me the courage to fake my way past the suspicious bouncer.

Places like Maxie's were where the real liberty action could be found, and the ratio of Marines to girls was more favorable than elsewhere. Females, young and attractive, or even unattractive, for that matter, were a rare sight in Oceanside. Wise parents sent their eligible daughters off to distant schools, to live with maiden aunts, or kept them under tight lock and key.

With thirty thousand Marines next door, most mothers figured they would have less to worry about if Attila and his Huns had moved into their previously sheltered neighborhood.

The rare, good-looking females we did see in Oceanside were married to officers or going with post troops. I wasn't mad about this deplorable situation, but I was jealous of their good fortune.

CHAPTER SEVEN

Back to the Grind

During a marching break one hot afternoon, a Marine remarked, "Screw all the training. I'm sick and tired of all this pussyfooting around. I want to get overseas and slap me a Jap!"

At the end of each brief liberty we always enjoyed the yoke of more training. Our earliest amphibious training was conducted on Ocean-side beaches and nearby San Clemente Island. We spent long, hard days learning that the Corps' famous slogan "soldiers of the sea" was meant literally.

To become one required torturous days under a hot Southern California sun while struggling in an angry surf. Days turned into weeks as we learned our new trade: how to launch cumbersome, eight-man rubber rafts in rough surf; how to climb cargo netting with full packs and weapons, the skills needed to embark, or disembark, into LCVPs (Marine-speak for "landing craft vehicular personnel").

If someone fell out of a boat, as we often did, he was in for an "ass-end-over-teakettle" ride. The Pacific's strong undertow could easily drag a large man helplessly along the ocean's bottom and toss him like a cork. Corpsmen were kept busy patching up unlucky men who took the underwater route back to shore!

Next was deep-water or open-ocean swimming. To learn this technique hands-on, we were ferried to a patch of open water on a rubber raft and told bluntly by Sergeant Windle, "Okay, you knuckleheads, try and make it to shore."

"Swimming?"

"Sure, unless you can walk on water!"

Lifeguards stood by—just in case.

Ocean training was very important to me. I distinctly remembered Corporal Tremulis telling about his eight-hour swimming ordeal in the Pacific after the USS *Yorktown* went down.

Countless simulated landings from LCVPs were top priority, and we knew why: Many of the bloodiest amphibious assaults made by Marines on the road to final victory used these reliable wooden workhorses. Probably we would, too.

Still, it wasn't all work and no fun during our maneuvers. We were bivouacked on one of California's finest beaches for days, getting paid to enjoy the ocean and sun.

California's golden sun was great for most of us, but one rifleman with a light complexion gave in to the temptation to get a suntan and overdid it. He received a serious sunburn and his recovery required missing important training sessions.

For punishment, the Corps docked him five days' pay—for misconduct!

His crime? *Abuse of government property!*

Training, training, and more training was changing us from commingled odds and ends of Marine Raiders, paratroopers, and other outfits into the semblance of a fighting unit. We were learning to respect and count on one another.

We did a lot of marching with full field packs to toughen us up. The first day we went on a twenty-mile hike, I learned what it meant to be a "foot soldier" when I inspected the large blisters on my heels.

KNOW YOUR ENEMY

Unleashing unrestricted mayhem against fellow humans was contrary to everything I had been taught by my parents and Sunday school teachers, but I was forced to justify the decision to be a Marine and learn to kill Japs.

My rationale at seventeen years of age was simple. I felt it was my first duty to protect my country and family from Japanese aggression. I would trust God to deal with the religious part of my internal conflicts. I felt that was *His* job! I also adopted a fatalistic approach. If the training we endured didn't kill us, the enemy would.

During a marching break one hot afternoon, a Marine remarked, "Screw all the training. I'm sick and tired of all this pussy-footing around. I want to get overseas and slap me a Jap!"

This remark was made in the presence of Sergeant George Lutchkus, who immediately cut him off, saying: "Hold on, Sonny! Let me tell *all of you* a thing or two about the Japanese soldier! Number one, he is not the caricature you see in newspapers with bombsight glasses and buckteeth. The average Japanese soldier has five or more years of combat experience. Their Army doesn't have a 'boot division' like ours. Don't forget, the Japs have already conquered half the nations in Asia. Remember Pearl Harbor? Not only are they better trained than you are right now, many are old hands at combat fighting and have a strict military code they live and die by called Bushido. Literally translated it means 'way of the warrior.' With their code, combined with their pledge to die for Emperor Hirohito, who they consider God, they will die before surrendering.

"Jap soldiers are well equipped and are experts with their weapons. They are trained to endure hardships, which would have most of you guys writing your congressman. I don't like Japs, but I respect them as fellow soldiers. I learned my respect the *hard way* on Guadalcanal.

"Japs are the world's best snipers, experts at the art of camouflage, and get by on a diet of fish heads and rice. They will never surrender and will commit hari-kari rather than be taken prisoner.

"Heck, they don't have corpsmen; if they are wounded, they are considered *damaged goods*. So, Sonny, mull all that over, and don't ever let me hear you complain about your training again. There will be a time when your life will depend on what you learn in the days ahead."

There was a new degree of seriousness in B Company from that speech forward! We started to worry a little about what fighting the Japanese would be like.

SNAKE IN THE GRASS!

Camp Pendleton was the ideal place to train Marines for combat. It had location, weather, terrain, and seemed to cover half of Southern California; plus it was near the Pacific Ocean, so we could learn water-borne aspects of our trade. It did, however, have one serious drawback: Pendleton was home to a million or so rattlesnakes, and they didn't like sharing their habitat with a bunch of Marines. When on field maneuvers, we had to watch our step lest we disturb one of the critters. At night, rattlers would seek the warmth of men sleeping on the ground by crawling alongside our bedding. Sergeant Windle didn't like snakes. No! Let me say he hated snakes, then Japs, in that order.

One day while on a field march through Pendleton's rolling hills, I came across a small rattlesnake. It had been run over by a truck, but was still in good condition, just dead. I placed it in my pack for a joke I wanted to play later. That night, after Windle had gone to sleep, I took the snake and coiled it up, lifelike, in front of his pup tent and placed a twig under its head to prop it up.

Next morning, I was awakened by sounds of cussing and someone beating the earth with a trench tool. As Steve and I peeked out of our tent, I could see one mad, redheaded Okie pulverizing one small rattlesnake to a pulp.

Man! *Was he excited!* He was still cussing the snake as he wiped its remains off his shovel blade. Steve and I immediately closed our tent flap, but Van, who was already up and about, saw it all and told us how pissed Windle was.

Van said our "mad Okie sergeant" climbed out of his tent, stood up, stretched, yawned, and looked down. Then he saw the snake.

"He must have jumped four feet off the ground, came down cussing, grabbed the closest weapon at hand, and started beating the snake."

Steve was the only one who knew what I had done, and I swore him to secrecy. Windle would have killed *me* with the same trench tool if he had known it was a *dead* snake and that he'd had Steve and me for an audience.

PARADE AND INSPECTION

After extensive field maneuvers, it was parade and inspection time for the 1st Battalion. Uniform of the day: khakis and field scarves, no packs, just cartridge belts and personal weapons. Sergeant Windle warned us to make sure we were "sharp," meaning everything had to be perfect. He carefully inspected each one of us to make sure the creases in our khakis were straight and our field scarves were tied to regulation. He even inspected our fingernails to be sure they were clean. He had us wait until the last minute to shave so no one had even the trace of a beard. Windle also checked our shoelaces to make sure we didn't have mismatched ends.

When we reached the parade area, Colonel Butler and his staff were waiting to review us. As each company marched by Colonel Butler, the company commander called "Eyes right!" as he saluted for his unit. After passing in review, each Marine stood at parade rest until the other troops passed in review.

It was hot and sticky on the parade ground, and we waited until it was B Company's turn for inspection. Colonel Butler, his staff, and our ex-football-star company commander, First Lieutenant Ben Sohn, followed Colonel Butler as he personally inspected each man's weapon. After a quick head-to-toe perusal of general appearance, deficiencies in weapons or gear were noted in a staff member's notebook. Company commanders would receive a copy of the deficiencies to be dealt with later. While we stared straight ahead, we weren't aware if anyone was failing inspection. A man three places away could have been stark naked and we would never have known it!

The highlight of the parade was when Platoon Sergeant John Basilone was called front and center. Colonel Butler announced to the assembled troops that John Basilone had received a promotion to the rank of gunnery sergeant, USMC. The next day John was transferred to C Company as gunnery sergeant for the machine-gun platoon. Because Gunnery Sergeant Stanley Kavato had joined B Company and machine-gun platoons rate only one gunny and C Company didn't have one, B Company lost its resident hero.

REAL BULLETS

After a lot of snapping in and dry-firing on the machine guns, we were ready to test our new skills with real bullets! This required a trip to a special firing range. Sergeant "Biz" Bissonnette taught a class in firing by burst. Firing by burst prolonged the life of a gun barrel and improved accuracy. By skillful manipulation of his right index finger's pressure on the trigger, Bissonnette demonstrated firing volleys of three rounds, then a succession of two rounds.

Then he got fancy: He showed us how easy it was (for him) to fire one round at a time. To demonstrate the accuracy of the Marine Corps' Model 1919A4 machine gun, Bissonnette lined up the sights on a target two hundred yards away. Gently tickling the trigger, he fired two rounds. Whammo! Right in the bull's-eye!

"Better than a rifle," Biz said with a smile. "A machine gun is like a woman," he explained. "You have to treat her kindly to get the best she has." Bissonnette was a Frenchman, so I guessed he knew what he was talking about when he described women.

When it came my turn to fire the machine gun, I hit the trigger hard and squeezed off a burst of twelve rounds. Bissonnette was quickly at my side, to coach me. "Like a woman, gently like a woman, *not a bear,*" he screamed in my ear.

WAITING FOR OUR TURN

In the summer of 1944, there was no end in sight for the war. From our point of view, we didn't know if it would ever end. When the Allies invaded Normandy on June 6, 1944, I felt things were going our way for a change after the bleak headlines describing the bloody combat of the 2nd and 4th Marine Divisions' assault on Saipan on June 15, 1944. We had a surge of pride in the accomplishments of the 2nd and 4th Divisions. By July 21, 1944, the 3rd Marine Division was fighting to take back Guam. Even though we were a division in training, we knew that we in the 5th would be next. But where?

In early July, we had the feeling something important was about to happen to our division because full-scale maneuvers to test the quality of our training began. As part of this program, our division staged a mock invasion of Camp Pendleton at Aliso Beach, which attracted the attention of our nation's commander in chief. A VIP witness to our exercises was the president of the United States, Franklin D. Roosevelt! As our amtrac went by the reviewing stand, I could see a figure in a black cape, sitting in a canvas chair, who I figured was FDR.

President Roosevelt had a personal interest in the Marine Corps. His son James "Jimmy" Roosevelt was a colonel in the Corps. While a major, he was executive officer of Carlson's 2nd Raider Battalion and personally participated in the raid on Makin Island, 1942. Later he commanded the 4th Raider Battalion.

Things really started speeding up when our 26th Regiment had its training schedule canceled. We knew a big operation was scheduled when, on July 22, 1944, the 26th shipped out to act as a "floating reserve" for the 3rd Marine Division's invasion of Guam. There were no orders for us yet, but we felt we would receive them soon. There was electricity in the air, and rumors were rife. We began packing our gear.

The 5th Division was to be ready to move, but to where? There was no immediate answer to that question; instead, leaves were granted!

CHAPTER EIGHT

Last Days at Home

My family patiently waited across the highway until I
caught a ride with a shipyard worker going south. They
all waved until I was out of sight. I had never felt so
lonely in my life.

For some, this leave would be the last chance to visit with loved ones.
Many good-byes said on this leave would be forever. Corporal Tom
Piper, from C Company, my hometown buddy, and I were granted
two weeks' leave and we decided to travel to Stockton together. It was
wartime, and all forms of transportation were in short supply.

We hitchhiked to L.A. and tried to get reservations on a Greyhound bus. We were put on standby for the next one, due in three
hours. While waiting for the bus to arrive, Tom and I went for a stroll
down the dirty streets of L.A. We passed greasy-spoon restaurants,
pawnshops, magazine stands, and workingmen's clothing stores.

Dressed to kill!

All this was of little interest, until we came upon a photography
studio with a small sign in the window advertising:

Photos of Service Men Our Specialty
Marine Dress Blues Available
Send One Home to Mother

I nearly tore the door down to get in to see what "Marine Dress Blues Available" meant. The studio had a one-size-fits-all dress blues blouse, which laces up the back like an undertaker's dickey. I couldn't give the man my money fast enough!

Tom laced me up to a good fit, then the photographer said, " 'Stand here," with "here" being behind a waist-high pedestal. I was handed a white dress cap (with an adjustable headband) and stuck it on my head.

The photographer didn't like the way I had his prop cover (hat) on, so he adjusted it to suit himself.

Total cost? *Eight bucks!*

I figured a picture of me in Marine dress blues would be worth its cost in girls. Tom, however, didn't surrender to vanity. We did have a picture of ourselves taken together in our dress greens, then had a hamburger and a Coke at a greasy spoon.

LAST BUS OUT

After eating, we returned to the bus depot and hung around the waiting room reading old *Collier's* magazines to kill time until the "gray dog" bus arrived.

When it arrived late, we were told "standing room only." Since it was the last bus for the day, we decided to stand all the four hundred miles to home.

There was *no way* we were going to miss seeing our families before leaving for combat. The wartime speed limit was, as I've said, forty-five miles per hour, and there was no danger that our battered, over-loaded Greyhound would exceed that limit, although I noticed we hit fifty going down the steep Grapevine Pass with a tailwind!

Tom said, "By the time we stop for every little town in the San Joaquin Valley, the war will be over."

Tom had a special girl waiting for him. When the bus stopped at Chowchilla, the driver announced a two-hour layover.

This made Tom mad. Being a man of action, he decided we could make better time hitchhiking. Our trouble was that this decision was made at three o'clock in the morning!

We managed to get picked up just as the bus was ready to leave. Our ride took us to Modesto, thirty miles from home. Luck was still with us, and we got a new ride almost at once, reaching Stockton at 7:30 a.m. The driver was kind enough to take us to our doorsteps. I arrived as my mother was putting breakfast on the table. Our reunion was perfect. I was home! It was the greatest feeling in the world after a long absence to be home with those I loved—and who loved me.

The first thing I did after eating breakfast with my family was to check on my car. My Ford V-8 roadster had been covered with a tarpaulin when I joined the Corps. Uncovering it, I discovered rats had made a nest in the seat upholstery and rust was in full attack on the frame and body. I tried to start it, but the battery had died a natural death from neglect. I didn't want to spend any of my precious leave money on another battery, so I covered my car again, "for the duration."

My leave went fast. It was strange being home this time, looking for friends and revisiting familiar places where I had hung out. Like me, most of my boyhood chums had signed up and gone off to war. Those still home seemed so juvenile to me now. But it was great to spend some time with my large family. I had two brothers, John and Dale, and three sisters, Audrey, Joan, and Mary.

When my mother married my stepfather, Orvil Sheaffer, I gained a stepsister, Bertha Lee, and two stepbrothers, Bert and Billy. We had pictures taken of me with my brothers and stepfather all standing alongside the family Buick. My brother Dale, dressed in a sailor's suit, was sitting on the fender-mounted spare tire, my brother John stood on the running board, and my stepbrother Bert posed next to the car. Other pictures were taken of me with my mother and my sisters. My sister Audrey was away at school in Sacramento, so she missed out. I never saw the snapshots until I returned from Iwo Jima. I finally met up with a close pal, J. R. Wyatt, who told me he was being drafted into the Army. I asked him, "Why not the Marine Corps?" His reply was, *"Are you crazy?"*

BROTHERLY LOVE

One day I thought I was alone in the house. As I started to step into the bedroom, which my brother John and I shared, I stopped short when I heard a noise. Peering into my room, I saw John standing at "attention" in front of the dresser mirror with my garrison hat on, practicing saluting.

I stepped back so he couldn't see me. The scene made me feel bad. The day before I had been mad at him when I discovered he had taken my Schwinn bicycle for a ride, wearing my Marine "low-cuts," (Marine-speak for "dress shoes") and cap. My bicycle had metal-cleated pedals and they had scuffed the sides of my shoes. Dress shoes were not part of our Marine clothing issue and were purchased out of my miserly pay. A pair of these Paramarine dress shoes cost a half month's pay and required a shoe-ration coupon. When I asked a shoe clerk *why* the coupon, he replied, "Hey, man! There's a war going on and that's why everything is so screwed up!" My brother John joined the Marine Corps after the war.

I had to cut my leave short a day. I planned to thumb my way back to Pendleton to save money. Already, my liberty money was gone, and my mother slipped me ten dollars *twice*. Orvil, my stepdad, drove our 1937 Buick Century straight eight to Highway 99. We parked at his brother Ira's Golden Eagle service station, to help me catch a ride.

Somehow my mother knew we were shipping out and told me, "Be very careful." I can still see the tears in her eyes as she kissed me good-bye. My family patiently waited across the highway until I caught a ride with a shipyard worker going south. They all waved until I was out of sight. I had never felt so lonely in my life.

SHIPPING OUT

Training at Pendleton intensified. We did it all: landings, night problems (Marine-speak for "missions"), marches, and compass training. We fired all the weapons we would be using, tossed grenades, and operated flamethrowers. We did combat survival swimming, launched rubber boats, and crawled under live machine-gun fire. The tempo was intense.

On August 11, 1944, the Word (Marine-speak for unofficial or official instructions or gossip) was to have our gear ready to ship out at 6 a.m. on the twelfth. Marine transport trucks rolled in—and B Company rolled out. Our destination was the harbor at San Diego, where Navy troop ships were waiting.

We boarded the USS *Baxter* (APA-94) at 1100 hours and set sail two hours later. The trip through San Diego Harbor took a little less than an hour. Tugboats pushed and shoved the *Baxter* through the harbor, past ships of all sizes being loaded for war.

After waiting in a line that wound through companionways and down to the mess area, a maneuver that consumed two hours, we were served hamburger steaks, topped with mashed potatoes and rich brown gravy.

In one compartment of my tray were peas and carrots. Hard as marbles, the peas were indigestible. The carrots were yellow mush. There was a sliver of cake with a small peach on it, dripping with a sugary liquid—like canned peaches. They tasted pretty damn good, even if they weren't locally grown!

I figured the long food lines were due to the Navy's having to feed an extra thousand hungry Marines. Sailors sure ate better than we did! No wonder so many guys wanted to be "swab jockeys."

RED SAILS IN THE SUNSET

After evening chow, we witnessed a beautiful sunset on the Pacific Ocean. It was a sight to enjoy; the sun had a reddish-orange ring around it as it sank below the horizon. I was aware that our ship was headed in a southwesterly direction because a deckhand told me it was.

The next morning it was announced over the public-address system that our destination was Hilo, the largest city on the Island of Hawaii. Our new home would be Camp Tarawa, near the Kona coast, on part of the mammoth Parker Ranch.

For most of us, this voyage was our first ocean trip. The rough water we encountered induced seasickness, with disastrous results for one older Marine. While heaving his guts out at the railing, he puked his false teeth overboard. He wasn't the only one at the rail; it took a few days to get our sea legs. The trip took seven days. After just two days, extreme boredom set in and overwhelmed many of us. We could eat, sleep, exercise, read a book, or stare at the bulkheads. We didn't have deck chairs and there were no provisions for shuffleboard. Nor was I ever asked to sit at the captain's table! Personally, I found the trip a real adventure.

We arrived at Hilo, Hawaii, territory of Hawaii, and disembarked on August 18, 1944. Here, we would conclude our final training for combat and receive the men needed to fill in the slots where we were short.

CHAPTER NINE

Hawaiian Interlude

My chamber-of-commerce brochure didn't mention that Hawaii had its own Gobi Desert. We discovered the "armpit of Hawaii" would be the location of our new digs. No wonder the 2nd Division had been so happy to invade Saipan and get out of Camp Tarawa!

The main island of Hawaii appeared like a huge hunk of green jade shimmering in the dark blue of the Pacific Ocean. It appeared lush, green, and tropical. In my youthful opinion, I was entering a volcanic paradise, one of Mother Nature's finest gifts to the human race, some "payback" for all the ugly places God scattered around the world; it still defies my feeble attempts to write about its tropic panorama.

At 11 a.m., the ship dropped anchor in Hilo's natural harbor, about a half mile from the smooth, white sands of the shoreline. LCVPs (landing craft) transported us from the USS *Baxter* to Hilo's sandy beaches. Assault personnel attack (APA) vessels like the *Baxter* had sixteen LCVPs hung from davits, eight on each side of the ship. These served as our waterborne taxis.

Boarding and disembarking an LCVP was a dangerous thing to do in smooth or rough water. Climbing down rope nets with full gear and weapons required the agility of a monkey, combined with the skill and daring of a trapeze artist, to avoid being slammed against the APA and being crushed by the LCVP as it pitched and rolled. Luckily, calm waters made our disembarking a relative snap.

Hilo, in 1944, was a quaint Hawaiian city, the second largest in Hawaii. We landed at a city park whose boundary was the shoreline. After being on an APA for seven days, we were glad to get our feet back on solid earth. We were instructed by Sergeant Kavato not to cross what later was known as Kamehameha Street or enter any small shops along the main thoroughfare. Some had signs written in Japanese and Chinese calligraphy like stores I remembered in Stockton. One offered fish; another was like a five-and-dime. I could smell bread baking.

The Word was that we were being quarantined in the city park because a Marine had been found to have come down with a rare ailment. If the rumor was true, it was my guess he had contracted it from a sailor. This presented a problem. One thousand Marines were stranded without a PX. We quickly ran short of cigarettes and pogey bait (Marine-speak for "candy").

One man was appointed runner and sent to shop for the rest of us. This solution made the Hilo merchants happy. Otherwise, they would have had to watch hundreds of potential customers so close yet so far away from their cash registers. I bet they could see dollar signs floating away on the breeze because of the quarantine. A battalion of Marines camping in a public park presented billeting problems the Marine Corps hadn't planned on, but they were equal to the task. Feeding us was solved when cooks set up field kitchens.

Weather during our three-day stay was a perfect seventy-five degrees, but it rained without notice, so pup tents were essential. Covered sleeping was provided when Marines joined their shelter halves together to make a pup tent. Slit trenches, or "1-2-3s" (Marine-speak for "outdoor latrines"), solved the sanitation problems. Slit trenches were one foot wide, two feet deep, and three feet long, and a modesty shield of tent canvas ringed the latrines. This was the standard Marine

Corps design, and one of the first things you learned to do was dig a 1-2-3 when on bivouac (Marine-speak for camping in the field).

To pass the time, we cleaned and oiled our weapons, did calisthenics, and policed the area, which encompassed several acres, keeping it neat as a pin. The rest of the time we sat and wondered how long we would be cooped up in the park. Finally, the Word came down to "pack up and prepare to move out." The quarantine was lifted and Hilo had been spared from the black plague or something worse.

We marched a half mile to a narrow-gauge railroad and boarded flatcars, which reminded me of the classic movie *Union Pacific*. The train's steam whistle signaled all aboard, and I asked Pfc. "Pops" Whitcomb, "Is this the Chattanooga Choo Choo?" Pops tried to hit me with his carbine. His hometown was Chattanooga. There were so many guys from Tennessee that at times I thought the entire state had joined the Marine Corps. I supposed that's why Tennessee was known as the "Volunteer State." Our squad leader, Corporal Whaley, was from Middleton. He was a really pleasant Marine with a soft, southern drawl. He was a good-looking guy, neat, and on top of that he was a good squad leader at the old age of twenty-one. I know some of my pranks had caused him extra concern, but I don't believe we ever exhanged a cross word. Not that that soft-spoken Marine wouldn't dress you down if you had it coming. Corporal Whaley always smoked a pipe and had the manners of a real southern gentleman. There were so many southerners in the ranks of the Marine Corps, I "reckoned" that at the end of the war I would go back to California with a southern accent.

The little narrow-gauge engine huffed, puffed, and chugged its way out of Hilo. We were on the way to a new home at Camp Tarawa, staked out on part of the Parker Ranch. My Hawaiian pamphlet said, "The Parker Ranch, which encompassed most of the Great Hawaiian Desert, was the second largest family-owned cattle operation in the world." My chamber-of-commerce brochure didn't mention that Hawaii had its own Gobi Desert. We discovered the "armpit of Hawaii" would be the location of our new digs. No wonder the 2nd Division had been so happy to invade Saipan and get out of Camp Tarawa!

Our train, with its cargo of Marines stretched out on flatcars, snaked out and wound through a nature lover's paradise. We had what amounted to a private tour and were treated to spectacular views of the countryside not available to those riding in truck convoys, which took the overland Saddle Road to our destination. The railroad route spanned gorges and traversed the sides of cliffs, which provided a close-up look at Hawaii's lava-based construction, testifying to the volcanic birth of the island.

My USO booklet explained briefly, "Hawaii is the youngest island and still growing with two sometimes very active volcanoes altering the landscape. The last eruption was May 1942." The most notable volcano was Mauna Loa at 13,680 feet, about forty miles from Hilo and the site of the famous Kalapana black sand beaches. Snowcapped Mauna Loa and Mauna Kea, 13,825 feet high, protruded into the sky. Snow was the last thing I'd expected to see in the tropics!

The vegetation we passed was mostly jungles of fern, whose lush green umbrellas dolled up the landscape. We saw tropical trees, twisted and torqued in every direction, laced with vines. Giant flowers lay at our feet. Other flora no one on the train recognized rushed by in a Technicolor blur. Rich greens blended with yellow to form new shades not seen elsewhere in my limited experience. Wild orchids were in full bloom. Cliffs with different strata of lava showed the full palette of nature's geological colors. It was a hot afternoon, but the time passed quickly as the train lumbered toward our destination. We soon entered a harsh environment, leaving the lush tropical portion of Hawaii behind us as the train started across the "Great Hawaiian Desert."

Camp Tarawa, with its grim name, was where General J. C. Smith's 2nd Marine Division came to replenish, reorganize, and rest after capturing the strategic island of Tarawa on November 23, 1943. A small atoll, less than nine feet above sea level in the Gilbert chain,

Tarawa was crushed by 18,660 Marines after seventy-six hours of horrific carnage for the defenders and attackers. Its capture, though necessary because of a strategic Japanese-held airport, was costly. Of the 5,000 men who attempted to land the first day, 1,500 became casualties. At the end of the three-day battle, official reports stated that the 2nd Division suffered 1,115 Marines and sailors killed or missing and 2,292 wounded in fighting for the islet. Japanese admiral Shibasaki and his 4,800-man defense force were annihilated. The only prisoners taken were 17 wounded Japanese and 130 Korean laborers.

The purging experience of Tarawa resulted in Marine and Naval strategists overhauling some of their techniques for amphibious assaults. Oceanography intelligence was flawed because observers relied on outdated tide and depth information they found on old maps. Bombardments, it was decided, needed accuracy improvement and additional time on target for "softening up." Fresh attention was paid to getting men safely ashore, and LVTs (landing vehicle tracked), also called "alligators" or amtracs, were used successfully for the first time. Hard lessons learned in the tragic Tarawa assault saved lives during the following invasions. After reorganizing and resting at Camp Tarawa, the 2nd Division trained and prepared for invasions of Saipan and Tinian—battles that were fought shortly before we arrived in Hawaii.

We knew about the invasion of Tarawa from newspaper headlines and a spellbinding documentary prepared by the Marine Corps. After seeing the bloated corpses of Marines on Tarawa's bloody beaches, with "The Battle Hymn of the Republic" played as a dirge behind the panning camera, I had second thoughts about joining the Marine Corps. I wondered to myself, *How could I get to Canada and join the Royal Canadian Mounted Police? There aren't any Japanese-controlled islands in Canada!* While in this reverie, I started to clean my "piece" and laid the parts in careful order on my shelter half. The bumpy roadbed made the train roll and pitch. During a sudden lurch, my carbine's hand guard rolled and dropped through a crack.

It was gone forever.

Now what in the world would I do?

My first thought was of all the trouble I would be in with Gunnery Sergeant Kavato. I already appeared prominently on his "bad list" because of a prank I played on him at Camp Pendleton.

THE BAD LIST

As the train clicked toward Camp Tarawa, I worried and stewed over my serious situation. Losing part of my piece would provoke the wrath of Kavato, who was always seeking revenge on me over the earlier incident, in which Pfc. Oriel and I had intentionally mismarked bullet hits when Kavato was bore-sighting the M1 rifle of our platoon leader, Lieutenant Dreger. Word had come down from the firing line to put up a fresh target for a bore-sighting test.

Kavato's first shot was in the second ring. *Pretty good,* I thought. However, I placed the marker just outside the target. His second shot was in the third ring, so I placed the next marker *inside* the target center ring.

Oriel and I were both laughing. The next six shots were all over the target because of the bum "dope" Oriel and I were supplying. I placed markers in new holes I made and ran the target up.

We heard an angry voice shouting, "Cease fire!"

Over the field telephone we received a call requesting, "The Marine pulling Sergeant Kavato's target report to the firing line with it."

Now what could we do? My gag was getting out of hand. The shit would hit the fan when Kavato found out what we had been doing. I decided to act fast! I told Oriel, "Take down the old target while I get a fresh one."

I laid the new sheet over the old one as a template. Then, using the marker, I punched eight new holes to match the ones I had misspotted. Oriel tore up the old target with *sixteen* holes in it and I took the altered one to the firing line. Kavato studied the target punctures in amazement. He couldn't believe what he saw. He *knew* something was wrong. Lieutenant Dreger and other officers also stared at the target sheet in bewilderment.

While this went on, I was, as they say, as nervous as a whore in church, and unconsciously wiped my hot brow several times. I was sweating profusely and promised myself, *I'll* never *go to Pottstown, Pennsylvania* [Kavato's hometown], *when the war ends."*

Sergeant Kavato kept looking at me intently and then asked, "Who was pulling targets with you Tatum?"

I replied quickly, "Pfc. Oriel, sir!"

Using steely eye contact as sweat glistened on his embarrassed face, Kavato said, "Hmm, I'll remember that, Tatum."

Oriel and I dug our hole deeper with Sergeant Kavato on the truck ride back to camp. We joined in an impromptu sing-along medley of Stephen Foster's "My Old Kentucky Home," "Swanee River," and "Old Black Joe." Kavato had an extremely dark complexion and his nickname was "Blackie," but it was whispered only behind his back. For the last song we added extra verses. None of us knew Sergeant Kavato was riding in front with the driver.

When we got back to camp, Kavato jumped out and met us at the tailgate. He told Oriel and me, "Stand fast!" He looked angry when he said, "I didn't like your singing. Meet me at the basketball court in ten minutes." Kavato showed up out of uniform and challenged Oriel and me to a fight. "I'll whip both of you at the same time."

I didn't believe he could beat both of us, but there was *no way* I would fight with a Marine gunnery sergeant, in or out of uniform.

We dodged the bullets by saying we meant "no harm" and "certainly didn't mean to make a racial slur."

He reluctantly accepted our apology, but still looked furious. I knew this wouldn't be the end of the incident. Kavato had a *long* memory.

Now, as we rode on the train to Camp Tarawa, I knew that when

I reported my missing rifle part to Kavato, he would have the perfect excuse to exact a full measure of pent-up revenge on me. I prepared for the coming wrath by telling Sergeant Windle first. He said, "Don't worry, draw another handgrip from the armory as soon as we get settled in."

Our expectations of finding a lush, green billet in a tropical paradise were shattered as the train rolled to a jolting stop.

A Marine who had served with the 2nd Division and fought at Tarawa told us the camp was called "the dust bowl." Now we knew what he meant as windblown, reddish volcanic dust greeted us. It was to be our everyday companion for the next six months.

Most of us adjusted to the dust quite readily, but Pfc. "Le Nose" Luman *hated* Camp Tarawa and *increased* his shower routine to the point where he wore a path from his tent to the head. His efforts, though, were futile. The incessant wind and gritty volcanic dust overcame his most dedicated efforts. I thought he was some kind of sanitary masochist for submitting his body to continual cold showers. There was *no* hot water at Camp Tarawa.

The entire Parker spread was leased to the U.S. government for one dollar per year, which seemed to me a gross *overcharge*. Surely it would be the subject of a special congressional investigation after the war! Rows of eucalyptus trees, planted close together, formed a windbreak against erosion. Daytime temperatures were hot and uncomfortable. The nights were cold, foggy, and often rain-swept. Dungarees with a field jacket were the uniform of choice at the camp, but sentries at higher elevations were issued sheepskin coats.

The Pacific Ocean was a twelve-mile hike, and to find the "comforts of civilization," our camp population of twenty thousand had to trek to the village of Kamuela, whose main attraction was the Aloha Sandwich Shop—a clapboard, galvanized, iron-roofed shack twelve by thirty feet. An elderly Japanese couple operated this "restaurant," where Marines could order bacon, eggs, toast, and coffee for less than a dollar. Food here was a nice break from mess-hall fare, and a hint of home.

As we assembled at our new area, Windle pointed out his section's tents, our new home. Our squad's was one of the more than 2,500 tents needed to billet the 5th Division. Each tent provided shelter for eight men, the basic squad unit in the Marine Corps. Using the pyramid style of design, each was twenty feet by twenty feet with wooden floors and a flap entrance. No windows. A bare sixty-watt bulb hung on the center pole, providing scant illumination.

Unexpectedly, Gunnery Sergeant Kavato called a surprise inspection with rifles before I could get to the armory ("settling in" hadn't allowed time to repair my piece). I presented my incomplete piece as he trooped down the line inspecting weapons. Ripping the carbine from my hands, he said, "Tatum, you screw-up! Where in the hell is the rest of your piece?" He was *really* pissed and I was nervous. I tried to answer, but was cut short when he said, "I'll deal with you later! I've got no time for your shit now."

Sergeant Windle, good noncom that he was, intervened on my behalf and told Kavato I had properly reported the loss and would replace it as soon as the armory opened. This intervention seemed to calm Kavato down, but I knew that deep down he was still pissed and I would have to work hard to get off that Marine gunnery sergeant's shit list.

No time was wasted. The day after our arrival, training schedules were posted and our purpose for being at Camp Tarawa was revealed. This was a serious training program designed to prepare us for battle.

FRESH CANNON FODDER

We also received replacements for the shortages in our undermanned formations. Our squad was short three members. One of our replacements was Private Lloyd Hurd. He was older, married, and came from the "North Pole," Sartell, Minnesota. All of our squad's "old hands" agreed that Hurd was an "okay Marine" and was a welcome addition. Hurd told me he was drafted. Surprised, I asked, "Why the Marines?"

He said he and a friend were slated to go in the Navy, but they would be trained at Farragut. In North Dakota. It was as cold there as it was in Sartell, Minnesota. When the Navy asked for Marine volunteers, he knew enough about geography to figure out the Marine base in San Diego, California, would be warmer than North Dakota.

Based on that assumption, Hurd and his pal stepped forward. The Marine Corps had two new converts.

The other Marines who joined our squad included Pfc. Lavor Jenkins, a quiet kid from Freedom, Wyoming, and Private Thomas Jeffries from Stonington, Colorado. Jeffries told me his birthplace was a boring little mining community, so he was "glad to sign up and get out of the hick town." With Hurd and Jeffries aboard, the 2nd Squad was up to strength.

Someone said as soon as the division was at full strength we would be shipped out to invade some Pacific target. It was apparent there were *big* plans for the 5th Division and speculation was rampant as to the supposed purpose for all our training. Scuttlebutt had it, "Truk might be hit." Then the Word was Okinawa. One rumor claimed "the mainland of China" would be the 5th's first combat site. We knew something important was in the works because we were placed on a combat alert status. That meant there would be no leaves granted for men in our division. Suddenly the alert status was canceled with no explanation. Rumors and more rumors abounded.

If you hadn't heard a rumor, it was okay to invent one. In the deep boredom of camp life, I decided to start one. Rumors had to be carefully crafted and told casually for best results. Mine went like this: "Hey! Did you guys hear all nonswimmers will be sent back to the States for retraining in combat swimming?"

"Where did you hear that?" would be the next question.

"I overheard two lieutenants talking about a bulletin coming out on it."

This was a very popular rumor with nonswimmers, and it spread fast. In less than a day I was being told my own creation by excited gossips.

BEACHES OF KONA

The sprawling acreage of Camp Tarawa allowed for every type of training—jungle warfare, tank formations, and even working with ground and air support. The nearby beaches of the Kona coast provided an ideal place to train for open-ocean swimming and launching small craft (like rubber boats). For practicing, we had our own tent city on the beach. The Kona area was the way Hawaii was *supposed* to be, lush and tropical. My booklet said, "You haven't seen Hawaii until you have seen Kona."

With full field gear it took three hours of hard marching to reach the Kona beaches. We would come back from exercises with tans rivaling those of the natives. Our beach camp was only a short distance from Napoopoo, where Captain John Cook lost his life in a dispute with a Hawaiian chieftain in 1779. The area's only other claim to fame, as far as we knew, was the Kona coffee bean. The USO book said, "Most of the territory's coffee output comes from Kona."

CHAPTER TEN

Camp Tarawa Capers

He cussed us for over an hour, yelling, "I will still be waiting no matter how long it takes. You can never come back to the company! I'll get you two [expletives] if it takes all night!"

In late October 1944, training underwent a dramatic change. There was always an assumption in our exercises and "combat problems" that we would fight in Pacific island jungles, but now the emphasis was on pillbox attacks supported with demolition men and tanks. These new tactics may have resulted from experience the 1st Division Marines gained at Peleliu. Japanese defenses there revolved around fortified caves and hardened positions, which had to be "cleaned out" one by one. These became a preview of the defense tactics used on Iwo Jima and Okinawa.

We practiced a lot of fire and movement drills. All exercises were simulations. We did a lot of moving, but no firing. One popular simulation was to form in a square, pretending we were in a boat. On a signal, we faked a beach landing by charging out and starting an attack on a pillbox (usually a large, red rock), each Marine performing his assigned task.

Our squad carried its machine gun, riflemen took up support positions, and demolition-squad members made dry runs using satchel charges of C2 explosives. Flamethrower troops moved forward to positions where their weapons could be effectively deployed.

All these activities took place under the watchful eyes of NCOs and officers. After we did an exercise, a critique was held. Mistakes were pointed out and combat veterans like Lutchkus and Windle would explain how to improve our performance. Then we would form up and do the whole exercise all over again. These were activities a platoon could do by itself or in concert with a company or larger formations. Sergeant Windle never talked about his role in earlier battles because he never talked about himself. I don't know if he had brothers or sisters, a girlfriend, or if his parents were still alive. The Marine Corps was his home and we were the better for his presence.

The only thing missing was a sandy beach and water. The physical perils we faced consisted of cactus clusters and sharp volcanic rocks, which cut knees and tore at our uniforms and hands. Overhead, a hot, sometimes blistering, Hawaiian sun beat down on our sweating bodies. We carried a light combat pack with C rations and a canteen (whose contents we learned to use sparingly, as we would be forced to do in combat), and were dressed in dungarees.

Our headgear was the standard three-pound steel helmet. Carrying personal weapons like an Ml or carbine and KA-BAR knife added to our loads. The training grind went on day after day until we could perform our jobs with smooth precision. Then we did it again and again, until it became second nature.

Daily simulations covered all aspects of living in the field, including the preparation of exterior toilet facilities (1-2-3 trenches) and the proper use of all weapons; we had live hand-grenade throwing practice, which was conducted from protected pits. It was fun to hear them explode.

We practiced handling C2s and shape charges after watching demonstrations, and learned how to use other high explosives. Using flamethrowers, bazookas, and rifle-launched grenades was also simulated. At different times we used live ordnance ourselves or watched while someone else did. The only weapon I didn't use in simulation was a flamethrower. I never wanted to carry that seventy-pound son-of-a-bitch "zippo" anyway.

"STOVEPIPE" ROCKETS

None of us knew when we would be called on to use these heavy weapons in combat, so we had to be prepared. The bazooka caught my attention. It was a simple but effective weapon whose official name was the 2.36-inch rocket launcher. It had the characteristics of a genuine rocket and could easily destroy a tank.

Made like a stovepipe, it was about five feet long, with aiming sights and handles attached. After the missile's release, the operator had little control over where the projectile went, so targets had to be large and close.

The drill for firing it was a quick but prescribed routine. The operator could be prone, sitting, kneeling, or standing. The assistant placed a shell in the tube and connected a magneto-type firing device. When the weapon was armed, the assistant tapped the operator's helmet. Because the rocket was easy to sight, launching was quick. It was finding concealment for a metal tube sixty inches long when firing the weapon that presented problems.

I remember the rocket left the tube with a big *swish* but had no recoil. It was also important for the assistant to remember to get away from the rocket exhaust blast! Otherwise, he could be a crispy critter.

It was fun controlling the bazooka's firepower. While on a field exercise, I got carried away and bet a bazooka man he couldn't hit an old tractor a hundred yards away in a cactus patch. His first shot took off a wheel. I lost the bet and had to pay a dollar. Then he bet me the same dollar that I couldn't hit the tractor.

I got my buck back when my first shot blew the radiator to kingdom come. This was *really* great sport! Five other guys clamored to take aim at the target. The tractor, a Fordson with solid wheels, was a pile of twisted, smoldering steel when the betting stopped (which only happened because we were out of rockets).

The last I heard, the military police were still trying to find out who used the tractor for target practice. This incident was the basis of a later claim by a Hawaiian farmer who owned it. It always amazed me how an old Fordson increased in value *after* it was bazooka'd to death.

GUNNY BASILONE

The total desolation of our camp must have pleased John Basilone. In our remote location, out of the glare of publicity and away from the celebrity status his fame had created, he seemed completely comfortable. He could concentrate on just being a Marine, not a war bond salesman. Somebody showed me a press clipping that seemed to explain his feelings: "I'm not a good speech maker, though they say I'm a fair instructor. But instructing a bunch of kids on machine guns and sounding off to a bunch of civilians in a war plant are two different things."

Camp Tarawa was a great place to train Marines, I thought—especially if one of the instructors was John Basilone! I was a confirmed Basilone watcher and saw him almost every day. When there was a battalion muster, all three companies, A, B, and C, fell out together, so Basilone was always on deck. I don't want my readers to get the idea I was a pal of "Gunny" Basilone (as fellow Marines, we were allowed to use this term of familiarity). The gulf between a Marine gunnery sergeant and a plain PFC is enormous.

But he had been our original sergeant in Baker Company and I still felt like I was one of "his" men. I wanted to pattern my career in the Marine Corps after his. Members of my squad didn't talk about this, but I always suspected other Marines had the same desire. I knew for sure he had half a million fans in the Marine Corps green! The men in his platoon worshipped him, and I think the feeling was mutual. So when I heard Sergeant Basilone's C Company machine-gun platoon (over fifty guys) shaved their heads in a bonding ceremony and took pictures of the ritual, it didn't surprise me.

Trying to outdo Basilone, our resident money loaner, Corporal Guy Brookshire, led his squad in another stunt even more "Asiatic" (Marine-speak for someone who is crazy). They started wearing *earrings*! Maybe this bizarre behavior was caused by Camp Tarawa's remote location. By virtue of its austere nature as a training base for unrestricted warfare, it was stripped of all forms of normal entertainment in order to keep us focused on our roles as fighting men. No radio, no newspapers, no books, no nothing. It's small wonder we resorted to peculiar ways of entertaining ourselves. At Camp Tarawa, the diversions Marines seized upon took many forms. Mine especially!

SHOCKING DEVELOPMENTS

As a boy, I found a hero in Thomas Alva Edison. The famed American inventor of the electric lightbulb, phonograph, and motion-picture projector captured my imagination.

My worship of Edison's creative genius fueled an interest in electricity stored in dry-cell batteries. I tried to build my own battery-powered crystal radio set and thought of many other uses for the batteries. When I found discarded batteries from our walkie-talkies in the camp dump, I was elated. I knew from previous experiments that discharged batteries, when left in the sun, could regain some of their lost power, maybe up to two or three volts.

With Steve's help, I carried twenty "dead" twelve-volt dry-cell batteries back to camp and hid them under my cot while I decided how to use their stored energy. My first experiment was to use copper wire scrounged from the battalion communications guys to wire the batteries in a series, then run a wire to a metal pie plate, then to a ground. I then placed a tin plate on a bench in a position that hid its wires. I was now ready for a victim to try my electric-shocking device on. My best friend, Steve Evanson, placed some cookies on the plate and invited Pfc. Oriel to enjoy one. As Oriel touched the plate, he jumped a couple of feet in the air from the shock and surprise. It gave him a real jolt.

I figured that with twenty batteries wired together, I had about sixty volts—not life threatening—but it sure as hell would get your attention.

From the height of Oriel's jump, I decided to lower the voltage and disconnected five batteries. This dropped the shock power down to the vicinity of forty volts. I touched the plate to test it and found that forty volts were stronger than getting shocked by an automobile spark plug!

It had a real wallop, but wouldn't permanently hurt you. We had great fun while it lasted, but our victims told others about the Evanson-Tatum "electric shocking plate" and we quickly ran out of unsuspecting people to electrocute.

RE-VOLTING BEHAVIOR

To improve the comfort of our tent, we had installed a homemade door constructed from packing crates. Our tent flaps were attached to the door framing, which allowed us to enter and leave our canvas abode without having to crawl through the flaps. We didn't have to tie them down each time we left either, an added convenience!

Corporal Whaley discovered some missing personal items and figured someone was coming into our tent and stealing them. To prevent anyone from entering our tent when we were gone, I decided to hot-wire our door. I accomplished this by hooking the hot wire from the batteries to the metal doorknob and then attaching a ground. It worked great! When I asked Steve to test it—he only jumped a foot!

"Goddammit, Tatum!" he shouted. "Are you trying to kill me?"

One night we were playing poker when the company's bugler sounded taps. It was a hot game and nobody wanted to quit playing. Hanging from the center of the tent we had a regulation, sixty-watt lightbulb. Using four blankets, we made a tent *inside* our tent and continued playing cards, secure in the knowledge that the guards couldn't see we had our light on. During the night, it started raining, but no one noticed or paid attention. Van Conkelberg was the only one not playing, because I was in the game.

The card game lasted until early morning. The last thing I did was hook my ground wire to the doorknob before hitting the sack. When reveille sounded we didn't hear it and overslept. Sergeant Windle came storming down the rain-soaked street, hollering, "You lazy bastards, get out of your sacks! Hit the deck!" Getting warmed up, he shouted, "It's six o'clock! Reveille, reveille!"

It was a morning ritual.

He noticed the lack of response from our tent and started to shake the door. I didn't see this, but Pfc. Ed Tucker told me later, "When Sergeant Windle reached for the doorknob, sparks leaped ten inches to his fingers and he jumped *two feet* in the air, *straight up.*"

When he came down, he was pissed. *Really* pissed! *So* pissed, in fact, that he kicked our door off its hinges and stormed into our tent, cussing a blue streak and screaming, "Tatum, I'm gonna get you for this stupid stunt!"

The first thing I knew, my cot was overturned and I was flat on the deck, staring at the maddest redheaded sergeant in the Marine Corps.

I thought I had heard all the cusswords used in the Navy *and* Marine Corps, but Windle invented a few new ones to describe his displeasure with me and my "[expletive] electric door!"

His anger was increased tenfold by laughing platoon members who'd witnessed his involuntary electrocution.

He calmed down enough to shout, "Fall in for roll call."

After morning chow, Corporal Whaley informed me I was to "report to Windle's tent on the double." I hated going, but knew I must face the consequences of my "shocking" misconduct.

At the sergeant's tent, I paused and said, "Pfc. Tatum reporting! Permission to come in."

A voice from inside said, "Enter."

As my eyes became accustomed to the semidarkness of Windle's tent, I saw he was seated at a makeshift desk writing something. Rising to his full five feet eight inches, he looked directly at me and said, "You are on permanent extra police duty."

My sentence was less severe than I had anticipated. From that moment forward, I would be assigned to any and all work parties Windle could think of, with no rotation.

But first, he had a few things he wanted me to do "at once."

One was to dismantle "that [expletive] electric contraption."

Next, "Take the batteries back to the dump. *One battery at a time.*" Inwardly I was relieved. The dump was *only* a mile away.

A warning followed. "Never screw up again or I'll have you up on office hours" (Marine-speak for appearing before a company commander).

I already knew Windle didn't like snakes and now I had found out he didn't like electricity either!

CHICKEN, TARAWA-STYLE

The day we had field cooking was the day that I thought the rest of my career in the Marines would be spent at the Mare Island Shipyard—not on duty, but in the Navy brig—housed as a "guest."

Field cooking was not one of my favorite drills, probably because

I didn't know how to cook. The raw ingredients issued for one exercise were mutton, potatoes, carrots, and a pot to boil the stew in. We were told to cook them over an open fire, two men per pot.

For this occasion, I was teamed with Pfc. Oriel, again. I hated the smell of mutton frying while we watched it sizzle in our pot. About this time Sergeant Windle called, "Tatum, front and center!"

What had I done now?

Our redheaded sergeant wanted me to "run to the battalion kitchen for boxes of salt and pepper, on the double." I hightailed it a quarter mile to the battalion mess hall.

While the mess sergeant was finding boxes of salt and pepper, I spied a dozen chickens being prepared for the officers' mess, plucked and gutted, ready for the skillet. I instantly decided to liberate one of them.

I didn't have a T-shirt on as I hid the cold carcass under my jacket. I don't think there is anything as uncomfortable as semifrozen chicken pressed against bare skin. Hurrying back to camp, I showed Oriel my newly liberated fowl *and a box of real butter.* We discarded the stinking mutton and cut the chicken in several large hunks. The pieces were soon simmering in the butter.

Our squad mate with the Clark Gable mustache, Pfc. "Tex" Thompson, stopped by. We bragged to him, "We are going to dine on chicken in butter sauce while the rest of this company of gyrenes is going to chow down on mutton." Other Marines stopped and someone asked, "Where did you get the chicken?" We explained proudly, "It was liberated from the officers' mess." Oriel added potatoes and carrots and the aroma of my soon-to-be version of chicken à la king filled the air (the only items missing were pimentos and mushrooms). The next move was to add salt and pepper. I allowed Oriel the privilege of doing this. Our visions of a gourmet feast were rudely interrupted when I saw Lieutenant John Dreger standing by our cooking pot. Next to him was an MP (military policeman).

The lieutenant said, "You are under arrest for chicken stealing, a court-martial offense." Apparently such a crime was even more serious if the theft was from the officers' mess.

I tried to explain that the tradition of soldiers living off the land by scrounging was okay (George Washington's army had often resorted to utilizing chickens found in their path). I glibly continued, "The chicken in question was only liberated in the traditions of our forefathers."

My story had no effect on the lieutenant. He did not buy it and said grimly, "You are under house arrest. Follow the MP back to your squad area. Don't leave your tent under any circumstances."

On the way I was thinking of the fix I had gotten myself into over a chunk of mutton. Would the court-martial be a "summary" (an officer serves as judge) or does stealing a chicken from the officers' mess rate a "general court-martial" (five-member jury and judge)? Knowing the Marine code of ethics and from the look on the face of the MP, I was sure it would be a general.

I had seen prisoners with a big white *P* stenciled on the back of their dungarees. This thought conjured up visions of going in chains to Mare Island, California, or Portsmouth, Virginia, for imprisonment. The MP reminded me sternly to stay in the tent. It was 10:30 a.m. I tried to read a book, but visions of bars on the windows and a *P* stenciled on my back were all I could think about.

How would I tell my mother her son was a common chicken thief? Time passed slowly and I was really hungry, but the MP had warned me, "Stand fast." The company returned about 2 p.m.

Corporal Whaley came for me and said, "Now you have gone and done it. I knew sooner or later your high jinks would get you in real trouble. Lieutenant Dreger wants to see you in his tent . . . *ON THE DOUBLE!*"

I reported to Dreger's tent and his somber look scared the heck out of me. The lieutenant had a big Adam's apple. It was twitching up and down really fast. This *was* serious. He said sternly, "Tatum, your chicken had too much salt on it for my taste, but Sergeant Windle liked it very much. In fact, he nearly ate the whole thing."

Dreger was using a toothpick to pry the last of my chicken à la king from his teeth. Motioning toward the tent entrance, he told me, "The pots are outside my tent. They need cleaning and to be returned to the mess officer."

Talk about relief! I was so happy that the nightmare was over I had forgotten that I was starving to death. The joke was on me for a change.

I went back to the tent and suffered the ribbing and kidding of my tent mates. Remarks like "Tatum is a belly robber for the officers' mess" and "Would you cook breakfast for the squad, honey?" and "Are you hungry?" and on and on.

Well, I did have it coming after all the tricks I played on the other guys. The ribbing I took was worse than a deck court-martial would have been.

THE GREAT COOKIE CAPER

Unrepentant, I played a dirty trick on Private Lawrence Alvino, a rifleman in the first platoon who was a "chow hound" of the first order. Anyone receiving a package from home could expect Alvino at his tent asking, "What did you get? Would you share a little?" He had given me a cookie at Pendleton, so now he figured I *owed* him.

I decided to put a stop to his begging once and for all. My Barbasol shaving cream came in a large tube and looked like cake icing. I had some stale cookies, hard as rocks, which I decorated by squeezing the tube, making nice-looking swirls in a figure-eight pattern. They looked great!

Alvino was invited to our tent, where he saw the cookies carefully placed on a dish so he couldn't miss them. Everyone pretended to be reading. Alvino wasted no time in asking if he could have a cookie or two.

I said, "Sure, help yourself."

He instantly gobbled up two or three of the cookies as we waited for his reaction.

"Goddammit," he said. "Your mother sure makes *great* cookies and the icing is the very best I ever had."

We were disappointed. "Cookie Hound" Alvino should have been foaming at the mouth by now!

As we stared in amazement, he left, saying, "Let me know the next time you get another package. Your mom *really* bakes nice cookies!"

MY LAST CAPER

With too much time on our hands, Evanson and I concocted a plan to scare the heck out of ammo carrier Pfc. "Gopher Gus" Henderson; to this end, we paid him a social call.

As part of his routine, Henderson was faithfully writing a letter home to his wife. He did this every day. He kept an unauthorized orange crate under his bunk to use as a desk. About dusk, he was seated on his cot, a simple V-mail blank and a wooden pencil at the ready, moistening the lead in his mouth while he was thinking.

He looked up, annoyed at our uninvited intrusion. Evanson and I said we were paying a casual social call—holding an illegal hand grenade. It was a twenty-one-ounce, M2K fragmentation version, not a practice one.

When detonated, the manual said, it had an "effective casualty rating of 15 meters, or 45 feet." I had deactivated it, I *thought,* by carefully taking out the explosive charge. In its present form, it was supposed to be harmless, but I actually didn't know if it was or not. Henderson didn't know I had messed with it.

To start a conversation we asked innocently, "Why do you write home so often, Gus?"

"It's none of your goddamn business," he shot back.

During this interlude I was messing with the grenade, holding the handle and pulling its safety pin in and out. Gus didn't like what I was doing and told both of us to "get the hell out of the tent with that [expletive] grenade." Clearly, we were making him nervous.

Evanson said, "Don't worry! Tatum knows what he is doing." Then adding, "Tatum, give me the grenade." This was my cue to "accidentally" drop it.

The safety handle flipped across the room—instantly arming the grenade for what our *Guidebook for Marines* said would be a "four- to five-second delay before explosion."

As the "pineapple" (Marine-speak for "grenade") lay on the wooden floor, it unexpectedly started spinning around, which shocked even me. I couldn't see Steve's reaction to this development—I was too busy watching the grenade's gyrations—and thinking, *Oh shit!*

The automatic countdown had started. Unless the present occupants of Henderson's tent made a headlong exit, our collective life spans would be less than five seconds. Gopher Gus was frozen. Transfixed with fear, he stared helplessly at the spinning grenade. In a few seconds the fuse assembly was spent. When the second fuse ignited, there was enough charge left to propel the grenade between Henderson's legs.

Gus sat motionless for a millionth of a second. Then, with a burst of energy, fired by the knowledge that the grenade would go off any second, he bolted over the orange-crate desk and opposite bunk in a single leap. Evanson and I were knocked aside by his desperate plunge. His exit maneuver was slowed a bit when he struck his head on a two-by-four railing that supported the edge of the tent. The beam was splintered as he hurled himself outside, landing in a trembling heap between two tents, entangled in the ropes, hands over his ears.

Evanson and I were rolling in the street, helplessly doubled over in laughter. Our continued enjoyment of Henderson's plight was stopped cold when we heard him return to his tent, followed by the ominous sounds of a bullet clip being slammed into a carbine and a round snapped home.

Gus leaped to his feet, ready for revenge, screaming comments on the legitimacy of our birth and awful things about our ancestry—our mothers included. Evanson was in the lead, with me right behind, as we hit the edge of the camp a hundred yards away, with Henderson in hot pursuit.

The enveloping darkness and the fact that Evanson and I were literally running for our lives (this was no drill) saved us. Henderson was firing on the run, shooting until he ran out of ammunition.

He cussed us for over an hour, yelling, "I will still be waiting no matter how long it takes. You can never come back to the company! I'll get you two [expletives] if it takes all night!"

At 9 p.m., we still could hear him cussing and searching for us as we crouched, shivering, in the cactus. We slipped around C Company's area and asked a Marine to alert Sergeant Windle. We wanted Windle to calm Henderson down and tell him we were just joking. We *were* sorry and wanted to apologize to Henderson for our stunt. We promised ourselves we would never do anything like it again. For good measure, we passed the Word that we would fix Henderson's two-by-four and get him another orange crate.

Fortunately, Gus wasn't one to hold a grudge. After we had apologized in front of everyone, including Sergeant Windle, things returned to normal.

Windle chewed me out good and told me *never* to bring a live grenade into the tent area again. I got more extra duty to remind me.

LAST DAYS IN PARADISE

In November, the Marine brass sped up our training. The latest scuttlebutt said the 5th was headed for a tiny speck of land in the Pacific called Iwo Jima. The clue came from an article in the *Honolulu Call Bulletin,* which said, "Increased bombing attacks on Iwo Jima, an island halfway between Saipan and the mainland of Japan, make an invasion likely."

The article indicated that the Japs were using the island as a base from which to bomb the U.S. airfields on Saipan and Tinian. The tone of the report made us think Iwo was a good bet for our division. Some of us stopped thinking about island "X" and focused attention on the possibility of Iwo Jima.

COMBAT READY

At that same moment across the Pacific, the Japanese commander of Iwo Jima, General Kuribayashi, toiled to convert Iwo Jima into a bristling underground fortress, impregnable to American assault. The Pacific Ocean would be his "castle's moat" as he waited for the Americans to attack.

In November, the entire division performed a three-day field exercise to test our combat readiness. We tested our full arsenal of weapons in a mock invasion. This arduous activity was designed to find flaws in our training and tactics. We passed!

The next thing was a full division equipment inspection that included everyone from General Rockey to the lowest private in the 27th's replacement draft. Everything we would use in combat was laid out. Any damaged or missing item, such as a canteen, mess kit, web gear, or marginal equipment was "surveyed" (Marine-speak for "replaced").

The 5th was combat ready! Our snapping in and field simulations were over. It was time to "fire for effect." By early December 1944, our 'Canal veterans sensed that "this was it." Having been through these preliminary stages before, they knew the routine and predicted solemnly, "A combat mission is just around the corner."

We packed our personal gear while we continued training with the LVTs. During field exercises, we continued our practice of knocking out pillboxes with demolition charges and flamethrowers—our methods of fighting the Japs were changing.

Our last hectic days at Camp Tarawa weren't all training, though, and time was allowed for recreation like baseball and football. Other games were organized. Our outdoor movie theater showed a flick every night. We hoped Bob Hope and his USO troupe would stop by, but Camp Tarawa was too remote. The last movie I saw there before shipping out was *The Song of Bernadette* with Jennifer Jones.

Two-day liberties were authorized in Hilo, the island's main city, for officers and all enlisted men. However, liberty to Hilo was set up on a rotating basis, since the town couldn't accommodate twenty thousand Marines at once!

A sixty-mile trip over Saddle Road in trucks was the only way to reach our liberty port. The journey could take more than four hours of bumpy, dusty jolting on hard wooden benches, making it a test of our backsides' endurance.

CHOW DOWN

Our food tasted good when you were as hungry as we were. On cold mornings, our SOS (Marine-speak for creamed beef on toast, profanely referred to as "shit on a shingle") congealed, leaving a thin coating of greasy lard floating on top. Instead of chipped beef, we were served mutton SOS—I wondered where all the lamb was coming from. We were on the biggest cattle ranch in Hawaii! It was another mystery, along with why we didn't get Dole pineapple juice, or pineapple—period.

Bacon and powdered eggs, potatoes and gravy, meat loaf and mutton stew were certain to stick to our ribs. Post Toasties and other dry cereals were offered, but they didn't go down well with powdered milk.

Understandably, some smart guys skipped these delightful meals, opting for more "sack time" (Marine-speak for sleep).

Coffee was bitter and strong. It was so powerful our spoons would stand upright in it. I doctored mine by adding condensed milk and three spoons of sugar. This was the only way I could force it down. Condensed milk isn't bad—really. The coffee was a real "sugar high."

Our "dining room" consisted of pyramid tents next to the mess building. Wooden tables and benches filled the space. No white tablecloths or napkins.

Mess kits were ingeniously designed for easy cleaning. The long handle, which held both halves together, was also used to suspend our knife, fork, spoon, and canteen cup. Hung on the handle, everything could be dipped in the boiling water safely.

Eating utensils were cleaned according to a prescribed Marine Corps "three-tub method." A huge garbage can was used first. We dumped our scraps in it. The boiling vat of soapy, hot water followed for heavy washing. Scalding-hot rinse water was next, and the final vat was more hot rinse water. Soap could give you dysentery, we were told, so extra attention was paid to removing it.

To feed our battalion of one thousand Marines three times a day, it was necessary to be assigned to mess duty on a rotating basis. Gunners and their assistants, like me, were excused; the Corps didn't want us to miss any training.

FIT IN MIND AND BODY

A form of military Olympics was on the schedule, with a competition between machine-gun squads. The drill was to see who could place a gun in action the fastest, including removing and replacing a barrel. Winners would be awarded a bottle of stateside whiskey from Lieutenant Dreger's private stash.

The drill went this way: A gunner and assistant stood at the starting line. When a whistle was blown, the two-man team ran fifteen feet forward and hit the deck. The gunner opened the tripod and his assistant put the machine-gun "pintle" (Marine-speak for the pivoting mechanism) on it, simulating going into action.

When the bolt was pulled back, there was a second whistle, a signal to go out of action and replace the barrel, then get the gun back into operation.

Steve and I had honed this maneuver with hours and hours of off-duty practice under John Basilone's watchful eye. Lieutenant Dreger reminded us our lives might depend on how fast we were able to do this drill under enemy fire, and we took his words seriously.

He knew the competition between our machine-gun sections in his platoon would build our confidence. We all viewed the event as deadly serious. Steve and I won the competition and company notoriety. We drank our winnings the next day with satisfaction, but most of all, it was a point of pride. I'm still proud of our achievement half a century later.

HOLIDAYS

In organized work parties, we began loading our supplies on trucks going to Hilo on December 20, 1944. We were given a break for Christmas, which we celebrated quietly. No Christmas tree, but the mess-hall cooks came up with a delightful turkey dinner.

Some Marines got their last packages from home.

There were no leaves and the normally joyous day was diminished by the ominous knowledge that mortal combat lay ahead. Being away from home and family made it especially hard for the married men like Pops, Gopher Gus, and Hurd. Hell, it was bleak for the rest of us, too! I confess to having been homesick. I'm sure I wasn't alone.

New Year's Eve was another holiday to celebrate, but with a lighter heart. The festivities roared into the new year and wee hours of the morning. Some Marines with musical talent entertained us with western music and folk songs. One of the more unusual renditions was the "Marines' Hymn" sung to the tune of the "Wabash Cannonball."

Spirits were available, three cans per man of a brand no one recognized. Bottles of stateside whiskey suddenly surfaced from seabags. "Five Islands Rum" (pure rotgut) mixed with Coca-Cola tasted like pure swill. But *all* the bottles were quickly emptied. There were also some homemade concoctions distilled from pineapple juice. The blender of this brew had found the recipe in his old pappy's "white lightning" still, somewhere in Kentucky. It even came in a gallon jug.

In celebration of the new year, demolition men blew up one of the heads for the "junior brass." Several officers murmured later, "It was a crappy deal."

The party was a good relief valve for the stored tension of the coming invasion. We didn't know where or when, but we knew it would be soon. It was at this time that we picked up a last-minute replacement for our machine-gun platoon, Private James Memory Martin, from Brookings, South Dakota. He was assigned to Corporal Brookshire's 3rd Squad. There wasn't much time to train him, so it was a good thing Jim was a quick study. He once told me that he was going to go to college and become a teacher when the war was over—if he made it through the forthcoming campaign.

CHAPTER ELEVEN

Home on the Seas

"Tatum," he said, "get something to eat, then go shine
up. We're going to hit Pearl harder than the Japs did!"

Loading out a Marine division for an amphibious assault was a mon-
umental day-and-night operation consuming our full time. The division began loading on ships December 27, 1944. While we waited our
turn, Camp Tarawa was almost vacant, its tent-lined streets strangely
silent. On January 10, 1945, it was our turn to board a convoy of
Marine olive-drab trucks for the twelve-mile run to Kawaihae Harbor.

We embarked on LST-634 and sailed on January 11 for six days
of maneuvers at sea with other ships. We disembarked on January 17
from Maui Island (territory of Hawaii) and immediately boarded the
USS *Hansford* (APA-186). The same day we set sail for Pearl Harbor
and Honolulu.

When we reached Pearl Harbor on January 19, we were in for a
real shock. As we pulled into port, I was awestruck by the spectacle
of what seemed, to me, like every ship in the United States Navy. The
scope of damage the Japanese had inflicted on December 7, 1941, and
the scars it had left, were still evident. I had a close look at the USS
Arizona (now the sunken tomb of a lot of brave American sailors and

Marines) as tugboats pushed and shoved the *Hansford* to its dock. It was good to know that some of the battlewagons damaged in the sneak attack had been resurrected. Refitted, they were on the high seas exacting their own sweet revenge. The specter of the Japanese attack and thoughts of our own impending baptism of fire was erased from our minds by the burning question: "Would there be liberty in Pearl?"

HONOLULU LIBERTY—"BUM DOPE"

Honolulu was every Marine's dream of liberty port, and the scuttlebutt was, we *would* have liberty!

Everyone was talking about what fun was to be had in Honolulu. Some told younger Marines tall tales of past conquests of voluptuous females and famous binges they had participated in while prowling the nightspots of Pearl. Small wonder some of the younger, less experienced Marines, including me, were frothing at the mouth in anticipation of our own chance to "pull liberty ashore."

I don't know why I was so excited. I had no clear idea of what I would do once I got ashore. With ten dollars left, there wasn't enough cash to "do" the port in true Marine fashion anyway. What the heck! Maybe I would get lucky in a card or crap game. Who knows what the future holds?

Living aboard a troop ship produced the very worst form of boredom. You can only listen to so many instructions or stand in so many endless lines. We had lines for the head, ship stores, chow, sick bay; there was a line for *everything* on our ship. Just when I thought I would go nuts, the Word came down—25 percent of the company could go on liberty at a time. Lloyd Hurd asked me, "Are you going on liberty?"

I said, "I only have ten dollars."

Hurd replied, "Don't worry, I've got money. I'll give you some," and he handed me ten dollars.

"Lloyd," I said, "I don't know when I can pay you back," remembering that he sent an allotment home to his wife, Amelda, and small son, Ron. He had even less money every month than I did. Lloyd, however, didn't gamble and eat pogey bait like me.

"Forget it." He grinned. "Where we're going, we might never need money again."

I was grateful for his generous attitude and he turned out to be a fine liberty buddy.

Pearl, however, turned out to be a *lousy* liberty town. The whole place was a gyp. Sleazy, "one drink and move on" bars, penny arcades with pinball machines, and wall-to-wall servicemen vying for its sparse entertainment.

The streets were packed with Marines, sailors, soldiers, and airmen. All of them were competing for expensive drinks and too few women.

MPs were everywhere, ready to arrest anyone on the slightest provocation or infraction of liberty rules. "No open containers, no spitting or speaking profanely in public." Our liberty regulation cards read, "Gambling or loud, boisterous, immoral or unsoldierly conduct is prohibited."

Sidewalks teemed with humanity and it was almost impossible to move along them. But anyone stepping out in the street would be hauled in by the MPs. Even Oahu's famous beaches were off-limits—they were strung with concertina wire to ward off any possible Japanese invasions! We strolled by the Royal Hawaiian, the fabled hotel of the "400 social set," but could only look at it from the street. The Royal Hawaiian Hotel was now part of the national war effort and was off-limits to us. It was serving as a rest-and-recreation center for submariners, officers, and pilots.

The highlight of our liberty came when Lloyd got an elaborate USMC tattoo with an eagle in its design, which took several hours to finish.

I had my hair cut by a Hawaiian lady barber for twenty-five cents.

One Marine told us he thought the ratio of men to women in Honolulu was one thousand to one. With two Marine divisions in port—forty thousand men—and thousands of Naval personnel from a harborful of ships, plus other military services stationed there, I could believe him.

I was *almost* glad to return to the *Hansford,* although it had been nice to be out and about.

UNWELCOME GUESTS

Boredom on a Navy ship in port was an inch thick. Complicating matters was overcrowding. With a thousand Marines on board, it was like having a hundred guests for dinner and no chairs. Every corner of the ship was draped with humans in Marine uniforms. There was no place to call your own—except our narrow, uncomfortable cots.

Marines weren't made welcome by the Navy. Most of the time we felt like the Catholic mother-in-law at a Bar Mitzvah. We had daily reminders of our status as unwelcome "guests," usually by the same bosun's mate on the ship's inner communications system.

The *Hansford*'s bosun I will hate forever. The shrill piping of his whistle grated in my ears when he announced over the intercom: "Now hear this! Now hear this! All Marines clear the decks, hatches, and companionways! A Navy work party is coming through!"

This happened several times a day. Each time it occurred, we had to "lay below" until the all clear sounded. As "guests" of the Navy, we were compelled by strict discipline to obey every order while on board Navy vessels.

Trapped in the hold of a steel ship that was docked in the tropics, with no air-conditioning, we were a mass of one thousand humans sweltering in hundred-degree heat and what felt like 100 percent humidity. Under these adverse conditions, I never understood what kept us from going bonkers and killing a boatload of "swab jockeys" instead of the Japs. After all, every Marine had a KA-BAR and some kind of personal weapon.

After the *Hansford,* I knew how immigrants felt when they sailed to America in steerage.

Aboard a docked ship, we had no set schedule, which made time pass even more slowly. We all knew we were going into combat and the waiting made the process even tougher. "Why not get going and get it over with?" someone groused.

While this depressed mood reigned, it was announced that liberty would be continued on the 25 percent rotation basis, as long as we were in port. This meant each group could go ashore every fourth day—if you had any money. Money or not, all cheered the good news. Pearl would be many a Marine's last liberty, and some must have known it, from the way they lived it up. Like Christians tossed to the lions, they had nothing to lose. You could kind of see it in certain guys who would say things like "If I don't do it now, I may never get another chance."

DUMMY PASSENGERS

On January 21, 1945, the Word came down. All liberty had been canceled! We were to sail in the morning! We *did,* in fact, sail—but where we went was right back to Maui!

The 5th Division was going to invade island "X" as a dress rehearsal, joined with the 4th Division, who would be practicing a fake assault of their own, on another beach.

The island selected for our mock maneuvers was supposed to closely resemble the Marine Corps' secret objective, a Japanese-held stronghold somewhere in the Pacific. Known as Kahoolawe, our practice objective was the smallest island in the Hawaiian chain, off the coast of Maui. We learned later that its geography strongly resembled that of our real objective and that it was four times bigger than our target—wherever it was.

The point of our rehearsal was mostly to give the Navy an opportunity to practice their landing-craft coordination. The first day was spent in tedious small-boat disembarking. The second day of maneuvers we used LCVPs to land on shore. We moved inland about three hundred yards and hung around until we got the Word to "Load up!"

Hell! So that's it? All that work just to load up and go back to the *Hansford*?

We were just dummy passengers for the Navy LCVPs' boatswains, who supervised the launching, and their coxswains, who served as the helmsmen who would one day deliver us to an enemy beach. We might just as well have stayed on board our ship! We spent the night on our seagoing "motel" and awaited developments.

We did a similar amphibious procedure the next morning, but it was different and more complex. We were issued K rations, enough for four meals. The extra food meant we would be onshore overnight. When darkness fell, we were told we would spend the night on our little rock pile. It was cold—no fires were allowed—and we almost froze our ears off as we shivered all night. It was unusual for it to be this cold in Hawaii.

"PISS-POOR PORT"

When we got back to Pearl, I was again down in the dumps. With only five dollars left in my pockets and the memory of liberty ashore with Hurd still fresh in my mind, I was not keen on going ashore again. I decided to save the five bucks for pogey bait and cigarettes aboard the *Hansford* when we sailed.

Gunnery Sergeant Kavato approached me while I was standing on the fantail wondering what it would be like if a division of Marines were *not* ashore.

"Tatum," he said, "have you got any money?"

I said, "No."

"Tatum, you are full of it! I just saw you rat-hole a fiver. Look," Kavato said confidentially, "I'm feeling lucky. If you give me the five, I'll split the winnings with you."

I had seen him lose about a hundred in a game I just left and knew he was desperate. Feeling trapped, I remembered Pfc. Jim Memory Martin telling me about a similar experience he had with Kavato.

"Sergeant Kavato is having a bad run of cards," Martin said ruefully. "He lost all his money and was going around asking squad members for a loan. Somehow he learned I had a couple of dollars—which I refused to give him. Boy, was he mad! He said, 'I'll get even!'"

At this point in Martin's story, I thought it was a classic case of "letting your mouth overload your ass."

With that thought fresh in mind, I said to myself, *Hell, what have I got to lose?* I gave Kavato the fiver and went below, resigned to the fact I would probably never see my five-spot again. All I was hoping for was that somehow Kavato would now finally take me off his personal bad list.

The next morning, Kavato found me in the chow line. He flashed a big roll of money and an even bigger grin. His hunch had been right! He hit a game for a *hundred and fifty bucks*!

"Tatum," he said, "get something to eat, then go shine up. We're going to hit Pearl harder than the Japs did!"

Gunnies and PFCs in the Marine Corps didn't normally pull liberty together, but, on the other hand, we were in fact "partners" and this was the *last* chance for me to go ashore. Now I could get something back from my investment. I finished breakfast in a hurry and got dressed.

There was no change in the scene ashore, with jam-packed streets and ever-present MPs. We shoved through the crowds and had a drink at the nearest bar, before moving on. We passed a theater advertising *Ecstasy* with Hedy Lamarr. We stood in line for nearly two hours to see Hedy run naked across the skyline. Given all of its buildup on the marquee advertising, it was a disappointment. It sure as hell didn't improve my sex education.

After the movie, Kavato suggested, "Let's get laid." When we finally found a "cathouse," we also found a line of Marines extending for nearly two blocks.

Even Kavato lost his appetite for sex when he contemplated standing in yet another line, figuring, the war would be over before we got to the front door.

So we went to a bar and swilled two more rum and Cokes. Then we went to a tattoo parlor where for fifty cents I had "USMC" tattooed on my right arm. It's still there.

Liberty ended before dark and I don't remember how much we spent collectively, but Kavato gave me my share of his winnings. I later "invested" the money in poker lessons with Corporal Brookshire and ended up with *thirteen cents* in my pocket.

I also didn't know if I was off Kavato's bad list, but I was fairly certain I had broken the ice with him. Maybe we'd get along yet.

Starting on January 26, 1945, the division's ships departed Pearl. I wondered if I would ever see these tropical islands again. I guessed only God knew the answer. By evening, they were all at sea, steaming toward our mystery battlefield destination, the mythical island "X."

I had made up my mind we were going to Iwo Jima. The Air Force hadn't bombed the heck out of it, and the Navy hadn't bombarded it for months to turn its surface into a sand hill, for nothing. I would have bet those last thirteen cents of mine that Iwo Jima was our destination.

IWO BOUND

On January 26, 1944, we lifted anchor for battle, our objective unknown. The second day out of Pearl, the bosun was up to his old tricks, blowing his stupid pipe over the intercom, his words grating in my ears like chalk on a blackboard.

"Now hear this! Now hear this!" (Who did he think he was, the town crier?)

"Shut up," a voice yelled.

"Blow it out your seabag," a cardplayer added.

"Pipe down!" I hollered. None of the Marine passengers on the *Hansford* liked these routine interruptions of our activities.

"All Marines! Stand to and listen!" the bosun called in a tone that made us more attentive than usual. Was this the announcement we had waited a year to hear?

Then the voice of Lieutenant Colonel Butler came over the ship's PA system. Speaking in a clear and confident tone, he said, "Our destination is Iwo Jima, an objective closer to the empire [of Japan] than any other to date."

The ship fell silent as each member of the 1st Battalion took counsel in private thoughts. "Grab assing," our favorite boredom-fighting occupation, was suspended as Colonel Butler continued, "The Twenty-seventh Regimental Landing Team ["LT 27" was stenciled on dungaree jackets] will be in the first assault wave."

There was no cheering.

Passenger quarters on the *Hansford* were *very* cozy and close. Bunks were stacked five high, separated by thirty-six-inch aisles. In this context, solidarity took on a new meaning. All personal gear—helmets, rifles, packs, web gear, and boondockers—was stored on your bunk. There was no other place to put them, unless they could be hung on the support poles. Our mattress was a taut canvas laced to a metal frame.

There was no provision for privacy. The man above was twenty-four inches away from my nose, and the guy below, the exact same distance from my butt. Canned sardines had more room than we did—and they were dead!

We prayed our neighbors didn't snore, suffer from severe gas attacks, and had bladders in good condition. Ventilation was poor to worse, making the troop quarters stink like a cheap Asian bathhouse. Belowdecks, the air was foul, stale, and disagreeable.

As a consequence of our living conditions, the irritability threshold was very high. Any invasion of personal space, i.e., your bunk, was cause for tempers to flare—even among friends.

Casually laying my helmet on a bunk next to me, I was told sharply by the owner, "Don't ever do that again, or it will cost your life."

Space was so cramped that a joker said, "You have to go on deck to change your mind."

Half your life as a Fleet Marine was spent standing in line. Standing in line was a twenty-four-hour way of life on the *Hansford*. One day a weary Marine told me, "I stood in a line for two hours before I found out it was an endless circle of men doing the same thing." He didn't seem too irritated by this realization. "I'm not going anywhere anyway," he said with a helpless shrug.

Life on the *Hansford* consisted of hours and hours of complete boredom, interrupted by hours of total boredom. As Marine Corps passengers on an ocean cruise courtesy of the United States Navy, we were denied the pleasures of playing shuffleboard, what with a thousand men sprawled on the decks. The use of deck chairs was prohibited, and no one I knew was invited to dine at the captain's table.

Since our trip to Iwo would be a long one, over five thousand miles, the Corps didn't want us to lose our fighting edge. And so right after morning chow, we had to do calisthenics. These were performed in gangways and on hatch covers.

We waited hours and stood in more lines to exercise, because all platoons took turns. The routine started at 8 a.m. and continued until 10:30 a.m.

As we were finishing one morning, John Basilone's C Company moved in and started their exercise regimen. I noticed that their hair was starting to grow out, making them look like Marines again instead of Buddhist monks!

MILITARY INTELLIGENCE?

Briefing sessions began as soon as calisthenics ended. An officer would take out relief maps and a large-scale model of Iwo Jima; we would gather around to listen. A warrant officer said the model was made of rubber. It was very good and seemed accurate. Captain Ben Sohn led the briefings I attended, assisted by now Captain Jimmy Mayenschein—no longer Lieutenant Jimmy—because he had been promoted on this voyage. Now B Company had *two* captains.

The briefings held our attention as we endeavored to learn all we could about the evil island we were going to attack. Each platoon's assignment was studied in exhausting detail. I knew Iwo Jima like the back of my hand before I ever arrived on its black shores. Optimism was high. Our leaders said, "There are five thousand Japs on Iwo, but it will be a seventy-two-hour cakewalk."

One day, a lecture was conducted by a regimental surgeon whose name was Commander Smith. According to him, Iwo Jima was "festering with every type of disease known to man." The black plague and the Chinese rot were two of the lesser forms of pestilence prevailing there.

The medical officer also discussed the use of a morphine syrette (a onetime, emergency syringe of painkiller) in each first-aid kit. The importance of inserting the needle in a large blood vessel was part of his presentation.

At the end of his presentation, he asked for questions. A smart-aleck PFC raised his hand. "What if I have to use the syrette on a wounded man in the dark?" he asked.

The "sawbones" (Marine-speak for "doctor") smiled. He loved questions like that. In his most authoritative manner, with a straight face, he said, "Sonny, it's simple. Unbutton his fly, pull out his pecker, and stab him in the head of his dick. All of the blood vessels meet there and you can't miss."

The PFC's face turned beet red with embarrassment, and the rest of us roared with delighted laughter. To practice using our syrettes, oranges were dispensed and we stabbed them with the needle. It might seem strange now, in a generation of promiscuous drug use, but I never knew of anyone using morphine as anything but a painkiller for the wounded. There was never any worry by officers that we would become dope fiends or become addicted.

One feather merchant (Marine-speak for "goofball") made this remark to the assemblage: "With all the medical problems on Iwo Jima, we should leave the Japs to die from natural causes, saving us the trouble of invading it."

The doctor didn't cover lead poisoning or combat fatigue, also known as shell shock, which many would suffer from after landing. Dysentery was discussed, and personal hygiene after sexual encounters was also on the doctor's agenda. He should have saved his breath. There was *no* chance of *any* sexual encounters with females on Iwo Jima. The few civilian women who lived on the island had been shipped out.

It was a relief of sorts; we wouldn't have to worry about killing noncombatants.

OFF-DUTY ACTIVITIES

For relaxation, we played cards, probably all known forms—pinochle, hearts, bridge, and most varieties of poker, with or without money. Matchsticks were the common form of tender when our cash ran out.

Everybody wrote letters home. On the *Hansford* we never knew when mail would be collected and forwarded stateside. I don't admit to being superstitious, but I had the gut feeling that if I *didn't* write aboard ship, I would make it back to the States.

Besides, I was a *lousy* letter writer, but one who liked to receive letters from home. My mother, Opal, was the one who wrote the most. Her letters kept me abreast of how the family was doing. There was strict rationing of all civilian necessities, she told me—shoes, butter, gasoline, tires, and coffee—and wages and prices were also frozen as a further economic measure. It wasn't any picnic back in the States. My mother never complained to me and her letters always ended with the tender caution to "be extra careful."

Shipboard boredom led to high jinks and literal "crappy tricks" we played on one another. Sanitary conveniences provided on the *Hansford* were totally public for enlisted personnel. There were *no* private toilets. The disparity between the ranks of enlisted men and officers was evident to me the day Windle ordered me to take a message to Lieutenant Dreger.

"Why me?" I whined.

He calmly reminded me, "Tatum, you are *still* on EPD" (Marine-speak for "extra police duty").

Sadly, I *did* remember, and obediently left on my errand.

When I entered "officers' country" in the *Hansford*'s superstructure above the decks, I enviously noticed Lieutenant Dreger's quarters had a "sit-down" porcelain toilet with a seat and even a lid. Our so-called toilet seat, by contrast, was a long plank suspended over a slanted trough with salt water splashing through it, which washed the foul waste overboard. An endless line of Marine asses hung over the plank day and night as men "took care of their business."

A favorite trick to play in the *Hansford*'s head was the "hot seat." The perpetrator took a position upstream on the plank, from where he could launch a burning wad of toilet paper, secretly set on fire with a quick flick of a Zippo lighter. As the floating firestorm sailed downstream, those innocently lingering in deep thought would suddenly leap skyward like spring-loaded jack-in-the-boxes, their butts on fire or feeling like they were. Perpetrators of this trick had to have their pants already up and be fleet of foot to escape angry retribution. Those with a practiced hand in the hot seat usually struck only at night—making a safe escape easier.

On the *Hansford* everyone needed to watch his butt! Literally.

Freshwater was at a premium. Shower water was pumped directly out of the Pacific Ocean. Salt water leaves the body feeling clammy and sticky. Unheated, it blasted out of the nozzles at sixty degrees or colder. Humidity intensified the feeling of discomfort. Even "Mr. Clean" Luman took short showers on the *Hansford*. Scuttlebutt had it that Luman was offering a half month's pay for enough freshwater to take a bath in. Regular soap won't work in salt water, so we were issued a special type. It wasn't really soap. Instead, it was a strange concoction that was *supposed* to work in ocean water, but it *never* made any suds. No matter how much we scrubbed, we never felt clean afterward.

CIRCULATING LIBRARIES

Some of us read books. Owning one was important. If you had a book, no matter what the subject, you could trade with someone else. Every book became an instant circulating library. Mine was Jack London's *Call of the Wild* and it was in big demand. Another of my favorites was Zane Grey's *Riders of the Purple Sage*. I *loved* reading. Hell, to stave off shipboard boredom, I would have read the L.A. *phone book* if one had been available.

A pocket-size copy of the New Testament was also well read. When I had it in my possession, I always turned to the 23rd Psalm. The Lord's Prayer was always a comfort to me; it seemed to be written especially for Marines. I think each of us had a favorite scriptural verse or comforting psalm we referred to on our journey to Iwo Jima.

Not one of my acquaintances professed atheism.

In my eyes, the Pacific Ocean was as beautiful at night as it was in the day. In the velvet darkness, it shimmered with a soft sparkle when moonlight danced on the wave crests. I suspected the glowing light was caused by phosphorus.

Flying fish often played in the ship's churning wake, and it was entertaining to watch their aerial acrobatics.

The *Hansford* was rigged with paravanes connected to the sides of the ship. These were torpedo-like devices hooked to cables, and they were used to cut the moorings of submerged mines, allowing the mines to surface and be destroyed. Set up on long booms from each side of the ship, cables tethered the paravanes. Each one had stabilizing fins to control direction and depth. Watching paravanes slither alongside the hull was an enjoyable time killer for me. Entertaining activities like this were hard to find; it didn't help that I have a short attention span.

CHAIN GANG

Trying to find something for us to do taxed the ingenuity of our officers. When they couldn't think of anything else, they had us guard things.

One night I was standing guard duty in the chain locker. As far as I know, there is no documentation of any Marine or sailor ever stealing an anchor chain from an APA—but if the Marine Corps said guard it, it would be guarded.

Awakened from a sound sleep, I was told to go on the 4 a.m. to 8 a.m. watch. It was roasting hot in the chain locker and quiet. I was dripping with sweat from the humidity.

Fighting off drowsiness, I remembered pulling my first guard duty at Camp Pendleton when we were issued Reising machine guns. The corporal of the guard posted me and another private to guard a large warehouse of foodstuffs. He warned us explicitly, "Don't screw around with the pieces [guns]. They are loaded with live ammo." Two hours into the watch, I heard the staccato sound of a machine gun and ran to the other end of the warehouse, where the civilian heads were located. The room was blazing with lights and inside stood the dazed private, holding his weapon with an empty clip. He mumbled in a bewildered voice, "I didn't know it was loaded!"

He had "killed" nine porcelain toilets and left the expensive tile walls pockmarked and shattered. A river of water was sloshing toward a center floor drain. I called the corporal of the guard. He surveyed the disaster and, looking straight at the private, said, "You have just put in for a transfer to Mare Island" (the Navy stockade). None of us saw the hapless private again.

The oppressive heat and rocking motion of our ship made me drowsy. I must have dozed off, but awoke when I heard footsteps on the steel ladder that led to the *Hansford*'s chain locker.

The officer of the day, a lieutenant from A Company, came down the ladder. "Who goes there?" I asked in my most challenging voice while blinking the drowsiness out of my eyes.

"Have you been asleep?" the lieutenant demanded.

"No sir!" I replied. "I haven't been sleeping."

"Then why were your eyes closed?"

I had to think quickly. Sleeping on guard duty was a court-martial offense. I replied, "Yes, sir, my eyes were closed, but just to keep this god-awful heat and sweat out of them, sir."

The lieutenant said, "That's a good answer, even if it is a lie. Forget the heat and keep your eyes open, or I'll put you up on a summary court-martial."

"Yes sir! I understand, sir." I didn't have any trouble staying awake the rest of *that* watch. Thoughts of the unknown fate of the private at Camp Pendleton haunted me the rest of the shift.

SPEED DEMONS

Speed is relative. The eight to ten knots the convoy was steaming was calculated to get us to Saipan on February 12, 1945. No increased speed was needed to achieve this ETA. At eight knots it would have taken us 192 miles in twenty-four hours. At ten knots we could go about 240 nautical miles. One day, to kill time, I figured and calculated all of this on paper and finally decided the captain of our ship was right on the money. *His* calculations would not have to be corrected.

Boredom again reared its ugly head at breakfast one morning. I had a gem of an idea for a trick to play on Theron Oriel. Taking a box of Post Toasties, I went below to our quarters. With Steve as lookout, I climbed to the top of our five-tiered bunks, pulled the blankets back, and emptied the cereal into Oriel's sack. After I restored his blankets to their former disorder, we went on deck to go about the day.

Steve and I purposely turned in early. At 9:30 p.m., Oriel appeared in the troops' quarters. He screwed around for a while before climbing into his bunk just after lights-out. The first words out of his mouth were, "Who the [expletive] has been [expletive] with my sack? I'm going to get the [expletives] who did this." He angrily kicked a cascade of Post Toasties on the men bunking below. A chorus of voices shouted, "Shut up!" and "Go to sleep!"

The next morning he was still fuming as he swept up the smashed mess on the deck. Later in the day, Oriel asked me suspiciously, "Did you have Post Toasties for breakfast yesterday?" When I turned in that night, I discovered that I had been short-sheeted (a prank whereby sheets are secretly folded so the victim can't fully extend his legs) by persons or parties unknown.

At night, the convoy was under a full blackout, but when the moon was bright, you could see ships of all types for miles fore and aft. It was an awesome sight and made me glad I wasn't a Jap. This might have been the largest single convoy in the Pacific war. I heard through the grapevine that there were over three hundred ships in our task force.

If a Japanese sub captain was watching our armada pass, I bet he pissed up his periscope!

A swab jockey I had begged to let me chip paint said, "Marines are not qualified. It's not in your MSO" (Marine-speak for "job description"), but he let me in on a secret. "The convoy crossed the hundred and eightieth meridian on January thirty-first," he whispered confidentially.

I wandered off in possession of some "straight scoop." It wasn't until fifty years later that I found out he was talking about crossing the earth's equator!

During daylight we watched the destroyers dart from position to position. The flank speed of these "greyhounds of the sea" in 1944 was in excess of thirty-five knots. The *Hansford* was hard put to make twelve to fifteen knots. The speed of an entire convoy was regulated by that of the slowest ship in the formation, which was usually an LST making ten knots.

LAST SHOT AT PARADISE

We arrived at Eniwetok Atoll on February 5, 1945. Refueling took three days. We had time to relax and were allowed to swim in the blue lagoon. It was a thrill to dive from the deck into the inviting water, twenty feet below. Eniwetok was small, more of an islet than an island, whose location in the Pacific made it a perfect refueling stop. It had been held by the Japanese, but the 4th Marine Division had captured it in a bloody battle starting February 17, 1944. The savage carnage ended five days later. It was a total holocaust for the defenders. A collection of 66 prisoners from General Mashada's defending Japanese force of 3,400 were all that survived. The 4th Division's losses were 300 killed and 750 wounded.

After refueling, we set sail for Saipan. This island had been conquered by the 2nd and 4th Marine Divisions back in June–July 1944. Saipan and nearby Tinian in the Marianas were bases for our B-29s' long-range bombing campaign. The "superforts" were raining death and destruction on heavy industries of Japan, turning them into desolate ash piles. Major objectives were the destruction of targets that would cripple Japan's war production capabilities.

THE USS *RUST BUCKET*

We arrived at Saipan on February 12, 1945, and took part in a mock training exercise off the west coast of Tinian that seemed to have been staged entirely for the Navy's benefit. We never set foot on Tinian and the whole mission was conducted with the same precision as a Chinese fire drill.

We then transferred from the *Hansford* to LST-10 (landing ship tank), which would transport B Company and its amtracs to Iwo. A and C Companies were loaded on other LSTs in the harbor.

Our new "hotel" was 328 feet long, 50 feet at the beam, and already loaded with the amtracs we would use to hit Iwo. Displacing 4,899 tons, it had a cargo capacity of 3,650. The tank deck was 60 feet long and 30 feet wide.

LST-10 could carry twenty-four amtracs and a reinforced Marine company of 250 to 325 men! Other passengers on board were seventy-five amtrac jockeys from the 5th Amtrac Battalion who would be our "taxi drivers" to the beach.

The ship's crew barely tolerated its Marine "guests." To the swabbies, we were just another cargo that ate food. Some of the resentment was centered on overcrowding and interference with their daily chores of running a ship on the high seas.

Amidships there were four LCPs (landing craft personnel) that could be lowered on davits for launching. An LCM (landing craft medium) was lashed to the forward deck, between the bridge and bow. LCMs were not oceangoing and had to be "piggybacked" to Iwo.

There were sixty sailors in the deck crew, forty in the diesel engine section, twenty-five in supply, fifteen in control, and ten gunner's mates. LST-10 was a floating warehouse capable of eight to ten knots at sea.

The sailors who crewed the LCM were not from the LST's company; they were temporary personnel who would be marooned once their craft was launched. As quickly as an LST was unloaded (if it survived), it left the beachhead. There was no possible way to get an LCM back on the deck without a large crane, so the boat and crew were abandoned, to be picked up later. (A majority of LCMs were blown out of the water by enemy fire, eliminating the need to retrieve very many of them.)

The bows of the "Rust Bucket" were huge doors that split open, allowing it to discharge trucks and tanks and to put men directly on a beach. Deep-draft ships were forced to stand offshore, where they unloaded cargo or troops or supplies into LCVPs or LCMs. LSTs had a flat bottom and a six-foot draft.

This was perfect for landing men and equipment on a flat beach, but in the open sea, the ship had all the stability of a lopsided cork because of its shallow draft and lack of a keel. It would twist and turn worse than a bucking bronco as we bobbed and rolled our way to Iwo. If there were any Japanese subs left, we had one important advantage over other ships—an LST's flat bottom would theoretically allow torpedoes to pass harmlessly under its hull!

LST-10 was old and weathered, and we affectionately named it the *Rust Bucket* as soon as we went on board. I won't go so far as to say that she wasn't shipshape, but the LST definitely suffered from deferred maintenance. USS *Rust Bucket* had seen service at Normandy, sailed halfway around the world, and survived the 1944 invasion of Luzon in the Philippines. Now she was on her way to Iwo Jima, with an operating schedule that left little time for repairs and upkeep. A second-class petty officer told me later that LST-10 had been taken out of service after the Luzon invasion, but a desperate need for ships to assault Iwo demanded that she return to service.

As I made my final step from the cargo net to the deck of the LST-10, my nostrils were assaulted by the acrid smell of diesel fuel. I would discover that the offensive odor permeated every crack and corner of our vessel, and it lasted until we left her on February 19, 1945. The pungent smell seeped into clothing and made our food taste like crude oil. While plentiful, shipboard meals were the worst I had ever tasted in the Corps. Some of my fellow passengers were so upset that they threatened to "break out our K rations if the food gets any worse." While trying to eat, I, and others, imagined that the LST crew was dining from an improved bill of fare. There sure were a lot of plump sailors aboard! It was small comfort to us bellyachers to know that we would only be slopping from the ship's troughs for three days. We saved the K rations for Iwo.

The LST-10's cooks observed the cherished Navy tradition of serving navy beans at breakfast, once a week. I looked forward to this "delectable" entrée. It was a hell of an improvement over synthetic powdered eggs and milk! I also liked "Spamwiches" and cold cuts. Sometimes we were given potato salad with meals—another treat. The ship's stores of pogey bait were soon exhausted as Marines queued up to supplement our Navy-supplied diet. "We're sold out, jarheads," an officer said. Suspicious, we thought, *Those "screws" are squirreling away goodies to keep us from getting them!*

DON'T TREAD ON ME

Small-bore defensive weapons were fitted on the ship. Two 40mm cannons were mounted on the bow, port, and starboard; amidship sections had 20mm antiaircraft guns, four each on the port and starboard sides. The stern bristled with twin 40mm antiaircraft guns and two 50mm machine guns.

Someone had proudly stenciled on the 'con tower two "meatballs" (Marine-speak for small Japanese flags), each one indicating a plane knocked down, proving that our LST wasn't a sitting duck and could defend herself. A salty petty officer told me, "One of the 'kills' was suspicious. It might have been an American TBM torpedo bomber!"

Living space was so tight that we were assigned "quarters" in an LCM landing craft on the ship's deck, instead of a rack with a canvas mat like those we had *enjoyed* on the *Hansford*! Our LCM was ready for launching directly from the deck on arrival at Iwo and was assigned to carry cargo from larger ships to the beaches.

We laid our ponchos and anything else we could find that was soft on the cold steel plating of the LCM to insulate our bodies so we could sleep. The diesel smell, rolling and pitching of our ship, and unyielding metal of our so-called beds made rest torturous. When we lifted anchor at Saipan on February 16, 1945, the weather was perfect. It looked like Mother Nature, at least, wouldn't impede our voyage to destiny.

THE ASSAULT PLAN

Indoctrination for the invasion of Iwo continued. We were told the approximate part of the island and beach where we would land. The plan for us in the 1st Battalion, 27th Marines, was to "cut across the island, turn north, and capture the western sector."

We were warned, "The beaches will be fiercely defended. Expect heavy concentrations of fortified positions and underwater barriers." One thing that really worried us was a prediction that "the Japs will explode gasoline drums in the water as we approach the shore." We were promised that on the day of the invasion we would be issued a cream for our faces as protection against flash burns. Our final admonition was to "prepare for a Banzai attack." The island was wide open and perfect for this kind of tactic. It had always been standard operating procedure for Japanese troops and was expected at any time during the invasion.

After the briefings, guess what? *More* physical conditioning. We were more crowded than ever, so platoons had to take turns again, and as a result it took hours to finish our exercises. In the afternoon, we cleaned and recleaned our weapons. We worked on our .30-caliber machine guns and carbines until we almost rubbed the protective bluing off them. Mortar men cleaned their 60mm mortars, riflemen polished their M-1 "Garand" rifles, and Browning Automatic Rifle (BAR) men "spit-shined" their light machine guns.

Steve Evanson spent hour upon hour sharpening his KA-BAR, using a personal whetstone with a special oil, spitting on it from time to time, drawing the edge to razor sharpness. When he tired of sharpening *his* knife, he said, "Tatum, give me that [expletive] KA-BAR of yours. It's so dull you couldn't open a K-ration box with it." He was right. I was never interested in keeping it sharp myself. Besides, sharpening it killed time for Steve. He didn't read much.

I noticed the serious look on the faces of people who had been in combat before. Veterans like Sergeants Windle and Lutchkus and, in my own section, Corporal Tremulis were somber and serious. Corporal Brookshire, also a combat veteran, told Van to "fold up the gambling operation." For those who hadn't yet tasted battle, apprehension was apparent in everyone's attitude. Joking around and dirty tricks were forgotten by everyone, including me.

As Iwo drew closer, each Marine gave thought to what the future held. The concern wasn't for life or death, it was, "Could I cut it as a Marine when the bullets started flying?" Early boot-camp training was working.

Confidence in the company ran high because of our experienced leadership. It was good to know we had more than "a few good men."

CONFESSION TIME

The passing of almost fifty years and the expiration of the statute of limitations now allows me to reveal a "dark" secret from my past. While on tank deck guard duty (why we guarded tanks in the first place has never been satisfactorily explained), I was becoming a little seasick from the heat and continual motion of the LST, so I sat down on some seabags stored on the deck to compose myself.

Sitting on the baggage was uncomfortable, so I began squirming a bit to find a better position when I made a discovery. A close investigation of a prominent lump in a seabag revealed the outline of a bottle of spirits! I confess, the bottle belonged to a lieutenant in the Marines—I know because the bag had his name stenciled on it.

My thought processes went like this: *If I don't liberate the bottle and the ship is hit by a torpedo and goes to Davey Jones's locker, nobody will get any good out of it.*

To prevent that from happening, I used my freshly sharpened KA-BAR to cut a small slit and liberate the bottle. It was a fine flask of Old Taylor bourbon whiskey. At the time I didn't equate liberating a bottle of libation with stealing. After all, the LST could be lost in the coming invasion. Many were! Those were the risks of war.

Hurd came up with two bottles of Coca-Cola from somewhere—I needed Coke to wash the whiskey down; I couldn't stand to drink it straight. This was my chance to repay Hurd for the ten dollars he had loaned me at Pearl. The next night Steve and I hosted a party on the tank deck of the LSM and invited Hurd, Sergeant Windle, and others to join us.

It was a wild party—as wild as it could be when one bottle is divided among seventeen men. It wasn't the "Last Supper," but it sure felt like it. Even though Windle knew we couldn't buy Old Taylor at the ship's stores, he seemed content not to ask where it *had* come from. Only Lloyd Hurd ever knew the truth (until now).

FIRST CASUALTY

Our squad suffered its first casualty when Van Conkleberg came down with a severely impacted tooth. His jaw swelled to the size of a cantaloupe, making him look like a fat chipmunk. There was no dentist aboard the *Rust Bucket,* so Van had to be transferred by bosun's chair on the high seas to an APA ship.

A ship-to-ship transfer in a bosun's chair in a wartime convoy is high drama. These maneuvers are done so the convoy doesn't have to stop. The receiving vessel shoots a line to the other ship's bow. This is used to haul a light hawser (rope) between the vessels.

The line is fastened securely to the receiving ship while the opposite end is held by fifteen to twenty sailors. This is called a "high line." Sailors pull on the rope in unison, acting as an adjustable tensioning device, moving back and forth as needed to keep the proper degree of tautness in the line.

The rope must be kept just right; too much tension and the ship's movements will break the rope from the sailor's grip. Too little and the passenger going across will get his feet or butt wet. It's a high-risk maneuver under the best of conditions, but in rough seas, it can be very dangerous.

The participating ships must adjust their speeds to each other as well as keep the same distance from each other. When the ships are about a hundred feet apart and their speeds synchronized, a transfer sling is pulled across, suspended on a pulley.

When all this was completed, George was ordered into the sling. Trying to make the moment lighter, I said to him, "Some people will do *anything* to get out of going to Iwo Jima!"

We waved good-bye and the mother ship's crew pulled him across using the attached pull line. Waiting hands reached out and secured my buddy aboard. I rated this drill "4.0" (Marine-speak for a job well done). B Company Marines sent up a cheer for George and the successful transfer. It was a good show, but I wondered when we would see Van again—he was badly needed in the squad.

My squad was down to seven men now. Losing Van meant that I was promoted to machine gunner and Steve became my assistant. I'd always hoped to be promoted to gunner, but not this way. Without Van, we were understrength, and it could mean trouble in battle. Everyone in the squad was worried.

Corporal Whaley, our soft-spoken squad leader, and the rest of us began to plan how we would deal with the loss—which was a serious handicap. A decision was made. I, the gunner, would carry a box of ammo in my pack and Corporal Whaley would carry *two* boxes. Each metal ammo box weighed twenty-two pounds and held 250 rounds. I would carry the tripod and extra ammo, plus my personal gear and weapons. Steve would tote the thirty-one pound gun, his personal gear and weapons, but no ammo.

We planned on using Whaley's two boxes first, freeing him to move around and lead the squad. The decision for me to carry a box of ammo would prove to be inspired. Later, the plan was amended and I carried two boxes.

OUT OF CONTROL!

The *Rust Bucket,* in her weakened state of maintenance, broke down and lost her steering apparatus on the night of February 17. We veered wildly off course, making a large curve to the right, passing through the main convoy, somehow avoiding a fatal collision as we ran amok. As a warning, our whistle blew a signal meaning "stand by for a ram."

Curious about the racket, Lloyd Hurd and I ran to the rail. I realized things had *really* hit the fan when other vessels took evasion action to miss us.

Our immediate concern was the danger of collision. Luckily, we careened through the convoy without fatal consequences. Now it was apparent that unless the situation was corrected, we might not make our tight schedule for the assault. As we silently watched the convoy disappear over the horizon, our apprehension grew.

On the eve of battle we were adrift, alone in the Pacific, except for a destroyer. Had our appointment with destiny been canceled? Like the proverbial dead duck, we were stalled in the water. By the grace of God, we were still afloat and safe, but our voyage to Iwo Jima seemed over—at least for the immediate future.

Since we had no power, the waves bobbed us to sleep as we drifted helplessly on the cold expanse of the Pacific. What else could go wrong? Were we jinxed? We had lost Van and now the LST's steering. "I wish they would stop buying these ships from the lowest bidder," a forlorn voice said in the darkness.

At dawn's early light there was no convoy in sight, but our guarding destroyer was a thousand yards off the starboard side. Scuttlebutt had it that our crew was trying to make emergency repairs to the broken steering apparatus.

It looked like B Company of the 27th Marines would be late for the invasion of Iwo. I couldn't decide if I should be happy or sad. During the day and far into the night of February 18, work crews were still trying to repair LST-10.

SERMON ON THE SEA

A nondenominational religious service was conducted that afternoon by a petty officer from the ship's crew. He read several Bible passages, but like I said before, my favorite was the 23rd Psalm. I found a large degree of comfort in its simple, dignified words. We sang familiar hymns from our 5th Division songbook during the devotional. One I liked the best was "Onward, Christian Soldiers." Others were "Nearer My God to Thee" and "I'll Walk in the Garden Alone." Some of our prayers were lavished on the quick repair of the USS *Rust Bucket*. Not everybody attended, but perhaps they should have.

To the everlasting credit of the United States Navy *and* the intrepid crew of the USS *Rust Bucket,* the sweating swabbies performed a mechanical breakthrough by jury-rigging a temporary steering control for the *Rust Bucket*'s rudder.

Reveille at 4:30 a.m. on February 19, 1945, found B Company at our appointed place in the convoy, anchored offshore from Iwo Jima! The briefly held thought of missing the battle had induced premature relief among some. I recall being pleased we had arrived and could now do our part, and I know the rest of my platoon shared my feeling.

CHAPTER TWELVE

D-Day, February 19, 1945
This Is It!

Everyone on the beach was caught in a giant sand trap of death. We were overwhelmed with white-hot steel. Blind fear and consternation swept the shoreline as men furiously dug into the loose sand.

We were two miles offshore, circling in our amtrac, as I watched three rocket-firing ships, LSMRs, running parallel to the beach, launching racks of five-inch, spin-stabilized missiles.

The shores of Iwo Jima erupted in smoke and flames when the screeching projectiles blasted an area between the island's volcanic peak, Mount Suribachi, and the main airfields of the island's three landing strips. The Navy's preassault bombardment was "zeroed in and firing for effect."

Steve and I were manning our 'trac's .50-caliber machine guns, anxiously looking for possible targets. Neither of us could see anything distinct. We did have front-row seats, however, to witness one of the greatest cannonades of World War II. Battleships' and cruisers' heavy guns added to the raging firestorm engulfing the island. Flights of Marine Corsairs and Navy carrier-based Hellcat fighters made bomb and napalm drops. They returned in low strafing runs that tore up the beach.

Mount Suribachi was under an especially vicious attack because the extinct volcano's sides bristled with hidden cannon and antiair-craft weapons pointed directly at our invasion beaches.

The crescendo of noise was indescribable. It was later estimated that eight thousand shells had blasted the beaches in a thirty-minute period. If successful, preassault strikes like this would allow nine thousand Marines to come ashore without serious losses in less than forty-five minutes.

The Japs would be facing a major immigration problem!

Our briefing officers on the way to Iwo had tried to reassure us, saying, "Our three-day bombardment will devastate the Japanese defenses and allow a quick victory."

Those guesstimates, it turned out, were tragically wrong. The bulk of enemy soldiers and their fortress survived the strike. Only a few beach emplacements were wrecked. Many were dummies to misdirect us and draw fire from real targets. (The shock effect of our preassault attack would allow our first three waves to land with little initial opposition. That much of our carefully detailed Iwo Jima assault plan worked.)

I looked at my watch. We, in the first wave, had been circling in an assembly pattern for twenty-two minutes and were still two hours away from hitting the beach. Without a war to distract me, I began daydreaming and thought of my previous interest in the tank service. It would be nice, I imagined, to be in a steel tank right now, sur-rounded by thick armor plating and in control of awesome firepower. I saw myself firing at enemy positions and smashing them with 75mm cannon shells or using the tank's hellish flamethrower.

My dreams of tank driving were interrupted by Sergeant Windle, who pulled the leg of my dungarees for attention. Distracted, I looked down.

"What the hell is happening, Tatum?" he demanded.

"The Navy is blowing hell out of the island, Sarge, but there is so much dust and smoke, I can't see the beach or most of the island."

I secretly harbored a comforting thought. The Navy might blow Iwo off the map and save us the trouble of a protracted fight.

To my left, I saw the line control boat and someone waving a signal flag. I wondered what it meant. Our 'trac revved up and accelerated toward the beach. We were heading into combat!

"Hey, Windle, this is it! We are going in," I yelled.

"Goddammit, Tatum, I told you people not to say that!"

I shrugged my shoulders. Windle was twenty-four years old and I was eighteen. Maybe he knew something I did not? Steve Evanson smiled like he knew the answer to some secret riddle. I looked at my watch again. It was 8:30 a.m.

No one said a word and I silently prayed for all of us.

The amtracs left the imaginary line of departure and headed to shore. Our assault wave, now formed in a line, followed. The two-mile trip to the beach was made at six miles per hour. This rate would put us on the beach at "curtain time," 9 a.m. We were in the first act. In fact, I reminded myself, we *were* the first act.

The drill for the amphibious assault was simple: Hit the beach and advance inland rapidly across Motoyama One, the main Japanese airfield. We had practiced this maneuver at San Clemente, California, on Maui, and on the high plateau and deserts of Camp Tarawa, Hawaii—endlessly.

Can we do it now when it really counts? I asked myself. Everyone in the invasion must have been asking himself the same nagging question.

How will I do my job? Will I live or die?

I recalled an earlier discussion I'd had with Pfc. Edward Tucker about surviving. Some had expressed the wish that they would be lucky and would make it home. Tucker didn't think he would. I told him, "You're full of it."

We were briefed to expect underwater snares that could rip the bottom out of a lumbering LVT before it could land. We would need periscopes to find our way to shore if our gator was sunk by traps.

Drivers were told to expect their churning tracks to set off exploding gasoline drums when we hit hidden trigger devices. To protect us from "Jap welcoming fireworks," we coated our faces with white flash-burn cream that gave us the appearance of Halloween ghouls.

We looked like ghosts headed for hell. We *were* destined for hell, the Japanese version.

At five hundred yards, Steve and I fired several bursts, testing our guns and venting our tension. We didn't see a single enemy soldier. Ahead, the LVTAs with their 37mm cannon were on the beach but couldn't move inland. They were blocked by sand terraces rising thirty feet in height with a steep fifteen-degree slope.

Poor traction and the steepness of the banks stopped the LVTAs in their tracks. Frustrated, the drivers returned to the sea, where they had better vision and could bring fire to bear on the hidden enemy.

The LVTAs would later come ashore after engineers managed to clear a path through the terraces.

ON THE BEACH

I heard the motor change pitch and felt our landing vehicle tank crawl to the black shoreline. The eighteen occupants of our tractor knew our "free" taxi ride was over. It was "time to hit the beach"!

Our ironclad haven would return to the sea, leaving us alone and naked. Adrenaline induced by sheer terror of what lay outside our steel capsule was surging through our veins. Our gator turned ninety degrees to the left. When the rear ramp clanked down, our boat team's exit to combat was completed in fifteen seconds.

Steve Evanson and I had an extra detail to attend to before jumping off. We had been ordered to cut loose the boxes of K rations that were strapped to the side of our gator and kick them overboard. After putting our KA-BARs to good use and cutting the straps, I threw the machine-gun tripod from the top of the amtrac to the wet sand and followed. Steve tossed me our thirty-one-pound, .30-caliber, air-cooled weapon. From the nine-foot height of the 'trac, it felt like a blacksmith's anvil landing in my arms.

There was no time to think. We reacted like the human robots the Marine Corps had taught us to be. Outside the gator there was no enemy fire coming in and we were in fine shape so far.

THE TERRACES

As I looked inland, all I could see was a mountain of black sand. I was surprised that our landing had been so easy. At Tarawa, Guam, and Saipan, enemy shore batteries had done their best to destroy the assaulting troops at the water's edge, and we expected the same treatment at Iwo.

I remembered the Tarawa documentary footage we saw at boot camp of wrecked amtracs and dead Marines floating in the surf. Why didn't the Japs blast us here? Where had they gone? I was puzzled.

The 'trac lurched ahead with the ramp closing, so we ran for the protection of the terraces as a stream of bullets ripped up the beach thirty feet in front of us, fired from a mortally wounded Navy torpedo bomber with a dead pilot at the controls. The plane flew over us before slamming into an LVT, turning it into a fireball some three hundred yards out in the ocean, causing airplane parts to rain down on the beach. Luckily, none of them hit us as we watched terrified, in the open, crouched on wet sand.

Steve and I moved inland to the first terrace, which looked like Mount Everest. Volcanic cinders sucked at our legs as we climbed. We were slowed to a crawl then halted by exhaustion. It was impossible to continue. Before D-Day came to an end, the looming black terraces would become a quicksand pit of death for hundreds of Marines. Did intelligence know about them? Were they surprised?

The second assault wave landed and began to close in on our heels. Colonel Butler had scaling ladders constructed to climb the terraces.

I recalled preinvasion discussions on their use and I remember some were placed on the assault 'tracs. I don't think they were used. No doubt these might have helped us in our struggles as we gasped for breath and felt paralyzed.

The muffled exhaust of the third assault wave's amtracs reverberated in the strange silence that reigned over the island. The offshore bombardment had ceased, and we weren't shooting at anyone.

The quiet was eerie and ominous.

When the third wave hit the beach, it would be jammed with thousands of Marines clinging to the impassable terraces. I looked around for our squad members.

MISSING PERSONS

Where are Sergeant Windle, Corporal Whaley, and Corporal Tremulis? I wondered. *Where is* anyone *from our platoon?* Without ammo carriers our machine gun would be worthless scrap iron.

I focused my attention on the back of a Marine four feet away. He had "C-1-27" stenciled on his gear. All around us were *C Company troops*! Steve and I were in the *wrong* place . . . or was it C Company that was in the wrong place? I didn't see a single person I recognized.

Sergeant Windle was going to be *pissed* when he found us missing. I had already made that redheaded Okie mad on other occasions, with the snake stunt and the electricity prank, and I didn't want a repeat now.

We *had* to find our own people and ammo carriers. With only five hundred rounds of ammo in two boxes, we had less than two minutes of firing time. Our machine gun was expensive junk.

I estimated our 'trac had moved about fifty feet after the first ninety-degree turn and we had run straight ahead after leaving it. Our driver had been in a big-ass hurry to get his hide off the beach.

So he must have driven us *farther* down the beach than I thought while we were trying to cut the boxes loose.

MIXED COMPANY

Whatever happened, we were now mixed with the Marines of Charlie Company and my hometown buddy, Tom Piper, was not among them. Maybe their machine-gun squad could lend us some .30-caliber rounds? We decided to ask them but couldn't find any members of their machine-gun squads.

Steve and I safely made it up the lowest terraces. The first three assault waves were on the beach and Marines were, as they say, thicker than fleas on a dog's back. As the fourth wave came ashore, the confusion increased.

Where are the Japs? I wondered.

The banshee wail of an incoming shell seemed to answer my question. The impacting sound and explosion were one and the same. A cloud of black sand indicated a hit in the middle of 4th Division Marines on our right.

Was it an enemy shell or one of our own? More shrieking salvos hit the 4th Division sector, revealing that the deadly fire was coming from Mount Suribachi, the commanding heights on our left.

We could see puffs of dust and smoke blown away by the wind from the sides and base of the extinct volcano. It was good to know we were not being shelled by our *own* Navy! A barrage of shells began exploding on the beach, and I knew Marines were being killed and maimed.

The concealed Jap guns couldn't miss!

Our artillery wasn't onshore yet and we were helpless to respond. Everyone on the beach was caught in a giant sand trap of death. We were overwhelmed with white-hot steel. Blind fear and consternation swept the shoreline as men furiously dug into the loose sand.

DIGGIN' IN

Frightened and not taking the time to grab my trenching tool, I used my shaking hands in an attempt to entrench myself. Steve was also burrowing as fast as he could, but for every handful of sand he dug out, two slid back where the hole was supposed to be. Lack of progress didn't slow our excavation efforts!

The tempo of explosions increased, most of the fire coming from Suribachi, where Japanese artillery observers had a panoramic view of thousands of helpless and exposed Marines stalled on the invasion beach.

The enemy used their powerful advantage of height and better visibility to pour fire down on us. Muzzle-blast vapor puked out of the scabbed-over, lava hide of Suribachi.

Instantly acclimatized to the sound of enemy mortars, I could tell that their peculiar *swish-swish* came from the right side of the island. Japanese shells were cascading from the sky. I tried to reach my folding shovel without rising up.

I quit in frustration.

Only partially buried in sand, I could feel the hard concussions of nearby hits. Fear was now a stark reality, as real as the hideous death and carnage occurring on all sides of us. Instantly, Steve and I knew we *had* to move, or we would be killed or wounded where we lay.

I looked at Steve and gave the nod, which silently said, *Let's go.* We moved out, crawling. It was the only option that seemed open to us. Reaching a flat area between the second and third terraces, we saw an explosion of sand ahead, followed by another hit. Japanese gunners had zeroed in on us and were "firing for effect." We saw two hits in the same place! We hit the ground again and started digging deeper into enemy-owned soil.

When I was a kid back in Oklahoma, my uncle had a wheat bin we played in, and I recalled trying to dig in it with no success. The wheat always slid back into the hole we dug.

On this black Monday, Iwo was the devil's own wheat bin. A third hit in the *same* spot confirmed my previous notion that Japanese gunners were bracketing us in this sector, shooting ahead of us to keep us pinned down while their other guns danced around behind and around us.

Looking back at the beach, I could see that the third and fourth assault waves were catching hell. Everyone I could see was hugging the deck, believing their survival depended on how close they could get to terra firma.

CHAPTER THIRTEEN

One-Man Task Force

I maintained short bursts aimed at the steel doors of the fort. When Basilone slapped me on the back, I quit and the demolition man charged within a few feet of the blockhouse.

I noticed a lone Marine walking back and forth on the shore, among hundreds of prone figures, kicking behinds, shouting cusswords, and demanding, "Move out! Get your butts off the beach!"

He gave the Marine Corps hand signal for "follow me." A group of men responded. Fascinated, I wondered why *he* wasn't digging in like the rest of us? As he advanced I recognized that the solitary Marine was none other than Gunny John Basilone!

C Company's living legend and the Marine Corps icon was headed toward me and Steve. His dungarees were freshly washed and ironed, his helmet strap was unhooked, he held a carbine in his left hand, and he had already ditched his cumbersome gas mask. Basilone wore a light field pack and showed no fear, as if this invasion was no more than a serious training maneuver. I also saw Colonel Louis C. Plain, the 27th Marines' executive officer. He and Basilone were the only two men standing up, shouting obscenities and orders. The forward surge of Basilone's group carried them to our position.

Only Basilone and Plain defied the firestorm raging around us.

"Move out! Move out! Get the [expletive] off the beach, you dumb sons of bitches," they screamed, kicking butts right and left.

What I thought was yet another mortar shell falling in the *same* spot as before exploded seventy-five feet in front of Steve and me. The blast's shock wave whipped up black dirt that pushed its way into my eyes and forced sand into my mouth—making me gag. It was uncomfortable and nasty, but my worry wasn't for myself: I hoped the dirt wouldn't foul our weapon.

Basilone ran up, whacked me on the helmet, and pointed to the area where what I thought were the mortar shells had been regularly hitting. Only, when the sand and dust cleared, I could see that Basilone was pointing at the aperture of a reinforced concrete bunker or blockhouse.

The structure probably housed a 75mm or larger cannon whose field of fire was directed down the beach to our right. It was a *big bastard,* with incredible killing power. Its shells were stalling the advance by killing men in the 4th Division. It may have been firing "tree bursts" (Marine-speak for explosions at tree level for antipersonnel destruction).

Basilone immediately directed Steve and me into action against the hardened concrete emplacement whose walls and roof had withstood our Navy's bombardment by fourteen- and sixteen-inch shells.

I slapped my machine-gun tripod on the deck and Steve snapped our weapon into place. I lifted open the breach and Steve handed me the ammo belt. I slammed the breach over the belt and pulled the bolt back, chambering the first round with an authoritative *click*. I tried to fire the first burst. Nothing happened!

The damn gun wouldn't fire because the breach was full of sand and grit. We had carefully wrapped our weapon in a protective green Marine bath towel intended to prevent crap from jamming the bolt.

It hadn't worked.

"Why in the name of hell did this have to happen *now*?"

I threw the breach open again and rolled over on my side while

Steve opened my pack and got the cleaning gear out. I used a tooth-brush to carefully clear away the sand fouling the breach. This took less than thirty seconds, but seemed like a lifetime.

Lieutenant Dreger, our platoon leader at Camp Tarawa, had drilled us endlessly on this procedure, forcing us to do it blindfolded. Now our training paid rich dividends for us.

I instinctively reloaded, closed the gun, pulled the bolt, and let it slam forward. I was relieved when this time it fired and I saw my tracers bouncing harmlessly off the blockhouse.

We weren't penetrating! My rounds ricocheted off the bunker's steel walls. Basilone knelt beside me, looking like he wanted to be the gunner. He watched me in frustration. When the machine gun was finally firing properly, he poked me as a signal to move to the right.

Running thirty-five feet to the spot picked by Basilone, our field of fire was now diagonal to the aperture of the blockhouse cannon. We opened fire again and the tracer rounds were right on target! Now I was *pleased*!

My bullets forced the enemy gunners to close the gun port. With the armored port closed, the front of the blockhouse was blind. Even though it was temporarily out of commission, I still wanted to fire at it.

GOING FOR IT!

Now I was settling in. I was excited but not nervous. Months of train-ing gave me confidence. But noticing that I was holding the trigger too long, I remembered to fire *short* bursts so I wouldn't overheat the barrel and burn up all our ammo. As long as I was shooting at them, the Japs wouldn't open the aperture and operate their cannon. We were saving Marine lives!

Basilone had found Corporal Ralph Belt's demolition assault team and directed a Marine to advance up the line of my streaking tracers toward the blockhouse.

He was a *brave* Marine!

I was shooting a stream of bullets three feet from his right arm—from behind. At any moment the Japs might spot his advance and open up on him, or he could trip and fall in front of our rounds and be killed or wounded. He carried a heavy satchel of composition C2, an explosive more powerful than TNT. I maintained short bursts aimed at the steel doors of the fort. When Basilone slapped me on the back, I quit and the demolition man charged within a few feet of the blockhouse.

Using the old underhand toss, he heaved his plastic explosives at the base of the closed metal doors. Without a pause, Belt's demo man whirled in his tracks and ran for his life while the satchel was still in midair!

We instinctively ducked for cover before the explosion splintered the blockhouse, blowing chunks of concrete laced with steel around the perimeter.

WHITE HEAT

Basilone signaled for me to commence firing again and directed a flamethrower operator, Corporal William Pegg, a Marine of imposing size, to repeat the precarious path taken by the demo man along our line of streaking bullets.

Basilone whacked me on the helmet to signal "cease firing." I didn't want to quit—everything was working perfectly. Why stop? I could see tracer rounds pounding into the building and felt extreme satisfaction with my accomplishment.

Nevertheless, I ceased firing as ordered, and Pegg, staggering under the seventy-pound weight of his tanks and equipment, cautiously moved close to the shattered bunker walls.

Sticking his flamethrower nozzle into the smoldering hole, he ignited his napalm, releasing 350 psi of pressure in his tanks. There was a loud roar of sound and it looked like a fire-spitting dragon's jaws had erupted. The unsuspecting and stunned men inside didn't know the horror that was about to engulf them. They were cast instantly into the center of a roaring inferno, an incinerating, searing hell.

I felt a surge of elation when the flames shot inside. It wasn't because of the gruesome conflagration and agony that were about to overwhelm the enemy, but because of our success! No one could live through Pegg's napalm pyre. Sergeant Basilone had directed this operation by the book—exactly the way we practiced it at Pendleton and Camp Tarawa.

SAYONARA!

As I lay prone, ready to fire again, Basilone stood astride my back, startling me. Bending over, he grabbed the machine-gun bail in one hand and, with a practiced motion, unlocked the tripod, releasing the gun.

He screamed in my ear, "Get the belt and follow me!"

Basilone ran toward the roof of the blockhouse. I grabbed what was left of the cloth ammo belt in my arms and followed him at a gallop up the slopes of the ruined emplacement.

Standing on top, we could look down on the rear entrance. There was a low area, thirty feet in diameter, where some of the Japanese defenders had run to escape the blistering inferno inside.

Basilone cut them down, firing from the hip. The machine gun vibrated in his powerful arms. He sprayed the enemy soldiers, helped by the "Basilone bail," a wooden handle fastened by wire to the barrel of the weapon that was inspired by Basilone's Medal of Honor engagement on the 'Canal when he was burned carrying a hot machine gun.

Without the bail, it would have been nearly impossible to control the blistering machine gun when it was taken off its tripod.

Mowing down the screaming Japs was purely a mercy slaying. Pitifully, the men were frantically trying to wipe away the still-flaming, jellied gasoline sticking to their tortured bodies. The putrid smell of burning human flesh nearly made me vomit.

Basilone's eyes contained a fury I had never seen before—his jaw was rigid, clenched hard, and sweat glistened on his forehead. He was not an executioner, but a true Marine performing his duty.

For me and others who saw Sergeant Basilone's actions during our assault, his leadership and courage were overwhelming. Meanwhile, C Company riflemen and Steve Evanson shot Japs as they screamed in agony. I noticed that a Marine from Baker Company had somehow joined us—Private Louis "Cookie Hound" Alvino. He was the rifleman whom I had fed cookies covered with shaving cream at Camp Tarawa. Alvino had been shot earlier and was still bleeding from three bullet wounds, but adrenaline kept him going throughout the action. He would stay behind as our group moved onward.

I counted nine dead Japanese soldiers outside and wondered how many Pegg's flamethrower had incinerated inside. Our group suffered no casualties.

"FOLLOW ME!"

Basilone handed back my scorching machine gun. I passed it to Steve and he gave me its tripod. Basilone signaled "follow me," and twenty others including Steve and me moved out on a sweep.

After the fight at the blockhouse, everyone took his own route toward the airstrip. Steve and I hunkered down in a trench the Japs had dug to reach their blockhouse, and we ran forward. Concealed in a "spider trap" (Marine-speak for a one-man hole with a camou-flaged cover that the Japanese often employed) next to our trench, a

Jap officer suddenly popped out, ready to kill us. A BAR man behind us killed the officer, who had his pistol aimed point-blank at our heads. The BAR man saved our butts. Possibly the Jap was in charge of the pillbox we had knocked out, or he was a forward observer for the guns on Suribachi.

After surviving this close call, we followed Basilone off the beach fringes to a small plateau at the rear of Motoyama Airfield Number One. From this plateau we advanced to a junkyard of wrecked "Zeros" and "Betty" bombers. The Japs had pushed them into heaps in order to clear the runways for operational planes.

We climbed the slopes leading to the vital airfield tarmac. As we surged onto the runway, I looked at my watch. It was 10:33 a.m. We had been on Iwo for an hour and thirty-three minutes. It seemed like a lifetime as images of the past morning crowded my mind.

We came under intense fire from gun emplacements on the slope of Mount Suribachi less than a mile away and took shelter in a crater made by one of our sixteen-inch guns or a *very* large bomb.

Mortar rounds fired from enemy positions at the north end of the runway started to fall in our immediate area. We *knew* someone was watching us. On top of everything else, we began receiving incoming fire from offshore *U.S. Navy* vessels! These were not misguided rounds—we had moved so far and fast that this rolling barrage was intended for the entrenched *Japanese defenders,* not for us! So now we were bracketed by Suribachi, by the enemy-held high ground to the north . . . and by our own Navy!

Of the three dangers we faced, I feared our Navy the most. I had already seen the destructive power that their shells caused when they pounded the Japs' beach defenses. I firmly believed we would be killed if we stayed in our giant shell hole. With what seemed to be instant common consent, everyone in our small group started to fall back. Basilone stopped the retrograde movement in our tracks by ordering, "Dig in and hold this ground, come hell or high water! I'll go back for more men!"

Manila John's professional combat expertise had broken up a human logjam on the beach and wiped out a major Japanese defense position; now his moral leadership would hold together a small group of green troops in an advanced position.

HOLED UP

Ours was a mixed bunch. Steve and I were the only machine gunners. We cuddled our gun with thirty rounds left on one belt, plus a full box (250 rounds), which I removed from my pack.

It felt good to unload my box of ammo. *No wonder I was so winded when we were still on the beach!* I was packing sixty additional pounds, counting ammo, an extra gun barrel, grenades, canteen, KA-BAR, gas mask, first-aid kit, carbine rifle, extra rifle rounds, cleaning gear, folding shovel, and a copy of the New Testament. Gunners normally didn't carry extra ammo, but at that moment I was sure happy that I did!

We had two Marines with BARs with almost full magazines and a group of riflemen. We had no officers. No one was in command except Basilone, and he had gone for reinforcements. It appeared to me that we were the spearhead for the *entire* battalion.

We had collected in a king-size foxhole and were safe for the moment. Even with seventeen men packed in it, the crater didn't seem too big. I wondered if the enemy soldiers on Suribachi could see me, personally. We all felt naked and exposed to unseen enemy eyes.

Pfc. Pegg and a corporal named Klobuchar took shelter in another hole close by. During the morning, both men had been wounded in the leg. Corporal Ralph Belt told them to "help each other back to the beach and send an officer to help us."

A veteran of other Pacific campaigns, Corporal Belt said, "We're taking TOT hits" (Marine-speak for shells that explode at a particular "time over target").

"Targets! Japs are trying to escape across the airstrip!" someone yelled. Checking his carbine, Belt discovered it full of dirt and fired it in the air to clear it. In the meantime, someone else picked off the fleeing soldiers.

The island's smoking rock pile, Suribachi, was to our rear, and the runways of Motoyama One in front of our position. When I carefully lifted my head, all I could see was the island's western beaches and the runway.

No other American troops were visible. It was obvious we were totally alone, halfway across the island, caught in a trap, exposed to artillery and mortar fire, in a big, open pit. But Basilone had told us to stay, and we were doing it. I was keeping my head down all the time. I remembered briefings at sea when we were told, "Jap snipers are good" (and they were).

TIME CHECK

Those shipboard briefings now seemed like a century ago. "What time is it?" I asked Steve, to make conversation.

He grinned and said, "Ten forty-five. Why, got a date?" We hadn't spoken twenty words since hitting Iwo. During Basilone's charge from the beach, we were on automatic pilot, reacting the way we had been trained to do, running low to the ground. There was no time to talk and nothing to talk about.

I gingerly peered from our position toward the landing beach. Seventy-five yards away, a group of Marines was advancing toward the runway with Basilone in the lead. I felt momentary elation— Gunny Basilone was coming back with more men!

Then I heard enemy rounds falling to earth. From the relative safety of our shell hole, I watched in horror as the explosions tore Basilone's party apart.

It was awful! It looked like Sergeant Basilone was down. Nobody was moving. The bombardment was creeping toward us and I ducked for cover. I felt the Japs were *really* trying to get us: We were a large group of Marines in the middle of their important airstrip with a perfect field of fire down the runway. We were an intolerable threat and they were trying to take us out.

Corporal Ralph Belt yelled, "They are really pissed at us!" Even as we cowered from the mortar shells, the thought that "our sergeant" might be dead or wounded was inconceivable. I figured now was a good time to "talk to the Man upstairs." I said a few words of silent prayer for *everyone*. I thought if I said prayers for everyone and not just myself, I would get a better answer.

LAST MUSTER

Unable to move, stuck in the shell hole, I don't remember when, but sometime that afternoon, the Word reached us: "Basilone is dead!"

America's hero dead?

My own hero, killed?

How could *he* be dead?

I couldn't believe it. The legend of Basilone, a legend born in the jungles of Guadalcanal, the hero I had read about in boot camp, whose stature had grown larger on the black and bloody sands of Iwo as I held the machine-gun belt for him—was gone.

We will all miss you, I thought as tears cut paths down my grime-covered face. I thought of Basilone's cocky smile, curly black hair, and the way he wore his hat at a jaunty angle over one ear. He had a unique personal style and charisma. For me at least, no one could ever be like Basilone.

America, the United States Marine Corps, and Charlie Company, 1st Battalion, 27th Marines had lost a hero, dead at twenty-nine.

Manila John Basilone's name, written on the sands of Iwo Jima, would now forever be engraved with the names of Marine Corps gunnery sergeants from other eras: Dan Daily, Lou Diamond, Mickey Finn, and John Quick on the Corps' roll of honor.

Basilone's death strengthened our makeshift squad. Resolve showed on the faces of seventeen Marines told to hold our position "come hell or high water." We were receiving fire from all quarters. The shells were pouring on us in a cacophony of shrieks and howls, shredding the earth around us.

Enemy gunners on Suribachi now turned their ballistic attentions on us, using observed and directed fire from their lava lair. Five-inch shells from ships mingled in the brew of devastation smashing across the landscape. Suribachi's defenders continued shooting at us while Japanese mortar men north of the airfield pursued their deadly pounding of the Marines along the beach.

The invasion area was a tangle of equipment and supplies, smashed vehicles and sunken Naval craft. Reserve and support units continued to pile up in a congested mess. Thousands of men—the dead, the wounded, the terrified, and those trying to unload supplies—swarmed over the black sand.

We were now targeted by our Navy's gunfire. I wasn't sure of the size and bore of the projectiles or if they emanated from a battleship or destroyer. But I did know that they chilled my blood as they came shrieking in.

I was learning to distinguish differences in ordnance by sound. Rounds fired from Suribachi cracked, mortars *swish-swished,* and offshore shells sounded like a freight train breaking the sound barrier. I had serious reservations about the security of our position and asked myself, *Should we stay put or withdraw?* Logic said, *"Get out!"* We had no radio or other means of communication with our commanders; we would have to decide when to leave without orders.

We would be safer if we withdrew to our established lines so that we would be *behind,* instead of in front of, the Navy's shells. But Sergeant Basilone had ordered us to stay, and that alone was sufficient reason to remain. None of us would disobey his direct order. We believed it was only a matter of time before others would reach us and we'd be free to move on.

CHOW DOWN

I glanced at my watch again; it was 11:30 a.m. Steve looked through his pack and yanked out a K ration, reminding me we hadn't eaten in six hours. Adrenaline had dulled my hunger, but Steve's eating made me instantly ravenous, so I gulped down some of my own rations, cold.

Naval support fire was rolling toward us. If it kept up, our little group would become "chop suey"! Offshore fire support usually lands six hundred feet in front of attacking troops. Did those gunners know where *we* were?

We assumed that the majority of assaulting troops were still to our rear and believed we were within the strike range of those monstrous sixteen-inch rounds. We were also concerned about being targets for our own aircraft.

Marine planes would strafe as close to advancing troops as possible. All Marine units were trained in the use of panel markers, which are laid directly in front of assaulting troops in order to identify "friendlies." Certainly *we* didn't have any and, still believing we were in advance of all other troops, we were properly concerned that we might be in *front* of the warning panels. Incoming rounds continued to fall from both Suribachi and the high ground to our north.

As the shells got closer, we decided to improve our position. The hole we were in was eight feet deep. I added three more feet; after all, it was my butt at stake. The M1 entrenching tool was my life insurance policy at the moment. Its wooden handle was twenty inches long. A large, wide nut locks the blade and handle together. You could say that mine was K-ration fueled and had variable speeds depending on the closeness of falling shells! I grew to love this ugly instrument on Iwo!

From the smoke and noise, we could tell there was one hell of a battle still going on at the beach.

MACHINE-GUN ALLEY

Where was Sergeant Windle, Corporal Whaley, and our ammo carriers? Were they still on the beach?

"Look at that!" someone hollered while I was pondering the disappearance of the other members of my squad. Two Japs were bolting across the airstrip attempting to escape the furious fighting and shelling on the beaches.

Steve seemed to be dozing or maybe just thinking, *What the heck is going to happen next?* With the sounds of commotion, he was immediately wide-awake.

We put our machine gun into action and tracers chipped at the heels of the enemy soldiers. We were joined by others. A BAR man got credit for killing both of the retreating Japanese.

We fired out our belt and loaded another one in order to be ready. When the next Jap sprang into view, trying his luck, a rifleman nailed him. Next, a group of six sprinted into the open. They were obliterated by our collective fire.

I reminded Steve that we had to conserve our rounds. With a firing rate of 450 to 500 rounds a minute, we were shooting too fast. We had no idea when we could be resupplied or when we would find our ammo carriers.

Soon more enemy soldiers made a run for it, probably driven from cover by advancing American forces. Sergeant Basilone knew what he was doing when he placed us in a forward position and demanded that we "hold it."

I was feeling good now and saw a clear purpose in my actions for the day. Gradually, however, my elation passed and I felt a twinge of fear as I heard the unearthly roar of firing rockets.

This new danger came from a Navy rocket ship sailing north to south. A full barrage of its deadly rockets cut loose. Briefly, I thought we might be in their impact zone. Luckily, the terror weapons landed in an area beyond the airstrip, which would be our objective the next day, D+1.

This new weapon was devastating. The impact covered an area equal to a couple of football fields. Clouds of dust filled the sky. I thought, *Nothing could live through an inferno like that.* I sure wouldn't want to be on the receiving end of it.

It was now 4 p.m. More Japs attempted a foolish dash across the airstrip. Conserving bullets, Steve and I left it up to the BAR Marine and rifleman in our shell hole to take care of them. We had decided to save our ammo for the long night ahead.

Above our heads, clouds gathered and it got very cold. We were definitely not in the South Pacific! Iwo Jima was seven hundred miles from Tokyo and it was February.

RELIEF COLUMN

Turning to my right, I saw an inspiring sight. Survivors of our B Company, with Sergeant Windle out in front, followed by Lloyd Hurd and the ammo carriers, were approaching us. What we were witnessing were the remnants of Baker Company. I didn't know what had happened to B Company on the landing beach, but I guessed someone would "cut me in on the scoop."

We were happily reunited with Hurd and the other ammo carriers, but were devastated by the news: Our company had suffered severe losses during the beach assault. We had seventeen men killed and fifty-one wounded, *26 percent* of the company's manpower when we hit the beach seven hours before. Missing and presumed dead from our squad was our squad leader, Corporal William Whaley, Pfc. Tex Thompson, and Private Thomas Jeffries, one of our Camp Tarawa replacements. I really admired Corporal Whaley and hated the thought that he was gone. He was a great leader who never quite gave me the heck I deserved. Besides that, we had lived together for the past year or so.

In the first squad, Corporal Tremulis lost his gunner, our platoon's muscleman, Pfc. Bruno "Spike" Mierczwa, and assistant gunner, Pfc. Loyal Leman, two best friends killed in the same shell blast. Five desperately needed men were gone from our section during the first few hours of the assault.

I didn't see Gunnery Sergeant Kavato, Lieutenant Dreger, or my buddy Pfc. Edward Tucker either. According to Hurd, they'd been "lost somewhere on the beach."

Remembering Tucker's premonition that he wouldn't make it through the battle, I hoped he and the others were only wounded. The machine-gun platoon had lost more men, but this was the best count we could muster in the confusion. News of our comrades' probable deaths was painful, but we didn't dwell on it. It was getting dark and we had things to do.

Steve and I were back in business. We had seventy-five rounds left in our last belt and night was approaching. Steve and I knew nothing about the debacle that had occurred on the beach after we left. We only knew we had commingled with C Company Marines and were carrying out Basilone's direct orders. Our 1st Battalion's (A, B, and C Companies') assault and advance was made with small groups, squads, and fire teams who, like ourselves, thought they were all alone. It was as if each cluster of Marines was operating in a war of its own.

This sporadic advance bypassed pockets of resistance. The reserve units and the battalion's support elements following the assault troops drove the enemy from their concealed positions. Because of our prompt advance across the island, we were in a place from which we could cut off their escape. We probably surprised some of them from our advanced emplacement on the airstrip as we sent them to join their ancestors.

SETTING OUR FIRST LINE

On a short list of one, we had to prepare for night fighting. A defense line was established and fields of fire set and aiming stakes driven into place. Our squad set up four machine guns.

Besides our air-cooled models, we had two additional water-cooled guns. The extra machine guns were needed because we *really* expected a massive Banzai attack and we wanted to be ready! We collected additional ammunition and dug our foxholes deeper.

Japanese officers were masters of the night Banzai charges. These were a simple maneuver—officers lined up their troops, filled them with sake, said a few prayers, and dedicated their lives to the emperor.

On a signal, they rushed the defending troops en masse with shouts of "*Hideki Banzai!* Marines! You die tonight!"

A Banzai charge was designed to terrify defenders and overrun their positions. Used by the Japanese throughout the Pacific, it was a bloody event and was usually unsuccessful. Costly in lives (for Japs more than Marines), it was nerve shattering for all participants.

D-Day night would be the most likely time for the Japanese to launch an all-out assault.

Our plan to repel them was also simple. Set a line of defense with dug-in Marines using interlocking fields of fire. Our supporting weapons—mortars and artillery—were preregistered and planned to protect likely avenues of approach.

When the enemy attacked, a curtain of fire would rain down, and the United States Marine Corps would make sure they would be given every chance to exercise their divine right to die for Hirohito, their God and emperor.

CHAPTER FOURTEEN

D+I, February 20, 1945
Zeroed In

"Can you make it to the beach? Can you crawl?" medics asked; they had no time to deliver wounded.
Stretcher bearers were dead or already carrying men.
"If you stay where you are, you'll be hit again," they
warned.

Mortar fire woke me from a restless sleep at dawn. I was happy to be
awake and still alive on this second day of battle. Steve had stood the
final watch of two hours.

The feared Banzai attack never materialized, so Steve and I opened
our waxed cartons of K rations and ate the contents cold. No fires
were allowed.

Mine was scrambled eggs and diced ham in a can. I used my
KA-BAR as a can opener. Compressed crackers (which, thanks to
some ingenious, scientific method, had absolutely no taste) were the
entrée. Our "food" was so dry that I swigged on my canteen of precious LST-10 water. It was now empty. I had enjoyed my last drink of
clean water for the next fourteen days.

A fog rolled over us on a damp cool breeze. Snipers in wrecked
Zeros and bombers near the airfield started firing. We grabbed carbines and joined several riflemen in an impromptu, unsuccessful
sniper hunt. Sergeant Windle chewed our butts out. "You dumb

[expletives]! You're machine gunners, *not* riflemen. It's your job to stay with the guns," he admonished us.

REGIMENTAL RESERVE

The 3rd Battalion of our regiment jumped off in an attack at 8:30 a.m. Our orders read, "1st Battalion will follow 3rd Battalion–27th Marines and 1st Battalion–26th Regiment (temporarily attached to the 27th)."

The men quickly passed through our lines and we were under way at 8:45 a.m. We followed four hundred yards to their rear. Meanwhile, the 28th Marines continued assaulting Suribachi with all three battalions engaged.

Our regiment's zone of advance covered the edge of the airfield, Motoyama One, and extended to the sea, which included the island's wide and flat western beaches.

The shore came into clear view as we advanced. It seemed to me these smooth beaches with firm smooth sand would have been easier to get across than the steep terraces where we were dumped on D-Day.

As soon as our advance started, the enemy reacted with heavy artillery and mortar barrages. Our first morning on Iwo, when we were pinned helplessly by mortar barrages on the black sand beaches, we were reminded of warnings by veterans who said, "The Japs are the world's best soldiers with a knee mortar."

Though chilling, those warnings weren't exaggerated. Even the blunt advice of the vets didn't convey the pure horror of an enemy mortar attack. It was pure hell to be caught in the open when the Japs opened up with a full mortar fusillade. The sound of mortars *swish-swishing* through the air froze my blood. Against these invisible missiles, there was no defense. If we were caught in the open, all we could do was hit the deck. A foxhole offered little protection from these high-trajectory missiles because they dropped straight down on us.

It wasn't a good idea to run. A mortar explodes on contact and sprays lethal fragments of hot steel in a 360-degree, fifty-yard swath. Most of the fragments never went higher than six feet off the ground, making them ideal antipersonnel weapons. *Yes sir! Jap mortarmen were as good as advertised,* I thought with grudging admiration. Our own artillery regiment, the 13th Marines, let their 75mm pack howitzers respond with counterfire, which dampened some of the Japs' enthusiasm.

By noon, the advance had carried forward two hundred tough yards. Following in reserve, we kept alert for bypassed enemy positions. These were frequent and deadly.

Fresh mortar rounds—the steel from hell—continued to fall sporadically. If the mortar kept firing from a fixed position, we quickly "zeroed in" and wiped it out. The Japanese were aware of this principle of Marine warfare and moved frequently in order to thwart us. Constant movement is also a standard procedure in the Marine Corps.

Being in regimental reserve didn't reduce our exposure to deadly enemy fire and casualties. On Iwo, there was no place anyone could go for relief from the crescendo of fire and shells descending on us from the sky.

A command post could be any depression large enough to hold five or more people. They were usually set up behind a chunk of concrete or a log, even a pile of junk. There are many instances of CPs being blown to hell during the raging battle for Iwo. Field hospitals and kitchens also received serious hits. Mom had no idea how hard it was to "be careful."

SHAMBLES

The rear areas, particularly the eastern or landing beaches where support forces were working, suffered a bloody pounding—but there were no lengthy pauses in the effort to keep us supplied. Adding to the torrent of mortar and artillery fire was a strong, cold offshore wind. The elements had turned against us. Work parties faced an unruly ocean and thrashing surf that soaked their bodies—but couldn't dampen their fighting spirit.

Sunk and broached landing craft piled up along the beaches. By midafternoon on D+l, it was necessary to close the island to further unloading until the weather subsided.

Our landing beaches were giant scrap piles; LCTs, LVTs, LCVPs, tanks, vehicles, and smashed DUKWs blocked access. Multimillions of dollars' worth of valuable equipment and vessels had been systematically wrecked by deadly, accurate Japanese shelling. Debris washed idly back and forth in the frothing surf.

Human wreckage—the wounded, dead, and dying—littered the cold sand. Engineers, Seabees, and shore-party personnel struggled to create order from the chaos. Doctors and corpsmen too often fought a losing battle against the Grim Reaper watching over our battlefield. Armed with simple field dressings and infusions of whole blood, they tried to stem the tide of human suffering and life's blood pouring into Iwo's lava hide. Our pharmacist's mate corpsmen, whom we'd jokingly called "shanker mechanics" (Marine-speak for a disease of the male organ) before the battle, now turned into masculine "angels of mercy." They saved hundreds of Marines daily and tried to ease the pain of the hopeless cases with liberal injections of morphine.

"Can you make it to the beach? Can you crawl?" medics asked; they had no time to deliver wounded. Stretcher bearers were dead or already carrying men. "If you stay where you are, you'll be hit again," they warned.

Casualties awaiting treatment or evacuation were sometimes hit a second or third time or even killed. If a wounded man could make it to a beach area, he stood a slim chance of evacuation, but at least there was hope. In spite of the high surf and dangerous conditions of the beach, heroic coxswains and DUKW drivers braved the hell onshore and the furious elements to rescue them.

PILLBOX BUSTIN'

Aided as we were by tanks, afternoon gains were better than those previously achieved; however, heavy fighting continued against stubborn enemy resistance. We were still receiving sporadic mortar fire as we pushed forward, overrunning active enemy positions as we charged.

When we attacked this way, behind the assault units, we made small rushes, slow walks, and crawls or sprints from one position to another.

Early in the afternoon, Sergeant Windle spotted an active pillbox and ordered us to take it out. As acting squad leader, I carried out his instructions and set up my twin machine guns thirty-five feet apart. Manning the nearest one was Steve and Pops Whitcomb. The other was operated by Billy Joe Cawthorn and Gopher Gus Henderson. Windle directed us to fire into the gun port while men from B Company's 2nd platoon advanced on the fortification to within grenade range. They hit the pillbox with grenades and TNT but came under strong fire from a concealed supporting position—another pillbox! Our attack stalled, but we were without casualties. Windle yelled, "Relocate Cawthorn's gun and attack the other pillbox!" It seemed as if Windle was everywhere all at once. He had the agility of a mountain goat and the heart of a lion. The next best thing you could have, next to God on your side, was the redheaded sergeant from Snyder, Oklahoma. Having him as your leader was better than a double insurance policy and a thousand good-luck charms.

Concurrently, Windle directed the riflemen to place both targets under direct fire. The infantry again maneuvered forward, accompanied by a demolition man who walked our line of fire toward the "new" pillbox. He reached it and threw a satchel of C2 into an opening, then ran flat out, back to our lines, seeking cover. The minifortress crumpled in a shattering blast that blew rocks, sand, and dirt over us. It was just a smokin' hole in the ground when I looked again.

Not waiting for the enemy to recover, we ran forward and uncovered additional positions like the smoldering pillbox. Captain Jimmy Mayenschein and Sergeant Windle set up this routine that we followed. As I passed the pillbox, I looked inside for dead Japs, but there were none. Windle said, "The Japs take their dead and wounded with them as they retreat." With more than 135 known pillboxes encountered in our zone of advance, it's no wonder we were taking all afternoon to move what seemed like only a few yards forward. Iwo's in-depth defense system was ominous. We were in for a long, brutal struggle.

This day's fighting had proved one indisputable truth to me. We could count our lucky stars that we had Windle, a crafty Marine sergeant, leading us. He personally picked good positions to fight from, since machine gun positions need good protection. The average life of a machine gunner in action was in the six- to twenty-minute range. Open fire with a machine gun and the entire Japanese defenses in that area would focus their attention on shortening your life span. To Windle, we were not expendable; we were his platoon and he committed us to battle like a precious commodity; our health and welfare were always his main concern.

QUITTIN' TIME

D+1's advance of seven hundred yards was one of the most significant made during Iwo's entire campaign. By 5 p.m., all offensive operations ceased and we started preparations for the night. We remained in reserve behind the 3rd Battalion, but dug in. A Banzai attack was still possible from any direction.

We set up our guns, including water-cooled .30s, which were kept and used primarily at night for defensive action. They were too heavy to move easily by hand and were usually moved on carts pulled by two Marines.

Sergeant Windle, a thorough professional, checked our positions and approved them. We had full confidence in this ex-paratrooper who had taken complete charge of the platoon. A machine-gun platoon was normally authorized by a lieutenant, gunnery sergeant, three sergeants, and six corporals. We were reduced to two sergeants and three corporals.

Someone said Corporal Frank Pospical, my L.A. liberty buddy, had been killed and "never made it off the beach." I felt Frank's loss very hard. A good-natured guy, he had nicknamed me "Tarzan" when I had worn a T-shirt that advertised my hometown football team, the Stockton High School Tarzans. I somberly recalled the L.A. liberty we had spent with the Weiss family.

As it grew dark, intermittent fire, ours and theirs, continued. Flares in the night sky cast flickering shapes and shadows. We alternated watches and shivered in a cold wind. Sleep, when we were able to achieve it, was fitful and short.

Dobermans were brought forward and their legendary alertness to infiltrating enemy soldiers enhanced our security. I would never go to sleep at night until the dogs were on duty. I hoped their handlers weren't feeding them K rations, and if they were, I hoped the dogs bit them. *I would be happy to share a steak with them if I ever see one again,* I promised myself.

Steve and I broke out K rations, which were still tasteless. I found a chocolate "brick"—it couldn't be called a bar. I nearly dulled my KA-BAR, which Steve had spent so much time sharpening, cutting slivers off so I could chew them.

Dying for a smoke, I found four Lucky Strikes in my K-ration pack, rather than Camels (my preference), which confirmed the ads that said, "Lucky Strike has gone to war." Sure enough! Four of their "coffin nails" were on the front lines with me!

Bored, I inspected the contents of my K ration: Item 1, a small can of cheese; Item 2, a small package of crackers; Item 3, a bar of hard chocolate; Item 4, a packet of powdered coffee (Nescafé); Item 5, a package of four cigarettes, gum, and toilet paper.

Eggs and ham from the breakfast pack was my favorite. The crackers in each meal were compressed to the hardness of granite. The chocolate bar was so hard a beaver couldn't chew it (I'm sure some of them will last until the next ice age).

In the defense of the chocolate, I can at least say that it wouldn't melt in your hand! In fact, a Seabee told me, "I couldn't melt a K-ration chocolate bar with my blowtorch." If its defenses could be breached, however, it would provide a good source of energy and made an excellent drink when melted in hot water, as did the powdered Nescafé coffee. Because they were low in bulk, K rations caused constipation. The most important item in a ration box was toilet tissue. I put two sticks of chewing gum in my jacket and toilet paper in my hip pocket.

After eating, I mused over my squad's losses. The Word had it that our soft-spoken squad leader, Corporal William Whaley, and our Tarawa replacement, Pfc. Thomas Jeffries—who just wanted to escape his Colorado "hick mining town"—had been wounded on the beach and evacuated. At least their clocks were still ticking. Pfc. Tex Thompson, with his Clark Gable mustache, wasn't so lucky. He never made it off the beach. Of our eight-man squad, there were only four of us remaining, since Van Conkelberg left us with his dental pains before we got to Iwo.

Fifty percent of the men I knew, trained with, and trusted were gone.

TALKING WITH "THE MAN"

I wondered about dying and wondered about killing Japs. I said a prayer for the dead and wondered if it was okay to pray to God during a war. I didn't believe God approved of war. I felt He should have given us an eleventh commandment: Thou shall not make war on thy fellow man.

Well, it doesn't matter, I decided, *because man wouldn't have obeyed that commandment any better than he did the other ten.* I also wondered what the Japanese God thought about the ghastly killing. I wondered if both the Japs and us had the same God. I wasn't having any trouble staying awake because of the close presence of the enemy. My adrenaline was working overtime! When my watch ended, I fell into a deep sleep for two short hours.

CHAPTER FIFTEEN

D+2, February 21, 1945
Yard by Yard

Strobe-lit human forms appeared directly in front. They ran low, crouched to the ground, screaming in a chilling, undecipherable wail. It was a Banzai charge!

Dawn on D+2 greeted us with a cold rain. I was stiff; it had been a miserable night. Steve and I faced our third morning on Iwo Jima with our fingers crossed. We were still next to Motoyama One Airstrip, so I figured we had advanced the grand total of a thousand yards from the beach in two days. At that rate, we surely wouldn't be arrested for speeding.

The terrain on which we found ourselves was flat from the edge of the runway to the western shoreline, probably the only flat ground on the island. The peaceful shoreline seemed less than five hunded yards away—an easy rifle shot.

The dark, overcast sky, filled with rain, soaked us and transformed the volcanic soil into a slick, gooey, and sticky mess. Vehicles and men struggled to move, then bogged down. On the landing beaches behind us, the chaos continued as increasing winds and rough seas smashed derelict landing craft.

Japanese mortar fire fell on men who were moving supplies to support the 28th Marine's attack against Suribachi. This fire came from the high ground north of Motoyama One.

Beaches remained closed to all but emergency traffic and wounded lay patiently in hastily prepared shelters while corpsmen and surgeons did what they could to save lives. Ammunition stocks were running low.

At 8 a.m., the frontal attack northward was renewed. We continued to be in regimental reserve, following the 3rd Battalion. The 5th Division's objective was the left flank of the island, the entire area between the runways and the beach.

We, the 27th Marines, occupied the right flank of the attack. In simple terms, our attack was running in a parallel line to the empty airport landing strips. As we had done the day before, we mopped up bypassed positions and consolidated the gains made. Progress was slow but steady. We were taken under fire by a bypassed pillbox, and the call came to bring our guns forward.

This tactic was routine—there were plenty of targets for everyone to practice on! I signaled Steve and Lloyd Hurd to move up their gun. Accompanied by ammo carriers, both moved into a firing position.

Corporal Tremulis (who aspired to run his family's flower shop after the war) had replaced Sergeant Windle as our section leader when Windle was promoted to platoon leader. Tremulis pointed out the target located in a clump of brush 150 yards away. Unexpectedly, a second supporting enemy stronghold took us under fire. This was the classic Japanese defense on Iwo, one strongpoint providing protection for another. Captain Jimmy Mayenschein, our company's executive officer, had warned Sergeant Windle that enemy defenses were triangular in depth—you would attack one pillbox and then be ambushed by another two that lay behind it to the left and right. From above, the enemy's defenses looked like the three points of a triangle, with each post designed to support the other.

In most cases, the emplacements were also connected by covered trenches or underground tunnels. The enemy could escape annihilation by falling back on his support position or moving underground to reoccupy a bypassed or previously destroyed location. This strategy frequently placed the advancing Marines under attack from the rear or flanks. Combined with the terrain and the Japanese soldier's tenacity and willingness to die in battle, this created the daily "hell of Iwo Jima."

I directed Steve's fire on the second fire point. Our first machine-gun section had already covered the primary strongpoint with accurate, probing fire. With both targets under direct attack, the infantry assault elements maneuvered forward, accompanied by flamethrower and demolition men.

Our advance worked like drills and we utterly destroyed the positions with explosive charges. The regimental advance continued at a good pace as we attacked and destroyed several more hardened emplacements.

As we moved forward, the 4th Division's 23rd Marine Regiment on our right came under intense resistance and made little progress. When a gap in the lines opened, Lieutenant Colonel Butler ordered our battalion to fill the void and link up with the elements of the 23rd Marines. B Company was directed forward and to the right. We moved out under mortar fire and fought our way forward to get on line. Somehow, during this movement, I found time to answer a call of nature. I had a tremendous headache after three days with no bowel movements. Physical exertion, adrenaline, K rations, and enemy fire had combined to delay normal body functions.

I found shelter from mortar explosions and scratched myself a small hole. (There is a Marine procedure for taking a crap, even under fire.) From the stench, it was apparent to me that the Japanese or Marines had used this place earlier. I didn't want to be hit with my pants down, so I hurried. Getting caught with your pants down on Iwo suddenly took on a new meaning! I covered my waste. I realized my headache was gone.

By 4:30 p.m., we were on line and tied in with the 23rd Marines. We were ordered to "dig in and prepare night defenses." A counterattack was expected. We brought up the heavy water-cooled .30-caliber guns and set our aiming stakes.

Our newly promoted platoon leader, Sergeant Windle, "walked the line," checking our field of fire, making necessary adjustments. Steve and I manned one of the water-cooled guns. A dog unit moved in and set up around our position. As I said before, the dogs were a vital defense against individual Japanese infiltrators.

Once we were settled in, the Word came down the line as to who had gotten killed that day. Officer casualties were running extremely high; we were running out of leaders. Our replacements were mostly fresh out of Officer Candidate School, and they had an unenviable task. Some just couldn't get the hang of combat leadership in the short time the Japs allowed them. Those with some savvy would learn to lead under fire from men like Sergeant Windle. Trying to take advantage of this opportunity was difficult, since combat-tested noncoms like Kavato and Basilone were being taken out on stretchers daily.

Iwo was a tough and brutal classroom in which to learn the art of war.

KAMIKAZE

As night settled over Iwo, air-raid sirens began to wail. We strained our ears and looked skyward. We saw flashes of antiaircraft fire and heard the whine of motors. Some kind of hellish action was going on. Fortunately the enemy didn't bomb the island—their target was our fleet. The attacking planes were suicide kamikazes that hit the USS *Saratoga,* killing 123 men and wounding 192. The valiant, thirteen-year-old flattop steamed away under her own power.

The *Bismarck Sea,* an escort carrier, fell victim to a kamikaze. Ten minutes after impact, the ship was dead in the water. Doomed by exploding planes on board, it slipped under the waves, taking 218 of her crew and all its aircraft to the bottom.

During the same night attack, torpedo bombers hit the *Lunga Point,* another escort carrier, but it suffered no serious damage. The *Keokuk,* a railroad ferryboat from San Francisco Bay, and LST-477 survived attacks against them in the same action.

All Japanese planes and their crews were lost. The Navy suffered 717 killed or wounded sailors.

Shortly after the air-raid alert ended, we settled into our nightly routine. Steve dozed off as I took the first watch. About 8:30 p.m., I woke him up. It was my turn to sleep. I felt a certain inexplicable restlessness, but managed to drift off into a fatigue-induced sleep.

Sometime later, the clatter of machine-gun and rifle fire jolted my senses and I was instantly awake. Flares fired from ships lit up the battlefield. The heaviest action seemed to be to our left.

I scanned the terrain in the flickering light. Shadowy figures seemed to be dancing on the horizon. Heavy fire had broken out to our right. Something big was happening.

I was tempted to train my gun in the direction of the firing. My heart hammered, but I reminded myself to maintain the assigned field of fire and keep within the constraints of the aiming stakes.

Strobe-lit human forms appeared directly in front. They ran low, crouched to the ground, screaming in a chilling, undecipherable wail. It was a Banzai charge! Instinctively, I fired, rapidly traversing my weapon through its assigned field of fire. In my excitement I failed to fire short bursts.

The barrel glowed red as I expended an entire belt of ammo. I threw open the breach and Steve quickly extracted and replaced the old belt. I slammed the cover, pulled the bolt back, and released it. Squeezing the trigger, I was back in business. This time I was calmer and fired short bursts, following the arc of tracers across my direction of fire. I stayed within my aiming stakes. Only if you could see an immediate danger was it okay to forget the stakes and traverse the gun widely. Alerted, our artillery responded, and exploding shells blanketed our front, falling in the midst of the assaulting Japanese. Flares continued to light the battlefield while we strained to see the enemy. They seemed to have evaporated.

What had happened was that they had gone back like rats, into their holes. I looked at my watch. It was 10:15 p.m. The attack must have lasted an hour. Steve and I were tense, and neither one of us could go back to sleep. We didn't know it, but our battalion had just turned back an estimated eight hundred Japanese.

Some infiltrators got through and were hunted down and killed in rear areas by reserve and supporting troops. There was also an attack on the western beaches, which had originated from seaward. This attack was also broken up.

Nobody can be sure because there are no surviving Japanese battle reports, but the Banzai attack of D+2 may have been hastily arranged when the Japs realized a gap in our lines had developed. The Japanese officers probably hadn't realized our 1st Battalion had filled the hole before dark, and were shocked at the hot reception we gave them.

ROLL CALL

I had the feeling that thousands of enemy eyes continued to watch our every move from higher ground, looking for a fresh chance to attack and kill us. In the attack's aftermath, I couldn't settle down; my mind was on overdrive and I thought about our losses.

I didn't know the total number of B Company's casualties, but I knew that our ranks of 246 men had grown thinner. Overall, we had been lucky. D-Day was costly, but we had not taken a casualty in my squad since February 19, despite some heavy fighting. No one took an official roll call; all we got in the front lines was word of mouth about our dead and wounded.

D-Day—February 19, 1945—on the beach at Iwo Jima cost the machine-gun platoon most of its leadership. The platoon lost:

Lieutenant John Dreger, DOW (died of wounds)
Gunnery Sergeant Kavato, DOW
Sergeant George Lutchkus, WIA (wounded in action)
Corporal Guy Brookshire, WIA
Corporal William Whaley, WIA
Corporal Frank Pospical, KIA (killed in action)

It was hard to believe that Lieutenant Dreger—who had been lenient on me after my chicken caper at Camp Tarawa—was gone. Or that we had lost Blackie Kavato—whose target I had messed with on the range and who took me with him on liberty at Pearl. And, it was hard to swallow the loss of my friend Corporal Frank Pospical, who had accompanied me on my adventure with the Weiss family in Beverly Hills. I wondered if his date, Marion, would ever learn of his death. I wondered if, unlike me, who had neglected to stay in touch with Ruth, Frank and Marion kept the ball rolling. If they did, their correspondence was to come to a tragic halt.

Among the wounded who would not return were our Guadalcanal hero Sergeant George Lutchkus; our faithful loan shark, Corporal Guy Brookshire; and my squad leader, Corporal William Whaley. These losses created a leadership void in the machine-gun platoon that would be hard to fill. Luckily, we still had the "Iron Okie," Sergeant Windle, and streetwise Corporal Tremulis, to lead the squads. Corporal George Chelf took over Brookshire's 3rd Squad. Chelf was a tall, blond, good-looking guy, from Denver, Colorado, who wrote letters home regularly to his girlfriend with great penmanship that looked like a printer's engraving.

From the squads, we were still missing Ed Tucker, who had told me his premonition that he wouldn't make it. I didn't know if he and some others were dead or wounded. I did know they were missing. We knew that Spike Mierczwa and Loyal Leman had been killed. There were more, but I had already forgotten. "If veterans like Basilone got killed, you can get taken out, too," somebody said apprehensively.

At some point, drowsiness overcame my thoughts and I passed out, bone tired.

CHAPTER SIXTEEN

D+3, February 22, 1945
Changing Places

I carried a picture of my sister Audrey. She was pretty, with coal-black hair and a smiling face. More than one lonesome Marine wanted to see my sister's photograph.

At daybreak on D+3, our battalion was ordered to stand fast. The 26th Marines moved forward to relieve us, the 27th Marines, and we reverted to "reserve." This should have meant rest for our battalion, but on Iwo, even the reserve units caught hell.

The 26th had already suffered heavy casualties in reserve. The 27th, meanwhile, was casualty-ridden, exhausted, and would need to reorganize and replenish our supplies. As the 26th Marines passed through our lines, there were no longer wisecracks like "You'll be sooorrrry!" Cracks like that had ceased to be funny on Iwo.

We moved rearward and settled down next to a disabled tank. Sergeant Windle told me, "Take a few men and go to the west side of the airstrip to pick up some K rations." I did better than he expected. I found "ten-in-ones," the rations of choice. Ten-in-ones offered a prime dining treat and ours included a can of beef stew. We made a small, smokeless fire with a chunk of C2 and cooked hot stew and coffee. This was our first warm meal since our preassault breakfast.

Our incredible feast was followed by a hot-water shave. I even brushed my teeth! I felt human for the first time in four days.

Reenergized by the stew, coffee, and the shave, I decided to check out the disabled tank, a Sherman equipped with a flamethrower. Resurrecting my old dreams of being a tanker, I lowered myself inside and positioned myself in the driver's seat.

My playing at being a tanker was interrupted by the returning tank crew, who said, "Get your ass out of our tank! It's repairable and we don't want you messing up our hardware!"

Later in the campaign, 1 came across a tank that had taken a direct hit and exploded. I peeked in the turret. The men inside had been burned to a black crisp. I never daydreamed about tanking or played in a disabled tank again.

"BLOOD AND GUTS"

We cleaned weapons and personal gear. A mimeographed news bulletin was passed around. GENERAL "BLOOD AND GUTS" PATTON ADVANCES 34 MILES IN ONE DAY! screamed the headline. Unbelievable—thirty-four miles? That's *seven times longer* than Iwo!

I don't think we had gone a mile yet! Patton had gone thirty-four—but he wasn't fighting the Japs here!

The northward attack continued and the contest for Suribachi wasn't finished. The Japanese *still* "owned" more of Iwo than we did! With each bloody day of action, more territory fell into our hands. We felt we would win—but what would be the cost?

Our whole area was subjected to a severe artillery and mortar attack. It stopped as quickly as it started. Steve and I used the lull afterward to improve our foxhole—by digging a lot deeper.

Private Lloyd Hurd was writing a letter home as we talked. He knew the scoop about what had happened to the squad on D-Day, when Steve and I were separated from the platoon.

I told him about our terrifying experiences on the airstrip and the action with Basilone. Hurd was a levelheaded guy with an eighteen-month-old son named Ron. He had shown me a picture of his wife, Amelda, and son on several occasions. He was sure proud of his family.

Steve was looking through his wallet and pulled out a small piece of paper, which he read and handed to me. It was the words from a song in the Broadway show *Oklahoma!*, which went, "Don't throw bouquets at me, don't please my folks too much, don't laugh at my jokes too much, people will say we're in love!" Steve then showed me his girl's picture. I had seen Steve read that note and look at his girl's picture more than once in the past year.

I carried a picture of my sister Audrey. She was pretty, with coal-black hair and a smiling face. More than one lonesome Marine wanted to see my sister's photograph. I should have written to her more often, as well as to my mother.

I checked my pockets and found thirteen cents; I threw a penny away to give me better odds. This was all of the money I had left from my last liberty in Hawaii. That *was* a liberty to remember and the reason I may have gotten off Gunny Kavato's bad list. I remembered him telling me, "Tatum . . . go shine up. We're going to hit Pearl harder than the Japs did!" My dungaree sleeves were rolled up and I could see my fifty-cent USMC tattoo. While I still wasn't convinced we'd "hit Pearl harder than the Japs," I knew the Japs were hitting us pretty hard right now.

Blackie Kavato never had a chance to prove his leadership in combat. He never made it up the terraces. Still, he trained us well. I gave silent thanks to Kavato, *thanks for the liberty and the things you taught us about weapons and about being Marines.* I guess Oriel and I shouldn't have misspotted his target on the range at Pendleton. It was wrong—but funny at the time. It was hard to believe Kavato was gone.

HELP ARRIVES!

We heard that the 21st Marines of the 3rd Marine Division were now ashore and would enter the lines to help take Motoyama Airfield Number Two.

Incoming mortar fire snapped me out of my woolgathering. Nearby, 75mm guns answered the Japanese and the Sherman tank crews went to work.

We continued cleaning our weapons and replaced the barrels of our machine guns. Maintenance of weapons was like eating—it was essential for survival. A well-maintained piece couldn't protect you from enemy ordnance, but it made you more capable of fighting back and gave the enemy less of a chance to take a crack at you.

The U.S. government sold each Marine a ten-thousand-dollar life insurance policy. Iwo Jima sure put a large dent in the balance of the GI Insurance Fund.

Before night fell, we moved into our positions from the night before, because our advanced line position wasn't defensible. The front lines had moved ahead by several hundred yards during the day. We were always alert for infiltrators or a breakthrough caused by a Banzai attack against frontline units. However, in our old foxholes, we didn't experience the tension and creeping fear of the front lines—it was almost like home!

CHAPTER SEVENTEEN

D+4, February 23, 1945
The Island Siege

Like it or not, the word was that the Japanese still occupied more of Iwo than the Marines. To prove that they were still the main landlord, the enemy sent a message via a concentrated artillery and mortar attack.

Our first night in reserve passed and we awoke to improved weather. The 26th Marines were preparing to jump off at 8:30 a.m. The Japs were alert and waiting. Our preattack bombardment was heavy but didn't last long—they never seemed to be long enough.

The enemy opened up as soon as our shells stopped falling. The 26th Marines' attack crawled ahead a yard at a time, smashing one enemy cave or tunnel entrance then *another* in a grinding fight.

There seemed to be no end to the Japanese defenses. Each small gain was consolidated, each yard forward paid for, with blood, sacrifice, and lives. Medics and stretcher bearers had worked themselves into exhaustion—but kept coming back. Their jobs were as hard as frontline fighting and they were taking severe casualties. As a matter of personal survival, no corpsman wore the Red Cross symbol. To use one would have been an invitation to be a special target. Japanese soldiers didn't observe international rules of war.

Our battle had become a *siege*. The enemy had no hope of escape or possibility of receiving reinforcements. There could be no resupply of food or water. Each Japanese soldier would fight with whatever arms and ammunition had been stored before our invasion.

When their supplies of ammo were exhausted, they would have to fight hand to hand, I figured. I'd heard Japanese officers charged with waving swords. I wondered how my KA-BAR would work if it came to man-to-man combat.

Steve always wanted a Japanese sword, but we never found any. If one *was* found, it could be a death warrant. Snipers were delighted to get souvenir hunters and scavengers in their sights.

Serious lack of water was the enemy commander's main problem and his troops were suffering from the shortage. Iwo had no naturally sweet water. There was evidence that the Japanese had attempted to find water by digging deep wells. American troops encountered a number of them. There was a danger of falling into one of the shafts in the dark—something the Japs didn't mind.

We had brought all our drinking water ashore in five-gallon "GI" cans. Our drinking water tasted like gasoline or fuel oil (which the cans were first used for), but slimy as it was, it was still water. I wondered what the Japs' water tasted like? Sulfur?

In traditional sieges, enemy water and food were cut off and whole fortresses were starved into submission. Sometimes water supplies were poisoned. We didn't have to poison the Japs' water; it was already contaminated with sulfur and who knows what else.

The ancient Japanese code of Bushido or "way of the warrior" dictates that honorable soldiers fight to the death. This credo was ingrained in Japanese children from an early age.

As Americans, we also had been trained to be patriotic from our early days, but our code was more flexible. We were allowed to live—if we could somehow manage it in this vicious situation.

MASTER PLANS

There was another mandate the Marines had to grapple with. Our operational orders dispatched from Hawaii to regimental commanders stated bluntly: "Land, seize, occupy, and defend Workman's Island"—Iwo's code name—"in order to use the island for future operations against the enemy. Destroy or capture the enemy thereon."

Thus the Marines were compelled to attack Iwo's defenders head-on.

Iwo's Japanese supreme commander, Lieutenant General Tadamichi Kuribayashi, and his men were determined to die on Iwo Jima. The general prepared his trap with line upon line of fortifications, "triangular and in depth," a blueprint planned to annihilate as many Marines as possible.

A genius in the design of fortifications, the general buried his entire garrison of twenty-three thousand in the favorable defensive terrain Iwo offered. He was a samurai warrior with a deep poetic and spiritual sense, and his life was totally committed, along with those of his men, to a last stand in defense of his homeland. Iwo was America's gateway to Japan.

"OUR FLAG UNFURLED TO EVERY BREEZE"

As the 26th Marines pressed their attack, enemy mortars began falling in our rest area. Japanese weapons were capable of firing from one end of the island to the other. With thousands of Marines crawling around in concentrated areas, it was an easy task to keep our advancing troops under fire.

From our reserve positions near the beach, it was possible to witness the battle raging for possession of Mount Suribachi.

Through Sergeant Windle's field glasses we took turns watching the upward progress of our men as they approached the steep rocky

slopes. It appeared that the 28th Marines were at the base of the volcano.

Haze from the battle obscured my vision, but we could tell that
one hell of a fight was going on. It felt sickening to be in reserve,
watching a battle where men were dying almost before our eyes. It
kind of seemed like watching a motion picture from the wrong end
of a telescope, if that makes any sense.

About 10:30 a.m., Steve slapped me on the back and pointed
toward Suribachi, shouting, "Tatum! Do you see that?"

I twisted around and saw our Stars and Stripes clearly on the peak,
waving in the breeze. The 28th Marines were now "kings of Iwo Jima's
hill"!

Cheers from thousands of Marines roared and reverberated across
the island. I felt a surge of pride. I was proud to be a Marine and proud
to be an American fighting on Iwo. But we weren't attending a picnic.
Live shells were still dropping on us and throughout Iwo. Steve and
I soon forgot the flag raising as we busily reengineered our foxhole,
digging deeper into "Mother Iwo."

UNWELCOME TENANTS

Like it or not, the Word was that the Japanese still occupied more of
Iwo than the Marines. To prove that they were still the main landlord,
the enemy sent a message via a concentrated artillery and mortar
attack.

In our reserve position in a flat area near the end of northern end
of Motoyama Number One, we were "naked as a jaybird," without
cover of any kind. The surprise barrage lasted for ten minutes. After
the shelling ceased, corpsmen started their gruesome tasks of tending
to the screaming wounded and removal of silent dead.

When division headquarters totaled up the 28th Regiment's losses
for the first four days, their figures were a staggering 2,057! We in B

Company had our fair share. Word quickly passed through our grapevine: Pfc. Theron Oriel—my buddy who had helped mismark Kavato's target and cook my stolen chicken at Camp Tarawa—had been hit by an artillery shell while in his foxhole. Severely wounded, he had been evacuated.

By the fifth day, fatigue was taking its toll; our bodies failed to respond to our demands. Little or no sleep had eroded the fine physical condition we were in when we landed. I suspected fear was as debilitating as lack of rest. I saw fear on every man's face and I'm sure my buddies saw it on mine.

The clean, salt air smell from the Pacific Ocean filled my nostrils, then the acrid smell of gunpowder, napalm, and burning flesh diluted its gentle zephyrs. The cold sweat of fear was on all our brows. Danger has a smell both sides recognized.

DEAD MEN'S PILE

My feet were sore as hell. Pulling off my shoes for the first time in five days, I removed my socks. They were disgusting and wretched. I had a serious case of toe jam and the tender skin between my toes was cracked.

My condition was not life threatening, but on Iwo, life depended on agility and being fleet-footed. Bad feet were a handicap against the odds. I carried an extra pair of socks in my pack, which I managed to keep dry.

Given the condition of my feet, I knew additional socks were imperative. My boondockers were constructed to allow for "breathing" and were fairly waterproof.

Needing additional socks, I asked Sergeant Windle for permission to make a run to the "dead man" or "casualty" pile to look for a pair. His approval came with a request to pick up a pair for him.

The dead man or casualty pile contained clothing, equipment, and weapons of dead or wounded Marines. I had to go a quarter of a mile, and as I hobbled there, I felt uneasy and a bit guilty about the prospects of being a scavenger.

But I had no choice. The demands and horrors of Iwo's battlefield left no other ready solution to the problem of resupply. I hesitantly picked up a pack only to drop it instantly. There was a bullet hole straight through it.

I found another one intact and slowly lifted it, trying to see the stenciled name of its previous owner. Curiosity got the best of me—it wasn't anyone I knew. Undoing the straps, I carefully removed the contents. There were two perfectly clean and dry pairs of green, wool socks.

A celluloid folder lay at the bottom of the pack and it fell to the ground as I shook out the contents. I opened the folder. A photo of a smiling girl beamed at me. "All my love to Joe, Marilyn" was neatly written across the bottom of the photograph. I carefully replaced the folder in the pack and said a prayer for Joe and Marilyn.

With no warning but their vicious *swish-swish* sound, mortar shells began raining down on me. I sprinted and dove for a hole, landing on a prone Marine captain whose body cushioned my fall. When the danger passed, I apologized and he said, "Mac, maybe you can do the same for me someday." He smiled. Constant danger had dissolved the formal line between ranks.

Needing something for my "dogs" (Marine-speak for "feet"), I checked in with our platoon corpsman, "Doc" Curtis Marsh, pharmacist's mate third class, from Cincinnati, Ohio. "Wash your feet and sprinkle them with this foot powder," he said, handing me a packet of powder. Doc was a good-looking guy with a good outlook on life in spite of his grim duty to battle pain and death itself. Following his instructions, I used my helmet as a washbasin to cleanse and powder my sore "dogs."

A former tool-and-die maker, Marsh had been drafted back in February 1943, shortly after his marriage to his high school sweetheart. He chose the Navy as his branch, received his medical corpsman training, and was thrown in with us roughneck Marines at Camp Pendleton. He had no say in the matter—the Corps needed corpsmen, so Marsh became a "directed volunteer."

Doc Marsh wore full Marine clothing, gear, and carried a .45-caliber pistol. The Navy supplied his black bag (medical kit) and it wasn't black—it was olive drab. For all real purposes, the corpsmen were considered Marines by the Marines and by themselves. They could wear either their Navy or Marine uniforms while on liberty, and in most cases, they went in Marine green.

Corpsmen trained with the Marines, but not as combatants, and they followed the Marines everywhere they went. A corpsman is technically considered a noncombatant. International law allows corpsmen to wear a Red Cross band on their left arm. Law or no law, corpsmen assigned to the Marines didn't wear the Red Cross Band. Who needs a target on their sleeve? Like I said, the Japanese didn't recognize the sanctity of this international symbol. Marsh was the equivalent of a sergeant and a typical Marine company like ours had six "docs."

BACK FROM THE DENTIST

Finishing the repairs on my feet, I looked up and there stood Van! Pfc. George Van Conkelberg was back from the dentist! "Where in the heck have *you* been?" I demanded.

"I've been trying to get ashore since D-Day to join you [expletives]! I had a hell of a time getting a ride to the beach. I have been trying to find you all morning."

Van sat in the hole with me and I noticed his dungaree jacket had "Tom Piper" stenciled on it. Corporal Tom Piper, you will recall, was the C Company Marine and close friend of mine from Stockton who had ridden the world's slowest Greyhound bus home with me. I had just been to the dead man's pile and knew spare clothing was being taken by anybody needing it. I was immediately depressed. Was Piper dead?

"Take over as the gunner on our squad's gun," I told Van. "Steve will be your assistant." I could tell he didn't cotton to the idea of me as acting corporal in charge of him *and* the squad. When he complained, though, Sergeant Windle told him in no uncertain terms, "Tatum has five days' combat experience and you don't have any."

NIGHTTIME VISITORS

We moved into night defense behind the lines and settled into a routine of sleep and watch. A quick firefight broke out near C Company. It was over as fast as it started. The Japanese moved at night, foraging, readjusting their lines, resupplying, and reoccupying previously overrun positions.

Whenever possible, they tried to kill sleeping Marines. At night, everyone *stayed put.* If something moved, it was presumed to be an enemy soldier. The frontline policy was to "shoot first and bury the results in the morning." D+4 was uneasy. We didn't rest well despite the fact that we were still in reserve and supposed to be resting.

CHAPTER EIGHTEEN

D+5, February 24, 1945
Frontline View

I awoke, looked down, and saw my filthy trousers,
creased and stained . . . My damp socks were matted
to my sticky feet; I was as crummy as a skid-row bum.
In short, I was a mess.

On the sixth day of battle, the 26th Marines advanced five hundred yards with what was described later as "moderate or reasonable casualties." For the dead and wounded, however, the terms *moderate* and *reasonable* would be misnomers.

Our 27th Regiment continued in reserve while the 21st Marines of the 3rd Marine Division on our right flank attacked Motoyama Airfield Number Two. This airfield was the "door" to the Japs' main defensive line of pillboxes, tank traps, blockhouses, and interlocking caves that cut across the width of Iwo. As the 21st Marines emerged on the airfield, they met fierce resistance.

Steve, me, and the rest of the squad had box seats for this frontal attack, which escalated into an epic battle for the 21st Marines. We watched eight Sherman tanks from our 5th Tank Battalion rumble forward to spearhead the attack. In less than ten minutes, five of them were taken out by fierce antitank fire and buried five-hundred-pound aerial torpedoes. Our riflemen threw smoke grenades, which laid a thick smoke screen to mask the withdrawal of the survivors.

Transfixed by the horror of units being ground to pieces before our eyes in the battle raging around us, each member of the squad understood that this chaotic scene was a preview of what was waiting when he took his place on the line.

SIGHTS FOR ENEMY EYES

It was easy for me to make out each of the men with the 26th Marines who were fighting for the airstrip, even from a long distance, because of the green color of their dungarees. Faded and dirty, they still contrasted sharply with the sandstone brown, gray, and black of the island's landscape.

In our dungarees, we Marines were easy game for Japanese gunners. We looked like ideal targets for enemy soldiers on an infernal rifle range. I knew if I could see our Marines, so could the Japs. It couldn't have been any worse if we had painted "Target! Target! Target!" on our chests!

Our green dungarees had served well in Saipan and other Pacific islands, but Iwo wasn't a "palm tree paradise." Where was our military "intelligence" on *this* screwup?

The Japs wore uniforms with a sandstone hue that blended into the terrain. Sometimes, an enemy soldier properly camouflaged, even a few yards away, was impossible for us to see.

The 26th Marines had plenty of work for their demo squads. Those guys used composition C2 like it was free. Working fast under fire with high explosives, they must have had "suicide" and "pleasure" mixed up. From my observations, I figured they enjoyed their work. Extreme danger has a certain degree of fascination for some Marines.

"CURTAIN TIME!"

We knew our rest was over. We would move forward to relieve the battered and exhausted units now on the attack. Dread and anxiety crept into our consciousness. It was clear the 27th Marines were going to shed more blood.

What happened to the "three-day cakewalk" we were promised? We had been here five days and this war was barely getting started! The prospect of dying had gone through my mind while on board LST-10. Then the possibility seemed distant and remote.

Now, fighting on Iwo Jima, I had become an unwilling witness to death all around me. Being killed, myself, had an obvious immediacy my mind tried to ignore.

"There ain't no combat virgins on Iwo anymore," Hurd told me. He was right. Now there were only veterans. Each of us experienced a deep sense of dread at the thought of being ordered back to battle. The odds of getting killed or wounded were against us and we accepted the fact.

I thought of a poem I had to memorize in school, "The Charge of the Light Brigade." The words I remembered were "Into the valley of death rode the six hundred . . ." Had the author of that poem, Alfred Lord Tennyson, written of Iwo instead of the Crimea, he might have said, "Into the valley of death rode the six hundred . . . again and again."

While we rested and mulled over the thoughts of impending combat, an order came from Corporal Tremulis: "Saddle up! We're going on a sniper hunt." Japanese sharpshooters had infiltrated our rear and set up shop by an embankment near the airstrip. Leaving our machine guns, we spread out in an infantry-style formation to comb the area. Our search for snipers was fruitless, but we did find a dead enemy soldier in a clump of bushes.

The smell of his rotting corpse almost made me puke. "The stench could gag a maggot!" Steve said. Bloated, the body was in a spider trap and almost unrecognizable as having been a human being. His uniform was so charred that I thought he might have been hit by a flamethrower.

Bloating had caused the tunic buttons of the cadaver's uniform to pop off. There was no skin on what had been the face, but the putrid flesh had scabbed over. Swarms of flies were attacking the torso and maggots were wiggling in the eyes. I guess we were lucky Iwo had no buzzards. A rifle lay beside the body. No one touched it. "It might be booby-trapped," Tremulis warned us, "so don't screw with it."

Later, resting in our reserve area, I looked at my watch, saw it was 3:30 p.m., and decided to eat a K ration. Seeing the bodies of dead Japs had become so commonplace I could erase this one from my thoughts. It had nothing to do with me. I had become as hardened to death as an undertaker.

BIG GAME HUNTING

Cutting my ration box open, I recalled a time when Van, Steve, Hurd, and I had gone hunting for wild boar in Hawaii. Hurd was designated our "outdoorsman" and leader of the expedition. He spent his boyhood in Sartell, Minnesota, where he had hunted and fished. He proved his weapons skills by firing "expert" at the rifle range in California.

For firing "expert," the Corps rewarded one with a metal clasp worn on the blouse and an additional five dollars' pay. Hurd sent the extra fiver to his wife and son in their allotment. Five dollars doesn't sound like much today, but in 1944, a "fiver" was equivalent to a 10 percent monthly raise for a private.

We had pushed off into the hills surrounding Camp Tarawa with food, pogey bait, and the camp's "no-name dog." After hours of working our way through the bush, we spotted a wild pig that our dog had flushed.

Hurd squeezed off a round. He missed the boar but accidentally hit and killed the dog. The pig disappeared over the edge of a deep ravine, where, Hurd said, "He probably killed himself." During the hog hunt, we camped out overnight, eating our rations of baloney sandwiches, and Steve had brought a surprise—marshmallows— which we toasted on sticks over the fire instead of roasting pork!

Drying my boots by the fire, I managed to burn the heel off one and had to limp twelve miles back to camp. On the way we found some piglets that we assumed belonged to the hog we'd chased into the ravine. We brought them back to camp, where they were tenderly cared for with plenty of help from the "country boys" in the platoon. When he found out about them, Lieutenant Dreger said, "I am forced to 'liberate' these swine since I can't reconcile pig maintenance in camp and Marine Corps regulations."

Maybe he took the piglets to the officers' mess, where they wound up on dinner plates. The hapless camp dog was never mentioned again.

Japanese artillery started falling and I was jerked back into the war as a flood of adrenaline hit my bloodstream. We were forced back into our deep holes to spend another long night of fitful sleeping and watching for infiltrators.

Fortunately, no Japanese picked on B Company during the night of D+5.

IWO BO

The stench of my body assaulted my nose, and I wondered if I smelled as bad to other people. I had never gone six days without a bath before. Subconsciously, my lack of sanitary measures probably triggered thoughts of washing in my sleep. The Pacific was so close; too bad the Japs wouldn't let us bathe in it!

While sleeping, I dreamed of taking a real shower under a water- fall of hot water with a king-size bar of luxurious Ivory soap, the kind

Pfc. Charles Tatum (left) and Pfc. Steve Evanson about the time of the infamous "snake in the grass." *Courtesy of Chuck Tatum*

The author's first job delivering the *Stockton Record*, 1942.
Courtesy of Chuck Tatum

John Willie Tatum, circa 1917.
Courtesy of Chuck Tatum

Pft. Tom Piper (left), boyhood friend of the author, Charles Tatum (right),
joined him on many adventures.
Courtesy of Chuck Tatum

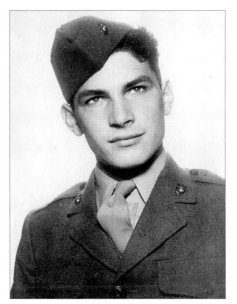

Charles W. Tatum, January 1944, Camp Pendleton, California.
Courtesy of Chuck Tatum

The author, Pfc. Charles "Chuck" Tatum, in a fake set of dress blues
taken sometime in July 1944.
Courtesy of Chuck Tatum

Camp Tarawa. Back row (left to right): Pfc. George Van Conkelberg, Cpl. Angelos Tremulis, Pfc. Charles Tatum, Pvt. Thomas Jeffries, Pvt. Lloyd Hurd, Pvt. Lavor Jenkins, Cpl. William Whaley. Front row (left to right): Pfc. Bruno Mierzwa, Sgt. Raymond Windle, Pfc. Charles Whitcomb, Pfc. Carl Thompson, Pfc. Billy Cawthorn, and Pvt. Ralph Jefferies. *Courtesy of Chuck Tatum*

The author demonstrates the proper way to shoot an M1 Garand from the kneeling firing position while at Camp Tarawa. *Courtesy of Chuck Tatum*

The author draws a 1911 .45 pistol while at Camp Tarawa.
Courtesy of Chuck Tatum

A snapshot taken from the front lines, March 11, 1945, D+20.
USMC photo

This Sherman tank crew escapes with only a damaged tread.
USMC photo

A Marine of the 5th Division runs past Japanese dead on March 3, D+12.
USMC photo by Col. William Rockey

Marine halftracks engage a Japanese pillbox from close range.
USMC photo

Feb. 19. 1945

Marines of the 5th Division landing on Iwo Jima. Mt Surabachi in background.

Lou Lowery

"Everyone on the beach was caught in a giant sand trap of death. We were swept with lethal, white-hot steel." —Chuck Tatum

USMC photo by Staff Sergeant Louis R. Lowery

Artillery spotters go about their deadly business as they take cover in a shell crater at the first Japanese airfield. *USMC photo*

Chuck Tatum at the wheel of a Tatum Special race car.
Tatum won his race at the Stockton Airport Racetrack that day.
Photo from the Chuck Tatum collection

The "Tatum Special" race car.
Photo from the Chuck Tatum collection

Family reunion (left to right): Dean Schaeffer (cousin), Machinist Mate 2nd class Johnson, Maude-Schaeffer (aunt), Elle Marie Wilson, PFC Charles W. Tatum, Wilman Jean Rogers (fiancé), George A. Schaeffer, friend of Wilma Jean Rogers, PFC Robert Ross holding small child, Mary Tatum (sister), Joan Tatum (sister), and Roy Schaeffer (cousin). *Photo from the Chuck Tatum collection*

John Basilone's fellow Marines of C-Company, in Hawaii, autumn 1944. This troop had attended John Basilone's and Lena Riggi's wedding on July 10, 1944. *Photo from the Chuck Tatum collection, courtesy of Lena Basilone*

Sgt. John Basilone and his bride, Lena, pose for a picture commemorating their wedding day in Oceanside, California. *Photo from the Chuck Tatum collection, courtesy of Lena Basilone*

Gunnery Sergeant John Basilone proudly receives the Congressional Medal of Honor for extraordinary heroism and conspicuous gallantry in action against Japanese enemy forces, above and beyond the call of duty. *USMC photo*

Gunnery Sergeant John Basilone.
USMC photo

Chuck Tatum with Tom Hanks, during the LA premier of *The Pacific*.

Photo from the Chuck Tatum collection

movie starlets on radio commercials swore *they* used. Maybe I even hummed some of the Ivory soap jingle, "Ninety-nine and forty-four one hundredths percent pure, so pure it floats."

Like most good dreams, it wasn't true. I awoke, looked down, and saw my filthy trousers, creased and stained. I hadn't changed shorts since D-Day and was afraid to inspect them for "nicotine stains."

My damp socks were matted to my sticky feet; I was as crummy as a skid-row bum. In short, I was a mess. Even so, my shower dream was a very vivid and comforting vision I hoped would come true.

PRIMITIVE HYGIENE

My primary daily concern was a bath to clean the accumulated dirt and grime from seven days of nonstop combat. Since landing, all I had been able to do was perform a daily ritual of washing my privates with canteen water. Since I wasn't circumcised, the latter act was a sanitary necessity. Anyway, the Marines, as always, had a prescribed procedure for doing it. It was known as the washcloth method, and we were given a full lecture about it by a Navy doctor; his theme was "sanitary precautions while traveling on trains."

Probably that same Navy doctor was now so busy in the operating tent that any thoughts of "washcloth" lectures were surely forgotten. Our 2nd Platoon corpsman, Curtis Marsh, didn't have an M.D.'s diploma, but he was our "Doc," and even though we called him a "pecker checker" in good-natured jest, Marsh was special to us. He used a mile of bandages fixing people on the beach the first day, saving lives and dispensing his own brand of tender loving care. On the battlefield, his only protection was the Colt .45 he had strapped to his leg. He told me confidentially forty-five years later, "I still had the same clip in my Colt when the battle ended in March. I never fired a bullet. The only shots I got off were from syrettes of morphine."

Marsh trained with us at Camp Pendleton and Tarawa. Wherever the Marines went, our corpsman followed. There was always a man getting hurt, a headache, a case of the clap, or blisters on a foot. A few complained of afflictions unknown since biblical times, trying to get out of duty.

Marsh's treatment? "Take two aspirins and see me later." If it was serious enough, he would send the ailing soldier to battalion sick bay. For that, you had better be good and sick! No gold-bricking (Marine-speak for "slacking off") under Doc Marsh's supervision!

Marsh and his fellow medics never let us down. Though Navy men, "Docs" were, in every sense, Marines and deserved the highest accolade we could offer: "He's a Marine!" By the time we reached battle, we completely trusted Marsh. I'm sure he appreciated our acceptance, but still grumbled that "being shanghaied into the Marines was only one click higher than working in a hospital ward with bed wetters and illiterates!"—his previous medical assignment.

CLEAN SWEEP

The 21st Marines' fight for Motoyama Airifeld Number Two was bloody and the progress slow. A bulge formed in our lines exposing the 5th Division's right flank, and we were ordered to hold up.

This allowed time to clean weapons, eat hot chow, and bullshit with our friends. In order to be able just to carry on, we avoided talking about lost buddies. Like most others, I believed "the Japs don't have a bullet with my name on it." During moments when I didn't believe that tired, old cliché, I prayed or dug my foxhole deeper.

Sergeant Windle assigned our squad to the 2nd Platoon for "mop-up duty." We were told, "Sweep the battalion area for bypassed Japanese positions and find and eliminate any infiltrators." We destroyed a number of empty emplacements with C2 and the only Japs we found were already dead.

Even in death, Iwo's Jap bastards were lethal. A corpse could kill or maim. Picking up a rifle, sword, or other interesting booty belonging to the Japanese was a no-no. A concealed wire or a strand of fine silk thread might be attached to an explosive device. Just lifting an object could trigger a blast, killing or maiming several people. Jap "dirty tricks" started on Guadalcanal and were used extensively throughout the Pacific islands.

We, as frontline troops, had neither the time nor the inclination to gather souvenirs. I never saw anyone in my section with Japanese gear. Nobody that I knew of was wounded from booby traps.

"CORPORAL PIPER, I PRESUME?"

Machine-gun and small-arms fire broke out near the embankment of the airfield. The fire was directed at a squad of Marines who were maneuvering near the edge of the airstrip. Hightailing across the airfield, they jumped over the edge of the strip and down the embankment.

As they approached, I recognized the squad leader. He was the corporal from C Company—Tom Piper—my hometown buddy! God! *Was I happy!* I thought Tom had been killed on the beach when Van showed up wearing his stenciled jacket.

I couldn't resist asking Tom how his dungaree blouse got into the dead man's pile. His answer was typical Piper. "When I came ashore, I decided I had too much stuff," he told me. An orderly person, he stacked his gas mask and extra gear neatly on the dead man's pile so they could be used by somebody else.

Tom was a natural leader and quick to show initiative. At Pendleton, during a training exercise, a brushfire was started by a tracer round and it gathered strength rapidly. It swept through a ravine and a lone Marine raced forward, ripped off his dungaree jacket, and began beating the flames. Behind him others followed his example, quickly formed a skirmish line, and knocked it down.

Lieutenant Colonel Butler arrived on the scene and wanted to know who had led the firefighters. Tom held back, but was pushed forward by his buddies. Colonel Butler asked his name. Hesitating for a moment, Tom answered, "Pfc. Piper, sir."

"No, not anymore. *Corporal* Piper," replied the colonel. Tom's spot promotion was the talk of our battalion for days.

LOGISTICS

Just before setting up for night security, Sergeant Windle ordered me to "take five men to the supply dump and bring back ammo." The trip was uneventful and we returned before nightfall with a full load of ammo.

We divided it up with other guns in the section. At night, Windle made sure each gun had fifteen boxes at the ready. A total of fifteen boxes of 250 rounds per box equaled 3,750 rounds or seven to eight minutes of fighting time at 500 rounds per minute. Before dark, Windle checked each gun's field of fire, making corrections as needed. His constant vigilance was like a shield. Our night defenses were the best. I don't remember any Japanese defenders infiltrating our lines at night, from the front at least.

In the darkness of a foxhole, I asked Van if he remembered our last poker game back at Pendleton. "Screw you, Tatum," he snarled. "You don't know [expletive] about poker." He was still pissed about our memorable poker game.

When Van asked if we knew what happened to his bosom buddy and our moneylender, Corporal Brookshire, we told him, "Brookshire got hit the first day on the beach."

CHAPTER NINETEEN

D+7, February 27, 1945
Dreading Dawn

Looming over us ominously, 362A's blocklike form was silhouetted against the sky, five hundred yards in front of us. Half the height of Suribachi, it was a dangerous obstacle to our advance.

Unvarying routine and the passage of time play tricks on your memory. My recollection of D+7 is hazy. The battalion prepared for offensive action and we spent the day repositioning for our assault role. Tanks surged forward and went into action along the division front.

This was the day we discovered that Iwo's Japanese had a few tricks left up their sleeves. When the enemy fired their secret weapon for the first time, we watched, fascinated, as a huge projectile roared overhead toward Suribachi. Their new weapon was a Jap copy of the hated German V-1 "Buzz Bomb," the world's first operational rocket-propelled bomb that had been used to strike London, and which the Japs were now launching in a north-to-south direction down the center of the island. The Japanese version was a 250mm rocket bomb that they fired from rough wooden chutes located in the hills just past Motoyama Number Two.

Trailing fire and smoke, the bombs made a screeching, whistling noise that could raise the hair on your neck. Fortunately, they couldn't be controlled with any accuracy and most of them missed the island

and fell harmlessly at sea. On occasion, they landed in the 28th Marines' area at the base of Suribachi or bounced off the mountain's rock-strewn sides.

Fortunately, the "ricky-ticky rockets" did little damage other than to shake the hell out of the island. As an offensive weapon, Japanese rockets were a failure—and a joke.

We employed mobile rocket launchers mounted on ships and trucks. Not as accurate as directed artillery and mortar fire, our rockets had a devastating effect on anything aboveground over a wide area when they hit.

Unfortunately, on Iwo, the Japanese had precious little of their defenses aboveground. Their mobile rocket launchers created a huge cloud of dust and smoke with their back blast, and drew counterbattery fire after launching so their crews would quickly withdraw.

Our artillery was frequently directed by spotter planes known as grasshoppers or OY-1s. Hovering over the battlefield, pilots spotted enemy positions and called in the 13th Regiment Artillery and Naval gunfire. Sitting ducks for enemy small-arms and antiaircraft fire, the pilots must have had balls as big as watermelons.

Iwo's condensed battlefield made it possible to watch the struggle for supremacy in all its dimensions. As action rose to a fury along the lines, we could see or hear the agony and hell being experienced by a nearby unit while we might be "enjoying" temporary safety.

Sulfur fumes, salt air, gunpowder, and death permeated the atmosphere with an evil smell. As the days wore on, our green dungarees absorbed the dust and grime of Iwo and we blended better into the landscape.

When daylight faded, we moved into position, preparing to open the attack on a hill called 362A, scheduled to start at sunrise. We were numb from fatigue and accumulated fear, but a new level of tension made for a restless night. Hill 362A was the northern anchor of the Japanese main defense belt running across Iwo, known as Tabor Zaka to the Japanese defenders, a name given in honor of a famed battlefield of the 1877 Japanese Civil War. This is where we would run head-on into General Tadamichi Kuribayashi's main defensive line for the western sector of the island. The cunning Japanese commanding general ordered all troops defending Tabor Zaka not to fall back from this position, to die at their guns. The odds were against anyone capturing this fortress of stone. We just didn't know how bad the odds were. We didn't know that Hill 362A had over three hundred Japanese defensive positions and over 1,200 Japanese defenders, all pledged and resolved to die. No one looked forward to dawn.

FORTRESS 362A

Following a soaking rain and uncomfortable night, we were up before dawn. The day broke cold and clear. Big things were about to happen. Lieutenant Lepre, leader of our 2nd Platoon, briefed us: "Landing Team 1-27 [1st Battalion, 27th] is to take the center of the line. On our right will be Landing Team 3-27 and on our left will be Landing Team 2-27."

The day had a funny feeling about it, like something would go wrong. Chilled and miserable, I smelled like an old billy goat, as did everyone in the platoon—except Pfc. Luman, our original Mr. Clean. Were Luman's dungarees starched with a secret potion to ward off dirt and scum? After eight days of combat on Iwo, he still maintained a neat appearance. Clean-shaven, armed with a bright, flashing smile reminiscent of a toothpaste ad in *Life,* he could have been a movie star instead of a combat Marine! Luman's appearance since D-Day defied nature and our war against Iwo's Japanese.

Waiting for our jump-off to begin, I observed the surrounding terrain. On our left, the western beaches joined a series of ridges that grew in height until they reached a huge rock with a sheer face resembling an ancient European fortress. Identified by its elevation, this was Hill 362A.

The high ridges between 362A and the shore were our regiment's objective. The ground before us was flat, but jam-packed with enemy "rat holes," caves, and connecting tunnels. Looming over us ominously, 362A's blocklike form was silhouetted against the sky, five hundred yards in front of us. Half the height of Suribachi, it was a dangerous obstacle to our advance. We could count on it being fortified and protected by heavy artillery support and mortar positions, waiting for us to advance.

Captain Jimmy Mayenschein briefed Sergeant Windle to "expect stiff resistance." It was obvious we would have an uphill battle to take this objective, with the Japs looking down our throats every inch of the way. But before we could attack 362A we would have to wreck the apron of concrete-protected, underground positions in our path to the hill. I worried that its approaches were mined. Even before that day, when we saw the hill on sector maps, Steve predicted, "We're gonna have to take that ugly sucker."

Our company would be in battalion reserve, following closely on the heels of A Company and Basilone's old C Company. But our reserve status would change quickly.

BETWEEN A ROCK AND HELL

After kickoff at 8:30 a.m., C Company, on the left, ran into a string of hidden pillboxes after going two hundred yards. They were quickly engaged in intense combat. Tanks, a 75mm half-track, demolition men, and flamethrower operators were called in to reduce the newly discovered, hardened positions. Nasty enemy fire disabled the supporting 75mm half-track and the crew took casualties trying to destroy a large emplacement.

By 11 a.m., C Company had pushed ahead and lost a number of men. Following closely, we received some small-arms fire and could watch C Company fight, a hundred yards ahead of us.

Three hours later, more concrete positions were discovered and tanks were called forward to blast them. Two men were killed and three wounded by the time C Company secured for the night.

While C Company had tough going, A Company advanced four hundred yards after their kickoff and moved to the top of a ridge near 362A in a sustained push, with light resistance. Pausing to consolidate, the men were hit with grenades, mortars, and machine-gun fire from their exposed flanks and rear.

Cleverly, the Japanese had sprung a trap. Mortar fire came from behind 362A. Caves in front of the cliff opened up and A Company's 1st Platoon was the hardest hit, incurring heavy casulaties. At 1:30 p.m., A Company had to pull back as quickly as the hail of machine-gun fire and bullets allowed. More men were lost trying to save their wounded. The work that had gone into arming and fortifying Hill 362A, the Japanese version of the Maginot Line in France, was awesome, and it was serving its designers' purpose: It was stopping the Marines.

At 3 p.m., Lieutenant Colonel Butler ordered those of us in B Company forward, in order to take on the objective. We quickly moved out, passing through A Company's shocked and bleeding survivors. I saw, in no uncertain terms, what I hoped wasn't a preview for B Company. A Company had suffered a terrible ordeal, and the ridge where their remaining wounded lay was named "Casualty Hill."

B Company followed closely behind the impact of supporting artillery fire. The shells blanketed the objective, churning up clouds of smoke and dirt, allowing us to snake very carefully forward. Section leaders gave the hand signal to advance. Moving out in clusters, we formed fire teams and began our ascent of the ridge. Again I had the feeling that unseen eyes were focused on our advance.

Clang! The trap sprang shut and we were in it! Japanese mortars winged in, greeting our attack. We took cover. Machine guns and rifle fire erupted from every crack and crevice in Hill 362A. The mountain was spewing death and destruction from every fissure in its volcanic hide. It seemed as if Tabor Zaka was alive! There was no way to fight back. We couldn't see our enemy. But they could see us, and they had us dead in their sights!

We scrambled over the rocky terrain without cover. Steve and Van carried our machine gun, followed by Pops Whitcomb and Lloyd Hurd, our ammo bearers. An orchestra of Marine and Jap mortars, machine guns, rifles, and artillery created a roaring, shrieking clamor, inducing terror throughout the ranks, stopping our forward momentum. With mounting casualties and nightfall approaching, we consolidated our positions and dug in. We were literally nose to nose with our mortal enemies.

Some of the enemy positions were less than forty feet in front of us. The day's fight had cost the battalion an estimated one hundred casualties for a gain of *two hundred yards* forward—a typical day's fighting on Iwo.

SILENT NIGHT

Weary but alert and tense, I took stock of our good fortune. Thanking the "Five-Star General in the Sky," I thought, *I'm grateful to make it through another day.* Anticipating the next day's fight, which would start as soon as I left my hole, I wondered, *Will we be chopped up like A Company?*

Steve had first watch. I tried to sleep but couldn't; my mind was running on overdrive. Lying on my back in the foxhole, I could see Steve's profile silhouetted by the white light of star shells descending to earth. His eyes were squinting, searching for movement or danger lurking in the inky darkness between flares. I trusted Steve to stay alert and ready when he was on watch. He felt the same way about me. We were great companions from Camp Tarawa—no, more than that, we were brothers-in-arms. Steve, from Opportunity, Washington, a small farming community near Seattle, was an "all-right Marine."

Steve's real name was Clifford Blaine Evanson. Even now, I think it was strange that we called him "Steve." I guess it had to do with the fact that joining the Marines gave each of us a great opportunity to be someone else if we wanted to. Lots of people shed names and other things not to their liking when they entered the service.

Drowsy, I thought of the liberty Steve and I had pulled in Hilo, Hawaii. We had done all there was to do in that town—which wasn't much. After we visited the tiny USO club, it was all downhill as far as entertainment was concerned. We spent a dull night at the YMCA, sleeping on cots (the same kind we had at Camp Tarawa), which made us feel at home!

On Sunday, we went back to the USO club and watched pretty "Hilo Hattie" perform Hawaiian dances. She became famous for her interpretations of native culture after the war. Bored stiff, we went for a walk, checking out the local stores, which ranged from a Chinese laundry and a tobacconist to a shop selling pots and pans. Some of Hilo's sidewalks were made of wooden planks, which creaked and groaned under protest from the pounding of our rough boondockers. The plain storefronts were made from the same rough lumber as the sidewalks. The effect was very quaint.

In a fit of exuberance, while strolling by a drugstore, Steve jumped and slapped at a Coca-Cola sign, making it flap on its rusted hooks. We had gone a few steps when the sign crashed to the plank walkway with a loud clatter. This racket was followed by the squeaky, high-pitched voice of the bearded "Fu Manchu" Chinese man who owned the store. He was screaming at the top of his lungs. *"Shur Patrol, Shur Patrol! You stay! You pay Marine!"*

Two Navy SPs arrived and tried calming the irate Chinaman down. It was clear he wanted money. "How much?" asked the petty officer in charge.

"Twenty-five dollar . . . cash please," replied the owner.

Steve and I had less than ten dollars between us. I had to do some fast talking. Calling one of the "swabby" officers aside, I told him,

"Look at the sign. The screws are rusted and he's lucky it didn't fall on someone a long time ago."

Nodding, the petty officer said, "Pay the old man *something.*"

I asked, "How about three bucks?"

"How about five?"

"Okay," I agreed.

The patrolman said, "Be quiet," to the screeching shop owner: "I'm holding a trial!" He asked Steve, "How do you plead?"

"Guilty," Steve answered.

The petty officer declared, "I hereby fine you five dollars for destruction of civilian property."

I handed over five bucks, and he passed it to the proprietor. Fu Manchu was still holding his hand out, wanting more.

"That's all you get," said the Navy policeman, ushering him back inside. The second shore patrolman led Steve and me away, saying, "It would be a good idea if you went to your assembly area and waited for a truck to take you back to Camp Tarawa."

I wondered if this incident was part of the "good old days" everyone was talking about. The last thing I knew, Steve was still looking into the dark night.

CHAPTER TWENTY

D+9, February 28, 1945
The Darkest of Days

Setting up the machine gun in seconds, they commenced pouring bullets and tracers into the opening. The rest of us used carbines and rifles to provide fire support. Van's gun suddenly stopped . . .

D+9 began like all the other days before it on Iwo Jima. I had the last watch and was awake when daylight came poking through the gray overcast sky. Steve and I were deep in our hole.

Steve was asleep and smiling. I supposed he must be having a nice dream. I felt the call of nature, but took precautions, something I had seen Roy Rogers do in a movie. I placed my helmet on my rifle and slowly raised it above our position. There was no response.

Now, when Roy had done this, the bad guys fired and gave away their position. Well, things always work better in the movies. Bending over to pick up my cartridge belt, I heard the sharp *crack* of a rifle and the near-simultaneous impact of a bullet on the dirt parapet above my head. Being lucky is as good as being smart on Iwo Jima!

Steve bolted upright, now wide-awake. He whispered, "What the hell is going on?"

"I've just raised a sniper. He has us bore-sighted—stay down, lie still," I whispered. We hunkered into the earth and didn't utter a word.

Time passed, the sun came up, and we could hear other Marines stirring. The sniper was quiet.

Convinced the sniper was gone, "holed up" from his night's work, Steve and I went about doing our toilet duties. In my case, it consisted of brushing my teeth with what was left of my toothpaste, splashing water in my face, and drying it with the sleeve of my filthy dungaree jacket. Once again I wondered how Luman managed to stay so clean.

I took our canteens and filled them with oily-tasting water drawn from a five-gallon GI can. It had previously been used for fuel. *Gag!*

DINING ALFRESCO

I headed back to our "dirt hotel." Steve was breaking out rations. Over a piece of C2, I heated my chocolate "rock" to make Iwo breakfast cocoa. I warmed a can of scrambled eggs and potted ham as the main menu entrée.

With the chocolate melted in my canteen cup, I opened a pack of hardtack crackers. I planned to soak them first rather than risk breaking a tooth, but I was so hungry that I gulped the rations down as fast as I could stuff them into my mouth.

Watching me, someone might've thought I was eating eggs Benedict from the Waldorf-Astoria! This meal, however, was courtesy of the famous French chefs of the "Café K-Raashoons."

After chow, I washed my face again and ran my dirty fingers through my matted hair. Damn! Even my hair hurt from the standard-issue helmet I wore—twenty-four hours a day.

My steel "lid" gave a false sense of security, because it wasn't bulletproof. If a round hit a helmet straight on, the occupant was a goner. A glancing shell fragment, though, was sometimes deflected. Still, the helmet did have one good use. If you took the liner out, it could be used as a washbasin.

OFF TO WORK!

Checking my carbine, I was ready for the day's fighting. Sergeant Windle passed out the "dope." We in the 1st Battalion were to take Hill 362A. He pointed to our objective—the ridge just to the left of 362A. B Company was on the right side of the battalion with C Company on our left, while A Company was still recovering from the day before and was being held in reserve. The ridge spine sloped toward the western beaches.

At 7:45 a.m., naval ships and the 13th Marines' artillery lambasted the hill and ridge for fifteen minutes. Close-in aerial assaults completed the softening up. Our planes took a stab at turning Hill 362A into a molehill.

Dust and explosions on the Japanese positions were so intense that we couldn't see the hill for a brief time. I hoped no one could escape from this engulfment of fire and flame. Following the prep fire, at 8:15 a.m., the signal came to "Move out!"

We rapidly advanced through a cluster of leafless saplings and scraggly brush dotting an ugly and lifeless landscape. No more trees, just rocks. The Japs greeted our advance with white phosphorus rounds exploding at treetop levels. Showers of white-hot fragments, which could burn through steel, filled the air. Fortunately, the enemy effort was weak and our company passed through the barrage.

The attack was barely moving when I heard the telltale *swish-swish* that says "mortar shells coming in." The concentration of shells pinned down our advance.

We entered a minivalley between two small ridges and were hit by both frontal and flanking machine-gun bursts. The most damaging fire was coming from our right flank. It wouldn't be suppressed until 3rd Battalion, advancing directly toward 362A, could overrun or neutralize the obstacle. The enemy had sprung an ideal ambush, taking our unit by surprise. There was no place to dig in. Piercing frontal machine-gun fire swept the ground. This, combined with mortar fire, caused B Company's advance to stall. I flattened myself against Mother Earth and prayed.

A CAPTAIN COURAGEOUS

I saw our company's second in command, Captain Jimmy Mayen-schein, crouched behind a rock. He was talking to our company commander, Captain Ben Sohn, by radio, relaying information and requesting artillery fire. To my relief, friendly high-velocity rounds whistled overhead and plowed into the forward ridge, hurling tons of rock into the sky.

Everyone took cover, no matter how thin. It was "Every man for himself!" We made excellent targets, frozen to the ground, trying to escape death. I didn't know where my squad was. I was so concerned with my immediate survival, I couldn't think about anyone else for a while.

Just then, a machine gun went into action to my left. It looked like Mr. Clean, Pfc. Luman, was "pouring it to 'em" from a small, earthen embankment. Riflemen and BAR operators joined with other machine gunners in suppressing the Jap fire.

Mr. Clean's machine gun was pumping out white puffs of smoke like an old Hudson with bad piston rings. Each puff said, "Look! Here's an American position!" Why in the hell didn't *we* have a scientist to cook up smokeless powder like the Japs used? And while he was at it, why couldn't he dream up some better K rations!

In agony, wounded members of B and C Companies found their way back to their starting positions and a measure of safety. Enemy fire slackened. We moved forward and secured a position at the base of the highest ridge. Starting a cautious ascent through a jumble of boulders and rocks, we seemed to be making progress when, again, all hell broke loose.

Mortar, machine gun, and targeted rifle fire tore into the company.

Men started dropping on all sides. Dirt ripped at my eyes and the clamor of explosions and bullets pounded against my ears. The ridge we faced was alive with an enemy that was impossible to see or kill.

Captain Mayenschein crept forward. He could see the chaos and disorder of our situation. Standing up, with a cool purposeful manner, he took charge. He looked as calm as though he was directing a training maneuver at Camp Pendleton.

Reorganizing the company, he directed a withdrawal from our untenable position. He seemed to be everywhere at the proper moment, personally assisting wounded, making sure everyone got out of the Japs' trap.

Captain Jimmy Mayenschein never ran out of courage, and his selfless, heroic actions saved B Company from destruction. But he did run out of luck. He was the last man still in the trap. When he attempted to withdraw toward our lines, Japanese soldiers used him for target practice, riddling his chest with multiple bullet wounds, killing him.

Reacting to the loss of our favorite officer, the company found a collective fury and determination. Reorganized, we rushed to the offensive. Because we were too close for artillery fire support or air strikes, the fight developed as a classic Marine infantry attack. Small clusters of men advanced by fire and fast movement until they found and obliterated each concealed strongpoint or individual enemy soldier. Our blistering advance made two hundred yards, a sizable gain on Iwo. Each forward thrust was made with a quick sprint, "heads up and asses down."

Lloyd Hurd, eight feet from me, looked concerned. Next to him, Van called out, "I see a cave!" Sergeant Windle pointed at me. He wanted my squad's gun to take it on, so I gave Van a hand signal to position his gun and fire at the cave entrance. Nodding, he and Steve ran to a clearing that offered a better firing location.

Setting up the machine gun in seconds, they commenced pouring bullets and tracers into the opening. The rest of us used carbines and rifles to provide fire support.

Van's gun suddenly stopped. Looking their way, I saw that he and Steve were down! Suddenly I was overwhelmed with rage, and all the anger I had stored up against the Japanese burst out. Without thought or hesitation, I sprinted to Van's position. Van had been hit in the back, near the right shoulder, and the round had exited his left side.

Steve had been gut-shot, twice, and was white with shock. By reflex, he was holding his hands to his stomach to stem the bleeding. Blood poured out around his fingers. As he pulled his legs into a fetal position, I could see the pain on his pinched face.

Knowing the Japs would shoot Steve and Van as they rolled around on the ground, I grabbed their machine gun into my arms and fired from the hip, like Basilone did, sending lead into the cave to suppress the enemy fire. I was in a hot rage and swiveled the gun about so its bullets would ricochet throughout the cave and decimate those bastards who shot my friends. Clouds of rock dust billowed from the cave's mouth. I poured fire into the cave's black mouth until the belt ran out. For a second I stood there, the .30's barrel smoking. The Japs who had shot Steve and Van were silent; nothing came from the cave, no Banzai charge, no moans, nothing. Just smoke and dust.

My senses returned. Dropping the gun, I turned to Steve and Van. I knew they were dying. I screamed, *"Corpsman!"* With the cave suppressed and the area safe, Doc Marsh ran to Steve and knelt over him, then turned to Van. Seconds ticked past, seeming like hours. I waited for Doc's orders.

Hurd ran out to join us and helped me and Marsh drag Van and Steve to cover. Marsh injected Van with morphine while I broke open Steve's first-aid kit and handed the syrette to Marsh. He shoved the needle into Steve's flesh. I screamed, *"Stretcher bearers!"*

When they came, the other medics and I lifted Steve as gently as possible onto a stretcher. They did the same with Van. Steve's face had the glassy look that accompanies deep shock.

Steve gave me a weak thumbs-up signal, as if to say he would be okay. I tried to smile as tears streamed down my cheeks.

The stretcher bearers left at a walk-run pace. Every second counted and my friends needed emergency medical treatment. *If Van and Steve live, it will be thanks to Doc Marsh,* I thought. I wanted to go with them, but Sergeant Windle denied my request. He couldn't spare the manpower. Windle had trained Steve, Van, and me. He had given us more than his personal attention and he deeply felt the loss. But he knew there was work to do.

Trembling with exhaustion and mental anguish, I *hated* this island. I *hated* the Japanese. I *hated* this war. Now the fight for Iwo Jima became a personal vendetta. *Someone is going to pay and pay!* I told myself. Never before was I more certain that this was the island God forgot and gave to the devil.

This day of violence, fear, killing, and maiming left me on the edge of despair. Sergeant Windle talked to me in a personal and Marine way. "Tatum!" he said. "Let's go, we've got a job to do."

I went obediently, but the rest of the day was foggy to me. Windle took ammo bearers Pops Whitcomb and Lloyd Hurd and made Whitcomb a gunner in place of Van, and Hurd his assistant, in place of Steve.

LOCKOUT

My mind slipped into a protective mode when events beyond my control took over. From that afternoon on, I purposely tried to avoid getting to know the replacement ammo humpers and the Marines filling the slots of those we had lost. I didn't want to know their names, where they were from, or see their girlfriends' pictures. I didn't want to get attached to them and suffer through the loss of close friends again.

The war was still going on—thirty feet ahead. I wanted revenge.

My squad consisted of Whitcomb, Hurd, and me. Before the day ended, Hill 362A claimed two more Marines from our machine-gun platoon. Corporal George Chelf, the leader of 3rd Squad, was shot in the head when he sat down to rest between firefights. Chelf was the tall, blond, good-looking guy from Denver who wrote letters to his girlfriend with penmanship like a printer's engraving. Lloyd Hurd and Jim Memory Martin were a foot away when Chelf was hit, and were splattered with his blood. We also lost Private Willis Daggett, a member of Chelf's squad, to a sniper. We never found where the fatal shots had come from.

Unseen, our enemy continued to punish us as we consolidated our gains for the day and attempted to clear the newly seized territory. A new private, a replacement, called me to the edge of a bluff. He had spotted enemy soldiers clustered in a pillbox and was trying to show me their location. I couldn't see what he had found and was sighting down his arm while he pointed, our heads side by side. All of a sudden a *crack* rang out, he jerked forward, and was dead before I could catch him. A sniper's bullet had hit him between the eyes. Instinctively, I called for a corpsman, although the man was beyond help. When the medic came up, he said, "I can't take it anymore. I can't go on. If they want to, they can just shoot me right now!"

The blood that covered the medic's uniform wasn't his own. Medics are considered noncombatants under international law, but the Japs didn't care about international law. After ten days on Iwo, he hadn't fired a shot—he was too busy stopping the flow of others' blood.

I didn't know what to tell him. I put my arm around his shoulders and said, "I understand." It didn't seem to help.

Staring straight ahead, he cried, "I just want out of this war!"

Then someone else yelled, "Corpsman!" The medic dried his eyes, picked up his kit, and left to go patch up another wounded Marine.

"BUNKIES"

At 7:30 p.m., we prepared our night defenses, running out our listening post, sighting our machine guns, and setting up our field of fire stakes. It was a routine that had become second nature.

When we wearily settled in for the night, a head count of B Company revealed that 17 men had been killed and 27 wounded. Of our original 250-man strength, almost 18 percent had been lost in one day. But our collective total was much higher—probably approaching 50 percent casualties.

My new "hole mate" was Lloyd Hurd. We had confidence in each other. He was a steady hand and a guy to trust with your life. We stocked up with ammo and were getting comfortable when Corporal Angelos Tremulis moved us to a new position to cover an area we had missed. Maybe we were getting a bit careless? Flares lit up the sky, casting a sepulchral glow over the landscape. Alerted, we watched for infiltrators—they were expected tonight. We forced ourselves to stay awake.

Desperate Japanese soldiers were foraging for food and especially searching for water. Their shortage of basic supplies was beyond critical. Maybe it was harder to die from thirst than to face death looking for water? A combat soldier can fight for days without food but will last only forty-eight hours without water. No wonder the Japanese took such desperate chances. The enemy's closeness and anticipated night activity kept our adrenaline high.

A firefight broke out on our left. Some enemy soldiers were attempting a penetration. I heard a voice saying in a whisper, "Stretcher bearers coming through." We could faintly discern their silhouettes, low and crouched. I thought the incident strange.

A BAR operator next to us opened fire, slicing them to pieces. We were dumbfounded. Sergeant Jay Laycock of 3rd platoon called, "What the hell is going on? Who fired on those men?"

The BAR man yelled back, "Don't worry, Sarge! Those were Japs."

No one ventured out to check. Shook up about the possible killing of Marine stretcher bearers, Hurd and I tried to settle down. Hurd took the first watch and I went to sleep immediately. My two-hour nap seemed like a minute when Hurd shook me awake.

The Japs had been firing artillery sporadically all night; there was an uneasy tension, so we talked for a while and I dozed off.

KING-SIZE FIREWORKS

Hurd didn't have to wake me the second time—the trembling, vibrating ground did. A massive explosion to the rear of our position had erupted. It seemed the enemy had blown up the whole island. An incredible display of fireworks followed. The entire southern end of the island appeared to be on fire. Unknown to us, a lucky enemy artillery round had found the 5th Division's main ammo dump. Amazingly, there were no reported deaths from the mayhem that followed.

The event provided a once-in-a-lifetime display of fire and pyrotechnics. An estimated million dollars in stored ordnance detonated. In our lonely foxhole, we imagined all sorts of possibilities, including a Banzai attack by Japanese troops from underground tunnels.

The explosion was followed by an air-raid alert. A lone Japanese plane flew over us, drawing fire from every AA (antiaircraft battery) afloat and ashore. Tracers streaked across the black sky. Hurd and I burrowed deeper into our hole, hoping we wouldn't be victims of spent 40mm and 20mm rounds falling on us. We felt naked and unprotected, accepting the theory that what goes up must come down. Other troops had been hit and killed by falling debris.

As if to add a coda to the night's events, the Japs fired a rocket at Mount Suribachi. Noisy and flaming, the inaccurate weapon lit up the whole sky briefly.

Somehow, in the early hours of morning, Hurd and I managed to enjoy a few hours' sleep. When dawn came, everyone wanted to check out the dead stretcher bearers. We discovered, to our relief, that the BAR man was right. Lying on the ground, ripped apart, were four Japanese soldiers in Marine dungarees. Covered with ponchos on the stretchers were several GI cans of water. Later, I asked the BAR Marine how he knew they were Japs. He responded tersely but with complete logic: "Marine stretcher bearers don't carry wounded to the front."

The *longest* night following one of the *longest* days was over. We had severely dented, but not taken, Hill 362A. The 5th Division was short 25 percent of its ammo supply because of a lucky hit by a Jap shell.

During our frightening day's fighting, our 1st Battalion racked up casualties of over a hundred men, dead and wounded.

CHAPTER TWENTY-ONE

D+10, March 1, 1945
No Answers

I missed the security of having friends like Steve and Van close by. Of the eight guys in my squad when we left Camp Tarawa, and the seven we landed with on D-Day, only Hurd, Whitcomb, and I were left.

Sergeant Windle called reveille early and I shook off the effect of a nearly sleepless night. My first conscious thought was of Steve and Van. Where were they? Were they all right? No one could answer those questions for me. I felt my squad mates were gone forever.

There was no direct communications between our unit and the field hospitals, so there was no organized way anyone could learn the fate of his wounded buddies. No officer would give me permission to leave the front lines.

Even if I walked a mile or so to an aid station or hospital tent without permission, none of the overworked staff could take the time to answer questions. Too many casualties were pouring into their facilities to think about individual men.

If Marines like Steve and Van were still alive, they would be transferred to a ship for further treatment. Frustrated, I tried to erase all thoughts of them. I was still in shock. My remaining squad mates and I "turned to" when Windle said, "Get your asses in gear! Prepare for unit passage."

The 28th Marines passed through our lines to renew the assault of Hill 362A. The 28th Regiment, Suribachi's conquerors, now rested and reorganized, would take on 362A's conquest, a job we had started at such a terrible cost.

While we were taking our turn in regimental reserve I knew what the 28th would be facing. Hill 362A was an objective that couldn't be bypassed. Regardless of the cost in blood and the number of lives sacrificed, orders for the 28th were unequivocal: "Take Hill 362A."

From where we "rested," I heard and saw deadly mortar and machine-gun fire ripping at the advancing men who were renewing the assault on Hill 362A. It was gut-wrenching to have to watch the slaughter of yesterday repeat itself.

Secretly, though, I was glad it wasn't us. Self-preservation, the desire to live, will always prevail in the human heart.

While shells and explosions raged, I wondered how many Steves and Vans it would cost the 28th before they secured that damned rock pile? By day's end, the 28th controlled the ridge. But the cost had been high. Scuttlebutt from a corpsman said *another* 224 Marines were killed or wounded. Almost *a full company* had been butchered!

As replacements arrived to join us, each of the remaining members of our squad, Hurd, Pops, and me, recognized a simple fact: "Our regiment had been shot to hell." We spent the day securing our gains and cleaning up the battlefield, which consisted of picking up stray weapons and gear. Hurd and I devoted a lot of energy to making improvements to our foxhole.

Reorganizing our battered ranks helped take my thoughts off Steve and Van. Darkness closed over the island as Hurd and I settled into our nighttime positions. Mine was the first watch. After Hurd fell asleep, I began daydreaming.

HOT RODS

I had always been crazy about cars, and as I settled in to my watch, I started indulging in an enjoyable fantasy: remembering my automobiles. My first car was a 1929 Model A Ford, purchased for the grand sum of twenty-four dollars. The body was shot, but it ran. My dream car was a coupe of the same model but without fenders and a rumble seat. While walking across a field in California one day, I spotted a 1930 Model A coupe body and frame.

The Ford's frame, front fenders, and radiator were totaled, but the cab was still in excellent condition. The Italian farmer who owned the wreck said if I removed it, it was mine.

With the help of two buddies, Aldrich Ross and J. R. Wyatt, I towed and dragged the hulk back to my parents' home.

My mother asked, "What are you going to do with that heap?"

I promised it wouldn't be in her yard longer than it took to change the body from one Model A to another.

My buddies and I were long on enthusiasm but short on skills and tools. But with youthful vigor and the help of a cold chisel, we cut all the bolts that couldn't be removed with wrenches and took the bodies off both cars. Our next chore was to lift the body of the coupe onto the frame of the sedan. It took eight of us to do it. We needed a lot of manpower because we didn't disconnect the steering columns. We just lifted the bodies over the shafts while they remained in place.

We hooked up the wiring and had my new/old car running in no time flat. Sitting so long in the field had wrecked the paint, so I decided it needed a new paint job. This was in the days before aerosol spray cans. For paint, the best I could afford was a seventy-five-cent can of "stove black." I took my stepfather Orvil's best camel-hair paintbrush and gave the car a coat of paint.

Guess what? No runs, but lots of streaks where the paint dried too fast. I also wrecked my stepdad's expensive paintbrush. But the Ford *was* black, and it looked great . . . in the dark.

Driving it was quite an experience. The shocks were gone, so passing over a railroad track could jolt your teeth out. The car had cable-operated brakes, so stopping was always a issue. I didn't care. I was *mobile,* free to come and go as I pleased (as long as I asked my mother).

I loved my Ford. For a fifteen-year-old during the 1940s, having a car was a *big* jump on life. Mine provided instant status and new friends, especially girls. Young women were more attentive to guys with wheels. However, I found quickly that I needed cash to make important inroads with women.

My part-time job at the local print shop paid twenty-five cents an hour. It couldn't support vehicle ownership. Gasoline in 1941 was fourteen cents a gallon. So it took over an hour's work to buy two gallons of gas.

Caught as I was in the grip of such economic realities, my car sat parked half of the time. When friends wanted me to take them somewhere, I demanded contributions! I learned about cars and friends as the owner of my Model A.

A succession of cars followed, including a 1934 Ford coupe and a 1932 Chrysler Royal coupe with *twin* spares in the front fenders, a rumble seat, and a little side door for carrying golf clubs. I didn't own any golf clubs, so I carried my tools instead.

The Chrysler was two-tone. Dark beige on the body, coffee-colored cream on the fenders. My Royal coupe drove good; the shocks worked and it stopped on a dime. This car had *hydraulic* brakes!

I sold the Chrysler for $125 to raise funds for my dream car, the 1929 Model A Ford roadster. What made this car special was an early-model Ford engine known as a V-8. It had plenty of power, but according to my uncle, it was a "death trap," an opinion that hardly pleased my mother.

It was probably fortunate my Ford had a leaky set of piston rings that constantly fouled the spark plugs. This circumstance slowed me down and prevented me from killing myself with speed before the Japs had their chance.

In my reverie, I had almost totally forgotten about the war, Iwo, and my daily exposure to death. My mind, now freewheeling, raced ahead to the modifications I contemplated undertaking when I returned home.

I planned to install an Edelbrock twin carburetor intake manifold and a set of Weiand high-compression aluminum heads in my Ford. I would call "Hot Rod King" Ed Iskenderian in Los Angeles and buy a high-lift camshaft. I didn't know what a camshaft did for an engine, but I had heard racing guys talking about special ones increasing speed.

I planned to replace my stock seventeen-inch wire wheels with the new sixteen-inch steel wheels.

FIZZLING SIZZLE

I was thinking what I would do with the brakes when an errant parachute flare nearly dropped in my lap. It was hot and fizzling when it hit the ground a few feet from where I sat. The burning aerial torch lit up an area at least three hundred feet across.

I crouched low in my hole to avoid its bright light. I didn't want to be a spotlighted target for a Japanese rifleman. While the flare fizzled and sputtered out, I forgot my cars and reentered the war.

I really missed the security of having friends like Steve and Van close by. Of the eight guys in my squad when we left Camp Tarawa, and the seven we landed with on D-Day, only Hurd, Whitcomb, and I were left.

Of our 1st Squad, we had Corporal Tremulis, Pfc. Billie Joe Cawthorn, Pfc. Gopher Gus Henderson, and our quiet Camp Tarawa replacement Pfc. Lavor Jenkins. Our ranks had grown frighteningly thinner. It was depressing.

CHAPTER TWENTY-TWO

D+11, March 2, 1945
The Badlands

My entire life was compressed into "right now." Forget about the past, I told myself. Don't dwell on the future. There may not be one for you.

There was no rest from battle even though we were in reserve behind the 28th Marines, who now assumed the assault in the final push to take 362A. Japanese mortar, artillery, and small-arms fire were still falling in our zone.

The battle for Iwo was running at full bore a scant few yards away. We had learned through painful experience on the front lines that each movement we made had to be quick and purposeful. A moment's carelessness usually resulted in death or injury.

At noon, we were advancing behind the 28th Marines when someone called, "Halt!" I decided to break out rations when I noticed an overpowering stench nearby. Looking for the source, I saw, ahead on the trail, lying directly in my path, a grotesque Japanese body.

The hideous shape looked like it would explode from bloat. It was stretched like an inflated balloon, uniform buttons popping, exposing an immense brown belly. I had seen other disgusting sights on Iwo, but this one took the cake.

Inured to human debris, I wouldn't let a grisly, overripe enemy soldier deter me from eating. I took cover across from the corpse and opened a can of cheese and bacon. My first mouthful was balanced on my KA-BAR when I heard Sherman tanks approaching. They were returning to rearm and load flamethrower napalm.

Staying on a marked trail to avoid land mines, the behemoths rumbled toward my "picnic." I had just enough time to jump clear of their crushing treads.

The lead tank rolled over the bloated Jap's body, exploding pieces of ripe flesh and fluids. A stream of fetid liquid splashed on my trouser leg.

I gagged, dropped my food, and ran to get away from the putrid odor. There was no place to go! Using my KA-BAR, I sliced away the fouled dungaree cloth. The smell pursued me the rest of the day and I was unable to eat.

We soon arrived at an open area near the unfinished Motoyama Airfield Number Three. This terrain resembled the Badlands of the American West, or more precisely "the devil's own rock pile," which Lucifer tossed from hell to Iwo. We were still following the 28th and looked gaunt and haggard, bearded, dirty, and red-eyed, just like the cartoon characters in Bill Mauldin's *Up Front*.

It was quiet for a moment and we paused. Silence on Iwo was uncommon. I automatically took cover in a small depression with a big rock in front.

"What the hell is going on?" I yelled to Corporal Tremulis.

"Don't ask me, ask Sergeant Windle!" he replied.

Leaving cover, I crawled to Windle's position.

"Tatum," he said. "Relax, we are just resting."

The Japs were also resting. The goddamn war was at a standstill. It was never officially confirmed that we had a truce—but it grew strangely quiet across the island.

KICK-STARTING THE BATTLE

After what seemed like hours but might have been only thirty minutes, the truce or whatever it was ended when the 13th Marines let go a thunderous barrage that kick-started the fight again.

The Japanese replied with mortars. The war was on again!

The sound of battle reverberated across the island. It was mind-numbing to realize our intense fighting and bleeding were in their *twelfth day.*

The winner's trophy, if you could call it that, would be a grim and ugly and hellish island named Iwo Jima.

Our sense of time was all screwed up. Each of our nights seemed at least twenty-four hours long except when it was your turn to sleep. Two hours of sleep seemed about a minute long—and two hours on watch could seem like forever.

The most important thing to do was to survive the next engagement on what some of us had taken to calling a "clapped-out, sulfur trap." I learned not to think about what I would eat (always K rations)— or when. Dinner was too far away and uncertain to contemplate. My entire life was compressed into "right now." *Forget about the past,* I told myself. *Don't dwell on the future. There may not be one for you.* The whole goddamn war for me was fifty feet wide and stood thirty feet directly in front of me. That was my personal chunk of it. My strategic planning consisted of two questions: "How do I make it to that big rock? How do I make it through the next ten minutes?"

Pfc. Pops Whitcomb found a rock he liked very much. In fact, he might have been falling in love with it—he was hugging it so tightly.

ENGINEERING A GUN PIT

The Word at 5 p.m. was dig in. We moved fifty feet to higher ground at the rear of our line. This would be easier to defend with better fields of fire. Hurd and I began setting up a water-cooled .30. At night, each machine-gun section operated four guns, which provided Baker Company with twelve machine guns on our defense line. For this night, I would be a gunner again.

Hurd and I started constructing a machine-gun emplacement. It would not be a haphazard project. We were not trained engineers, but we could "hold school" on foxhole design if asked, and we had a proven mental blueprint to follow.

Since we would spend twelve hours or more in foxhole, it would have to be large enough for one of us to sleep in. The dirt we shoveled out was piled around the edges to make the sides higher. Most of the excess sandstone and volcanic crap we were mining went to the front, forming a kind of parapet.

We set our machine gun behind this breastwork with only the barrel peeking over. This way we could sweep everything in front of us without exposing ourselves too much.

We were a little short on power entrenching tools. The Seabees were using all the bulldozers and "drag lines," so we fell back on our collapsible shovels. I had mine set at a ninety-degree angle. In this hoelike position, it clawed through the hard-packed dirt better.

Hurd had his set in the shovel position so he could toss earth out of our new home. We were building this temporary structure as if our lives depended on it. Darkness came fast on Iwo, and we were in a rush to finish our construction project.

We had ammo placed at the ready and within easy reach—we couldn't be scrambling and hunting for it in the dark if the Japs decided to storm our positions. We relaxed a little once our machine guns were settled in, with our fields of fire selected and aiming stakes set.

All toilet arrangements were made before nightfall. Answering a call of nature after dark could get your head blown off by friendly fire. "If it moves, shoot it!" was our unspoken rule. I took many a piss in the bottom of my foxhole. I wouldn't venture out of my space and attract a bullet just to relieve my bladder.

CHAPTER TWENTY-THREE

D+12, March 3, 1945
Attrition

"I'm sure glad to be at the front," a young replacement about my age said.

Incredulous, Buckland responded, "Are you crazy? No one in their right mind would say that."

March 3 was a bad day for replacement officers. Lieutenants Garcia, Harrington, and Leach, all assigned from the 27th replacement draft, were killed in action.

With almost no experienced commanding troops in combat (or anywhere else), second lieutenants had been cranked out of Officer Candidate School in Quantico, Virginia, wholesale. The Marine Corps created its new leaders with assembly-line speed.

Harrington and Leach were commissioned officers for five months when they were told to lead platoons in deadly combat. Brave, inexperienced pinch hitters or substitute quarterbacks in a game of death, they never knew the men they were trying to lead.

Green officers like Harrington and Leach were forced to push forward in hellish circumstances. Often they replaced popular leaders like our fallen captain Jimmy Mayenschein and Lieutenant Dreger. Those men had commanded since our days at Pendleton and the presence of replacement officers was not immediately accepted.

The first task of new officers upon assuming command on Iwo

was to survive long enough to learn the names of the Marines they commanded. Lucky ones entered platoon structures, which, hopefully, had a surviving sergeant to assist in the transition.

Eager beavers didn't last long if they ignored the seasoned sergeants who, on top of their natural talents for command and combat, had learned tactical skills on Iwo that couldn't be learned in Officer Candidate School.

I know of no quantitative data on the loss ratio of new officers in Iwo Jima's incredibly tough command assignments, but Sergeant Jay Laycock said to me, "I lost two replacement officers in my platoon in rapid succession."

"Don't send me any more green Second Louies," he told headquarters, exasperated. "I don't have time to look after them!" New officers on Iwo were knocked out of action so fast many never had a chance to prove their mettle in battle.

Because Marine units kept fighting with near-total dependency on replacements during the battle, it was a testimony to the training and esprit de corps of our branch of service that cooks, bakers, shore-party details, and rear-echelon personnel who were sent forward were able to effectively fill the ranks of the assault units. There are no non-combatants in the Marine Corps. Every man was trained to fight first—and only *then* received a specialty classification or assignment.

It was only near the end of the battle, when replacements grew scarce and 60-man platoons became squads of sixteen and companies of 260 Marines became platoon size, that units were finally rendered combat ineffective.

"GUNG HO"—"WORK TOGETHER"

Early that same day, D+12, Sergeant Buckland, who now commanded B Company's 1st Platoon, received three replacements. I overheard his warning: "Be very careful and keep your heads down—Jap snipers are having a field day."

"I'm sure glad to be at the front," a young replacement about my age said.

Incredulous, Buckland responded, "Are you crazy? No one in their right mind would say that."

"Sergeant, try to understand," the Marine said earnestly. "I came ashore on D-plus-1 and unloaded supplies for five days and nights straight. My next six days were spent doing the most gruesome task on Iwo—working on the burial detail. Sir, some of the men had been in the sun four or five days and were *really* ripe. The stench of rotting corpses would run a raven off a gut wagon. I wore my gas mask to ward off the ghastly odors. My job was cutting off one half of the dog tags to nail on each white cross.

"Sir," he finished sincerely, "I joined the Corps to fight, not to be a flunky!"

"You'll get a bellyful of action—if you live long enough!" Sergeant Buckland promised.

On a trip to the rear I noticed a Marine, wrapped in a poncho, who was sleeping in the daytime. He was holding the chain leash of an alert Doberman. The dog looked tougher than a master gunny sergeant with a rash on his butt.

I guessed both of them had been up all night guarding the front lines against infiltrators. I couldn't help wondering if the Corps gave out dog tags to their mutts.

That Marine could sleep all day—as long as he was up all night with his K-9 partner. The dogs were "recruited" as part of the national war effort. Pet owners donated dogs like those I saw on Iwo to the Marine Corps—knowing they would never see them again. If they weren't killed in combat, the dogs, who couldn't be returned to the States, would be destroyed. This was just another reason why the whole war was so lousy.

In the late afternoon of that day, Sergeant Windle ordered Lloyd Hurd back to the rear, despite Hurd's strong protest. Physically and mentally spent, he had begun spitting up blood, which was caused by mortar-shell concussions. It was tough to lose Lloyd. That morning he had said, "I hope my wife and son are all right back in Minnesota. I miss my family. I hope to make it off Iwo and get back home someday."

After thirteen days, we were all on the edge of exhaustion, each of us with a different threshold. Sergeant Windle was still in full control of our dwindling platoon and was quick to spot a man who couldn't go on. The sergeant was like a mother hen; everyone was under his wing. Leadership by example was his style. I guess the best thing that Windle did was to give us the courage to carry on day in and day out on Iwo Jima. After all, who would want to let the sergeant down? He wasn't letting us down.

Hurd had survived D-Day, the western push, and Hill 362A, fighting aggressively and valiantly, never backing off. Now he was exhausted, no longer able to continue.

COOKING WITH STEAM

Pangs of hunger gripped my gut. It was C-ration time! The area we were camped in was above a sulfur field—so the ground was hot. If you dug deeper, the temperature increased. The heat was almost distracting. Not hot enough to actually burn you, but it got your attention.

Before Hurd left, we had buried our rations in the bottom of the foxhole. Now I had *two* beef-stew dinners—both more than warm—*almost hot*. They sure tasted better this way than cold, out of the can. Next, I buried my canteen so I could make warm coffee. When it was ready, I decided to fix hot chocolate. The water wasn't hot enough, but I carved slivers of chocolate bar into the canteen cup and drank it anyway.

While I gagged down crumbs of compressed crackers, thoughts of meals past filtered through my mind. What wouldn't I give now for a plate of SOS? My lips were smacking at the thoughts of dinner composed of that concoction. Marine cooks used hamburger submerged in a sea of flour-based, white gravy, served over toasted bread . . . I longed to sink my teeth into a slice of real bread. Damn those crackers!

Better yet, bread with a *large* slice of SPAM. Greed overcame my imagination. I wanted *two* slices of bread and a chunk of SPAM. I wished it was Wednesday morning aboard ship so I could have a bowl of navy beans.

The aroma of my Nescafé instant coffee couldn't match my memory of the smell of real coffee—the kind of smell that would invade your nostrils while you stood in a chow line in the galley on a Navy ship. The warmth of a galley would have made for a nice change after enduring nearly two weeks of Iwo's chilly nights.

The constant heat from Iwo's sulfur fields had a way of invading your body. I folded my poncho several times to shield my ass from the penetrating heat of the foxhole. It would be a long, hot night on Iwo. I twisted and turned, trying to get comfortable. Discomfort from the heat was almost as bad as the cold. I wondered, *Isn't there any way to get comfortable on this ghastly island?*

I don't know who I shared a hole with that night, but I do remember that before dark, Sergeant Windle told us, "Intelligence still wants prisoners from here on. Don't go around plugging the wounded, the big brass wants them for interrogating; but don't get killed doing it. Savvy?" It was good, in theory.

I was feeling gloomy and fighting off sleep when a noise shook me from my stupor and sent my pulse racing. I felt a string tightening around my neck. I reached inside my jacket to see what it was. My dog tags had slipped around, choking me. I pulled the string to the front and checked to see if both were still there. They were. It may have just been Sergeant Windle's talk that spooked me.

There was a reason why we carried those two pieces of rectangular stainless steel with rounded corners tied on a string around our necks. Each pair was pushed inside a rubber ring to keep them from jingling together (jangling dog tags on the front lines could be pretty fatal).

If we screwed up and got killed, the burial detail cut one dog tag off and nailed it to a prefab white cross. I thought bitterly, *How many crosses did the Corps bring with them? Probably not enough for all the men we're losing.*

When Marines were "planted" in the bulldozed trench, each cross was placed exactly over the body. The other dog tag remained with the corpse as a final identification of the remains.

My tags, like everyone elses's, had the following general statistics stamped on it: "TATUM, C. W. 522829 P Type-A. 1/44 USMCR."

Sleep, when it came, was short and fitful. I could hear Pops Whitcomb shifting his gear in the next foxhole. With Lloyd gone, it was just Whitcomb and me from the original squad. Of all the guys, it was Pops who remained, the same guy who thought I was a screwup. Thankfully, combat had made us closer.

IWO QUAKE

That day of March 3 had been eventful, but it was far from over. Earlier, a lieutenant in the language section interviewed a captive Korean laborer he had coaxed out of a cave. The man was talked into going back with an offer, giving the Japanese troops inside a chance to surrender.

He was reminded that the entrance to the cave was slated to be sealed with C2 in an hour. The Korean returned promptly with the enemy's reply, "No surrender, ever! We will blow ourselves up tonight." That did it! The entrance was blasted shut by a couple of engineers, as promised.

So far, on Iwo, we had faced danger from the sky, sea, and land. Now we were threatened with a new peril—explosions from *beneath* our feet. No one thought there was any hazard from Japanese soldiers buried in a cave.

We set our night defense line on a ridge above the closed-off cave. At 11 p.m., we learned never to scoff at a Japanese promise. I don't know what happened first, whether I felt the upheaval of the ground in the bottom of my foxhole or heard the sound of a tremendous earthquake erupting with me in the epicenter. I do not know. The enemy soldiers had blown themselves up and with some *heavy* TNT!

The night sky was suddenly filled with rocks, dust, and dirt. Flames and smoke belched from crevices in the earth. The main blast seemed to be on my right. I found it difficult to breathe and my mouth was full of grit and dirt. Men were up and running everywhere—mass confusion reigned. When I checked myself out, all my body parts seemed to be in good working order, but I was covered with a thick layer of dust.

My carbine would need to be field-stripped and cleaned. The bolt wouldn't retract. I gulped a big swig from my canteen to wash away the impacted dirt in my mouth and throat and then took a couple of drinks to calm myself.

I don't recall anyone from B Company being killed by the underground Japs who blew their asses sky-high. But we learned again to heed a Japanese vow when they promised to "die for the emperor!"

CHAPTER TWENTY-FOUR

D+13, March 4, 1945
The Morass

Rolling up my trouser leg, I hoped I might have a million-dollar wound. Every guy on Iwo wanted one bad enough to get off the island—but not serious enough to die from. I wasn't so lucky.

When I awoke, Tremulis tapped me on the shoulder. He wanted a chunk of C2 in order to make a cup of coffee. He didn't look good to me. Skinny as a rail to begin with, he now seemed like an example of the living dead.

"Corporal Tremulis," I said, "you look like hell."

"Screw you, Tatum," he snapped. "Have *you* looked in a mirror lately? You look like crap!"

The only thing that improved my exhausted condition was to brush my teeth, which I did whenever I had the chance. I was out of toothpaste, so I vigorously scrubbed away using the last of some oily water from a GI can nearby. I noticed the can had three parallel handles and asked, "Corporal Tremulis, why do all these cans have three handles?"

"You don't know anything, Tatum. When they're full, each one weighs forty pounds and the handles make it easier for two men to carry."

Probably upset over my stupid effort to make conversation, Tremulis assigned me to a water detail. Before we left, he pulled my sleeve, cautioning softly, "Look out for snipers."

With several others I set off to gather GI cans of water from regimental supply, stockpiled two hundred yards behind our lines. "Be alert. Let's not get our asses shot off hauling water," I warned the others.

We found water stored behind a cluster of rocks. I assigned each man a can to carry. Remembering what happened to Basilone's group on the airfield, I hollered, "Stay spread out, don't bunch up."

I carried a can on my shoulder. Feeling threatened by snipers and infiltrating enemy soldiers, I yelled, "Move out on the double to our position."

When we got back, Tremulis said, "Put the water down, Tatum, and get your gear together. We're moving out."

"What about the water?"

"Leave it. Someone will use it."

Pissed off at exposing ourselves to Japanese fire to get water I wasn't even going to have the chance to use, I deliberately took my time refilling my canteen and throwing cool water in my face. When I was finished, we moved out immediately.

Windle directed us to fill a gap in the lines. On the way we came under a brief mortar attack that seemed like it lasted thirty minutes. The 5th Division's 13th Marines replied with a horrendous barrage. When the fire slackened, we moved out again.

We found ourselves in the rubble of the third airstrip. This was the second time we had been in this godforsaken area. The ground was open and level but strewn with small rocks. The airstrip was unfinished because of our bombing raids. To me, this area had the appearance of a prehistoric landscape. Flat tones of sandstone brown made it look to me like a dinosaur might step from a boulder at any time.

JAPANESE POSSUM

I was walking on a ridge, several paces behind one of the company's replacement riflemen. I didn't know his name. I didn't want to. He had been around a couple of days. We passed a Japanese soldier sprawled in a shallow trench below. Glancing at him, I thought he looked dead.

From the corner of my eye, though, I saw him roll over and throw a grenade. He must have been wounded, for it was a weak toss, but it was enough for the grenade to make it up to where we were walking. Jumping backward, I rolled down the hill on the side shielded from the enemy soldier and was near the bottom when the grenade detonated above me. Its blast smashed me in the back.

I blacked out, becoming conscious a few seconds later. I still held my carbine—I think this was accidental. The Marine rifleman was twenty feet to my left, sitting and wiping dirt from his eyes. His Ml rifle was near the top on the ridge; I noted, with satisfaction, that I had hung on to mine.

He was hollering, but I couldn't hear what he was yelling. My ears were ringing. A silent sound like a drum beating or bell chiming was throbbing in my head. I felt something warm running down my right leg. Rolling up my trouser leg, I hoped I might have a million-dollar wound. Every guy on Iwo wanted one bad enough to get off the island—but not serious enough to die from. I wasn't so lucky. I had a bad scrape about eight inches long and a sixteenth of an inch deep. The blood was already clotting.

Slightly disappointed, I popped open my first-aid kit and sprinkled the wound with sulfa powder. The rifleman seemed okay. Picking up his piece, he wiped it off. I checked my own carbine. I didn't give a damn about the Jap and didn't go back to find out what happened to him.

BELLS START RINGING

I was pleased during the roll down the hill that I never let go of my carbine and was okay except for my ringing ears and a splitting headache. I felt dizzy and didn't give a damn. I wanted to sit down where I was, so I did. After a while I got up.

The rifleman had left me and I didn't see anyone else. I started in the direction I thought my platoon had taken, toward the front line. I found some Marines who pointed me to the Baker Company sector and I was soon back with the squad. By way of greeting, Tremulis said, "Where the [expletive] have you been, Tatum?" He was probably the only guy who'd noticed I was missing—and cared. Strangely enough, for all his streetwise toughness, Tremulis was becoming my buddy.

That night, our platoon gained a new hero. At the close of fighting that day, the lay of the land and luck of the draw placed Baker Company in a poor defensive position with rocks and obstructions in front of us. Fields of fire were *thin* and *none*.

Sergeant Windle surveyed the topography and ordered the placement of machine guns for nighttime defense. Windle was the cement that held the formation together. I went where he sent our gun squad.

Farther down the line, on his own initiative, Private Ralph Jeffers, a Camp Tarawa replacement in our platoon, placed *his gun* on a precarious ledge in order to deliver overhead fire in support of Baker Company's front lines. Jeffers's exposed position made him an inviting target, and the Japs reacted with an enthusiastic and concentrated effort to shorten his life span—with concentrated sniper fire.

When this strategy didn't do the job, the enemy resorted to shooting at Jeffers with a heavy, dual-purpose antiaircraft gun. In spite of the obvious danger, Jeffers resolutely refused to leave his almost untenable position.

After a long night of enemy harassment, daybreak on Iwo found Jeffers crouched at his gun, facing fifty enemy soldiers who were massing for a counterattack. Jeffers's skillful handling of his weapon dispatched most of them for an early meeting with their ancestors. The Japanese who did survive his assault fled to the safety of a cave. Everyone thought Jeffers deserved a medal—if he lived to receive it.

CAPTAIN SOHN'S LAST "DOWN"

I don't clearly remember the details, but sometime after I rejoined the company, I saw our ex–football star/company commander, Captain Ben Sohn, get hit. He was kneeling with his back to the front lines and his position hidden by an outcropping of rocks. He was eating a C-ration stew while using a walkie-talkie and looking at a sector map spread on the ground—Sohn wasn't the kind of commander to waste time! Nearby, noncoms waited for orders.

Watching the group from thirty feet away, I saw the skipper suddenly grab his left arm and fall forward. Simultaneous with this came the sound of a rifle *crack* from a cluster of rocks to our front.

Someone screamed, "Talullah!" (Marine-speak for "corpsman," used in combat. This code name was to keep the Japs from decoying a corpsman to their position—because the Japanese couldn't pronounce the *l*'s.)

It was now hard to tell which got to Sohn first, a medic or another sniper round. The second bullet hit him in the left leg.

Applying first aid, the corpsman shouted, "Stretcher bearers!" Big Ben Sohn had run out of "downs" and luck on Iwo. He waved the stretcher men away and walked off without help, just the way he did from the New York Giants football field after taking a hard hit. Sohn was determined that his men were not going to see Big Ben leave the front lines flat on his back. Baker Company loved the big Marine who had trained and led us since April 1944. It was hard for me to forget Benjamin Sohn. The story was that on the day of the Pearl Harbor sneak attack, December 7, 1941, he had been playing in a football game and, as a Marine Reserve officer, was called to active duty on the spot. He would be hard for the Marines to replace and the New York Giants would have to draft a new lineman after the war.

NEW COs

With the skipper gone, Sergeant Windle took command of Baker Company. Now Windle's combat experience was put to a new test. Only one Camp Tarawa officer was left, Lieutenant Thrower.

Squad leadership was now up to the man with the know-how and the man who was also one of the last sergeants standing—Windle. When our new company commander, Captain Edmond O'Herron, arrived, Windle consulted and worked with him until he was acclimated to battle conditions.

Windle helped O'Herron become familiar with his new command's strengths and weaknesses. Captain O'Herron would use Windle like an executive officer. Windle was at regimental headquarters when they got word that Captain Sohn was okay and he shared the news with us soon after. Probably trying to make me feel better, he also let me know that Hurd, after a day's rest, had volunteered for one of the most dangerous jobs on Iwo: carrying ammunition to the front lines. He never returned to the squad, but he was still in the fight.

We were all pleased to hear that our captain had survived his wounds and I was personally thrilled to hear that Hurd's injuries from the mortar concussion had mended.

Captain O'Herron was originally assigned as the divisional staff's chemical officer, but grew restless with inactivity and requested a frontline assignment. When our battalion supply officer was wounded, he came on board as a replacement. A short time later came the call to take over Baker Company. Captain O'Herron, with no previous experience commanding a line company, took over our casualty-riddled unit. We were in the middle of a bloody campaign, which wasn't halfway over. O'Herron depended heavily on Windle to lead the company. Lieutenant Thrower assisted him with supply and administration. Captain O'Herron was a quick study under Windle's tutelage and we respected his style of command. He would be on Iwo until the last day of battle, and Baker Company continued to make important contributions to the fighting.

Under O'Herron, we were again nose to nose with the enemy. Our movement during the day on D+13 brought us back to the front lines. In Europe, where the fighting still raged, there might be a buffer zone of a mile or so between the armies. On Iwo Jima, this traditional no-man's-land did not exist. There simply was no neutral ground. The separation between advancing troops and Japanese defenders was frequently no more than a few yards. Our enemy could sometimes be heard moving underground, underneath forward positions. An attack began when we left protected positions and moved the first foot forward into Japanese-held territory.

Darkness approached and we dug in. Sergeant Windle wisely continued to warn of a Banzai attack during the night. There had been a few in other places, none of them successful. The enemy's situation was steadily deteriorating with each day's fighting on Iwo.

It was beginning to look like *we* now owned more of Iwo than its original landlords did! There were strong expectations at headquarters and in the field that our compression of the Japs into smaller areas would force them to attempt a last, spectacular, desperate assault.

On Saipan in 1944, when hope was lost, the Japanese commander had ordered a final Banzai charge. I wondered if *Banzai* and *suicide* in Japanese meant the same thing?

"Tomorrow will be a rest day," Windle told us. This was wonderful news. The three divisions of the 5th Amphibious Corps were scheduled for a rest in order to "regroup, reorganize, and replenish line units." The division had been subjected to intensive combat for four-teen days—and it showed.

FLOWER SHOP MARINE

My head still ached. I felt nauseous and my ears kept ringing and Tremulis had the "terminal craps." His endless rectal malfunctions, however, did not impair his job performance or keep him from giving me orders.

"Here's some rations, Tatum. Pass 'em out. I need to take care of some business. While I'm gone, dig us a foxhole."

I gave him the finger, but "turned to" immediately and started digging.

When he returned I said sarcastically, "If you waited a little longer, I would have installed hot and cold water for you,"

We laughed, but I could see he was ragged out. The craps were dragging him down fast. We settled in for the night.

I asked, "Are you going to stay in the Corps after the war?"

"No [expletive] way, Tatum. If I make it off this rock pile, I'm going back to Chicago and get my own flower shop."

He told me his dad and uncle had a flower store in Rockford. Illinois, and a sister ran one in Chicago. "I'll work for my sister until I have enough money to open my own." I somehow couldn't imagine this battle-hardened Marine running a flower shop of all things. He was the same guy who, while stationed on the carrier, USS *Yorktown*, had manned a 20mm antiaircraft gun that had "splashed" a couple of Japanese planes. When the *Yorktown* sank, he abandoned ship by leaping thirty-five feet from its flaming carrier deck. He swam and treaded water in oil-slick seas for eight hours until he was rescued. After recuperation, he signed up for paratrooper training. When the Paramarines disbanded, he ended up in Baker Company's machine-gun platoon. After fourteen days of the toughest fighting in the Pacific

and five years in the Corps, he tells me, "I want to open a flower shop."
What an anomaly!

À LA RAASHOON CAFÉ

My stomach growled: "Chow time!" I wondered what delectable treat
was in the K-ration box the chefs of "À La Raashoon Café" had so
carefully prepared for me.

Slitting the waxed box with my KA-BAR, I dumped the contents
on my poncho. Guess what? Cheese and bacon again. On the spot I
decided I was going to switch restaurants. Rear-echelon troops were
eating C rations or maybe a *hot meal,* I surmised.

I traded Tremulis my cheese and bacon for his chopped ham and
eggs because he said he hoped the cheese would "plug him up."

Tremulis took the first watch and, exhausted, I slept fitfully. When
my watch started, I woke with a splitting headache. Feeling depressed,
I couldn't explain my uncharacteristic mood. I was melancholy and
didn't give a good goddamn about *anything.* I wanted to shut the war
and the loss of friends out of my recollection processes. Normally
upbeat and cheerful, I figured I had held up pretty good so far.

Off duty, Tremulis fell asleep immediately. I wanted to visit a
little, but I knew it wasn't safe to talk. Voices carried a long way and
might reveal your position.

Through weary eyes I peered at Iwo's landscape of jumbled rock
and weird forms lit intermittently by falling flares. In this surreal
setting, I thought of my parents' home and its comforts. I missed my
mother's cooking, especially biscuits and gravy for breakfast and her
devil's food chocolate cake. I wondered how my brothers and sisters
were doing. How were their grades? Did my sisters have new boy-
friends?

Despair about my situation on Iwo Jima left me knee-deep in a
never-ending morass of death and cries of wounded Marines. Silently,

I hummed hymns I learned in Sunday school: "I Walk in the Garden Alone," "The Old Rugged Cross," and "Onward, Christian Soldiers." I recited my favorite biblical verse, the 23rd Psalm, from memory. I prayed, "God, please save us all."

I pictured my large family of three sisters, two brothers, two stepbrothers, and one stepsister in my mind. I remembered each of them, lovingly turning their images in my mind's eye.

When I joined the Marine Corps, it provided a small economic relief for my parents. Gone to war, I was one less mouth to feed. Before the war, times had been difficult, but my mother had said in a recent letter, "Your stepfather's wartime employment has improved family finances, so things are on the upswing . . ."

An artillery round exploded, distracting my thoughts. I suddenly felt sick.

I hope I'm not getting Tremulis's diarrhea, I thought. With scattered human limbs and bloated bodies strewn across the battlefield and ninety thousand men taking craps where they stood, it wouldn't have been surprising if *everyone* had diarrhea or "Chinese rot" like the shipboard sawbones had warned us about. Iwo was probably the most densely populated battlefield in World War II, with seventy thousand Marines and support troops in the attack against an estimated twenty-one thousand defenders in an area covering eight square miles.

Thank God, tomorrow would be a day of rest! I yearned for dawn.

CHAPTER TWENTY-FIVE

D+14, March 5, 1945
The Cut Grows Deeper

My head pounded and I gulped down canteen water
until my stomach was upset. My legs felt paralyzed,
like a childhood nightmare in which I wanted to run
but couldn't. The company moved out, but I stayed
where I was.

By midmorning, word swept through our ranks: "Colonel Butler has
been killed!" Butler had been riding in a jeep to a conference at the
regimental command post in order to save time. Along the way, he
decided to check out the terrain he anticipated would be his men's
next objective when the vehicle approached a trail junction near an
old sugar mill. His party took a direct 47mm-round hit from a Japanese antitank and he was killed instantly. The driver and NCOs
accompanying him were seriously wounded. It was another Iwo trag-
edy but not the last.

Shortly after Colonel Butler's death, a sniper killed my squad mate
and a Camp Tarawa replacement, Pfc. Lavor Jenkins of Freedom,
Wyoming, as he rested between assaults. His casualty report said,
"GSW [Marine-speak for 'gunshot wound'] head." Lavor was eighteen
days short of celebrating his first year in the Corps.

Jenkins's loss meant the 1st Squad was down to three members,
Billy Joe Cawthorn, our "baby-faced Marine"; Gopher Gus Henderson;
and Ralph Jeffers.

When Colonel Butler had visited our B Company lines the night before his death, Pops Whitcomb was on "listening post," alone, and got spooked at the colonel's surprise appearance. As Whitcomb remembered it, "Colonel Butler visited my position the night before he was killed." He said, "I was very tense and alert. The colonel's inspection startled hell out of me." Butler had asked how Whitcomb was doing and had some specific questions about the current situation and position.

"I may have been the last man on the line to talk to Colonel Butler and the news he was killed shocked me to the core," Whitcomb told me. Butler's visit was in keeping with his style of leadership, i.e., frequently on the line, checking things out, and showing his concern and respect for the men in the ranks. His honest feelings for us were felt and returned.

We were fortunate that our 1st Battalion's leadership was passed to Lieutenant Colonel Justin Gates Duryea, a former Paramarine and 'Canal veteran. Moving directly from Regimental Operations to take command, Duryea had helped form our battalion at Pendleton and was well known to us—particularly to the paratroopers.

SELF-RELIANT REMEDY

During our day of rest, my headache grew worse and I consulted a corpsman. "My ears ring," I told him.

Not impressed, he answered, "It's normal for ears to ring in combat." He gave me some aspirin for my headache and asked, "Anything else wrong?" I showed him my leg wound. He jokingly said, "Too bad your wound isn't deeper—if it was, you would have a ticket off this damned island."

The aspirin didn't touch my headache; it grew worse. My ears rang constantly and I felt nauseous. I was getting weaker and knew it. I had caught Tremulis's craps, but not as bad. When Tremulis gave me hell about something or other, my mind was hazy and numb. I didn't answer him.

Corporal Tremulis had been living with the runs for days when he asked a corpsman for something to stop the condition. "Eat more cheese," the pecker checker told him. In frustration, Tremulis took a soft bandage, coated it with petroleum jelly, and pushed it between the cheeks of his butt. His shorts held the remedy in place while he waddled about, carrying out his duties. The Marines I knew were tough and self-reliant.

To stay busy, I joined Pops Whitcomb in cleaning a machine gun. At age twenty-seven, he was the oldest man in our squad. We shared the same first and middle names, which made us closer. I liked to listen to his refined southern accent as a change of pace. Working on the machine gun, I felt spent, like the empty shell casings lying around us. I was going through fundamental motions like a robot, not focused on what I was doing.

Of the eight original members of our squad, Pop and I were the only ones who were still on board. Six down and two to go? Additional Japanese "purging" of Marine ranks included another officer, Second Lieutenant Dunbar Jones, of Denver, Colorado. Jones was another "2nd Louie" attached to our Headquarters Company before head-quarters sent him to us.

"Jones got it while calling in mortar fire on a walkie-talkie," Pfc. Gunnar Johnson, a fellow Okie, told me. "He was hit in the head by a Nip bullet when he raised up to take a better look at the front lines." Johnson, who'd been crouching next to him, remembered, "A shot cracked the air and Dunbar's helmet went spinning. He was probably dead before he hit the ground. It was so quick! He was alive a second ago . . . now he was dead."

Jones had been wounded on D+9 but returned to duty the same day. He was the *seventh* officer of the 1st Battalion to die in combat on ugly Iwo.

DAY OF "REST" ENDS

About midday, the Word came down: "Move out!" Our day of rest was over, I reckoned ruefully. We formed up to move out in a spread formation and immediately began taking mortar fire.

"Take cover!" Windle hollered, and we scattered like a covey of quail seeking refuge. A round hit a few yards from me. My pulse raced and my battle senses told me to move. Sprinting, I ran for a rock outcropping thirty yards away. When I was halfway to its safety, a close round knocked me to the ground. Mortar and artillery shelling had scared the hell out of me since D-Day, but the fear I felt now was different. My hands trembled. Fortunately, the barrage stopped quickly. I chain-smoked to settle down.

Able and Baker Company men were wounded by the attack and it took a while to reorganize. John "Gopher Gus" Henderson, the victim of my practice grenade prank at Camp Tarawa, was down and wounded.

My head pounded and I gulped down canteen water until my stomach was upset. My legs felt paralyzed, like a childhood nightmare in which I wanted to run but couldn't. The company moved out, but I stayed where I was.

All I could think was, *F— the war, f— the Japs, and f— this whole island!*

A flood of other "f— everything" surged through my tangled thinking processes. Then awareness that I was alone and the fear of becoming a sniper's target prompted me to move. There was another conclusion: If I stayed where I was, the Marine Corps would shoot me as a deserter.

Self-preservation instincts kicking in, I told myself, *Get off your butt and start moving.* I looked for my vanished company. Eventually I heard someone calling my name.

Through hazy vision, I saw Sergeant Windle walking toward me.

When he was close enough he looked at me. "Tatum, are you okay?" he asked. "Look, let's join the company, and don't worry, you're going to be okay—you're going to make it."

I followed him without argument or objection.

BACK TO RED BEACH TWO

Before we set in for the evening, at 3:30 p.m., Windle said to me, "Tatum, I'm sending you back." Glancing at Tremulis, he added, "You're out of here, too! You're *both* finished. Get the hell back, both of you."

The trek to the rear and Red Beach Two, our starting point fifteen days ago, took an hour. There were no tears in my eyes. I had combat fatigue. Was I *leaving* Iwo Jima?

Tremulis and I followed a trail to a crude sign that marked a freshly bulldozed road that improved as we got farther from the lines. As we took the long walk back from the front, I was hoping that some goddamned Jap we had passed by didn't pick me off as his last chance to dispatch a Marine to that big battlefield in the sky. As a kind of verbal talisman, I recited the 23rd Psalm in my mind, *"Yea, though I walk through the valley of death, I shall fear no evil for the Lord, My God, is with me and surely goodness and mercy shall follow me all the days of my life!"* I wished now that I had paid more attention in Sunday school and knew all the words.

We walked without talking. What was there to say? Each step improved my morale. No one told us where to go, we were just going back to where we had been. Just back—anywhere was better than the front. Our last push had killed off the big guns that used to shell the rear areas. But Iwo Jima seemed different. The debris of war still littered the landscape, but as we walked, there were changes that appeared before our eyes.

At Motoyama Airfield Number Two, we passed some dozers and

rollers roaring back and forth. Seabees were flattening the ground where the 21st Marines had bled only a week ago in a bitter engagement. Silently, we passed clusters of tents and giant stacks of food and ammo. We saw sailors, mainly Seabees, swarming everywhere.

We passed a large cemetery filled with small, neat, white crosses, a mute testament and reminder of the price being paid in young lives in order to own Iwo Jima. Each Marine division had a cemetery. The 5th Division's was located closest to Suribachi.

We passed a water distillation plant where we guzzled water without any fuel-oil taste for the first time since landing. After filling our bellies and canteens, we trudged on. Soon we saw a forlorn Korean laborer crouching by the roadside. Clad only in a loincloth, the man was probably one of hundreds brought to Iwo by the Japanese to construct their underground tunnels and fortifications. I guessed he was awed by the power he saw around him and the rapid transformation of Iwo from battlefield to American bastion. The Seabees had already built a road to the top of Suribachi—something the Japanese had never succeeded in doing.

At Airfield Number One, we saw a few B-29s sitting on the newly improved runways. The first one, *Dinah Might,* had landed on March 4, 1945. We were inwardly thrilled to see clusters of transports, P-51 Mustangs, and a few Marine "grasshopper" artillery observation planes. The B-29s were beginning to use Iwo as a refuge on the long flights from Saipan, Guam, and Tinian in the Marianas to Japan and back.

The Stars and Stripes flew proudly from the top of Suribachi, surrounded by rotating radar domes and antennas that scanned the skies in all directions.

As we passed the airstrip, we encountered an amphibious DUKW or "Duck," as the vehicle was affectionately called. Its driver was a black soldier from the Army's 471st Amphibian Truck Company who had picked up some Marine slang: "Where you all going, Mac? Give you a lift?"

He was headed to an offshore destroyer to pick up a load. Tremulis, the former seagoing Marine, didn't hesitate. We climbed on board and the DUKW rumbled down to Red Beach Two on its six "donut" wheels. We passed the spot on the south end of the first airstrip from which I had watched Basilone die and where I spent a good part of D-Day. The DUKW effortlessly passed over the black sand dunes where our innocent blood was first shed on Iwo, and eased into the choppy ocean.

Our seagoing DUKW jockey was a smooth operator. He maneuvered the vehicle through stiff breakers and into the open sea. In a brief time, we pulled alongside a destroyer a mile offshore. Sailors rigged a cargo net for us like those we used debarking from APAs in Hawaii. This time our climb was shorter and we weren't burdened with a ton of gear and weapons. Even so, we were weak and shaky. We welcomed the eager hands that pulled us on board. The swabbies were anxious for news about what was going on and figured combat Marines would have the "straight skinny."

They anxiously pummeled us with a thousand questions, but the most welcome one was, "Are you hungry?"

"Hell yes!"

They took us down to the galley for a terrific feed, but I don't remember what we ate. I *can* remember chowing until I felt like bursting. I do remember washing my hands with soap and hot water, a nearly forgotten ritual.

But the best thing of all was the hot shower. I felt fifteen days of filth flush off in clouds of wonderful, steaming water. My shower was an hour long and I didn't give a damn that it was salt water.

Our "Good Samaritan" sailors found clean navy dungarees and underwear for us, too. I suppose the swabbies threw our fouled uniforms overboard. We were shown to spare bunks and lay down at 5 p.m. "just to rest." In an instant, we were locked in deep sleep.

CHAPTER TWENTY-SIX

D+15, March 6, 1945
Heaven After Hell

Our wounds were to our minds and there were no bandages that could be applied to them. There were no
drugs we could take that would erase the images of
war that filled our heads.

We awoke to a rolling ship, well under way. The Navy let us sleep until
8 a.m., which worked out to be fourteen hours. The only reason they
woke us was to keep us from missing morning chow.

It was great to get star treatment. Breakfast was steak and eggs. I
ate *four* eggs, sunny-side up, *eight* pieces of toast, and drank cup after
cup of coffee. We even enjoyed orange marmalade on our toast. I had to
pinch myself to make sure it wasn't a dream. Had I died and gone
to heaven? If this wasn't heaven, it was definitely the next best thing
to it.

Our destroyer was under orders to go on patrol. "Can we go with
the ship?" Tremulis and I asked.

"No," came the answer, "the ship isn't coming back to Iwo."

Instead, we would be transferred and were taken to the USS *Doyen*
(APA-1) anchored a half mile off the eastern shore of Iwo Jima. As we
climbed the rope ladder to get on board, we could hear distant sounds
of battle and see the explosions of artillery and mortar fire. Tremulis
and I were safe, but our buddies from Baker Company were still in

harm's way. I said a prayer for them. Standing on the deck of the *Doyen,* we saluted and asked permission to come on board.

The officer of the deck told us to "report to sick bay." The sick-bay office was two decks below and nearly empty. When we got there, the corpsman on duty asked, "Are you Navy or Marines?" (We were wearing Navy dungarees donated by the friendly sailors.) The corpsman asked if we were wounded.

Tremulis said, "Yes! Tatum has a leg wound that's almost healed, not much more than a scratch, but he is suffering from a blast concussion and has been acting funny."

Next the corpsman questioned Tremulis: "Are you wounded?"

Tremulis snorted. "In the butt hole."

The corpsman said, "*Butt hole?* How did you get shot there?"

"I wasn't *shot* there. I have the Iwo Jima runs . . . you know, the craps. My butt hole is as big as a silver dollar. I need medicine to plug it up before I crap myself to death."

The corpsman told us a doctor had to look at us before any medicine could be prescribed. Pretty soon a Navy doctor took a look at my leg, cleaned it up, and put a dressing on it that stung. Then he told me, "It looks good. You'll live." He prescribed paregoric for the dysentery that was racking Tremulis's butt.

Filling out a lot of forms, the doctor started a paper trail and casualty report on each of us.

CANNONADE FROM THE NORTH

The *Doyen* was anchored off Blue Beach Two, where the 4th Division had landed on D-Day. After our noon chow, Tremulis and I went topside on the foredeck with other "ambulatory Marines" (i.e., the walking wounded) as the Navy called us.

The deck was covered with patients on stretchers because the main sick bays were full. This was the overflow. APAs didn't have large sick bays and all ships at Iwo were doing double duty by serving as hospital vessels.

The sound of incoming fire sent a chill up my spine. I couldn't believe it! Two shells sent splashes across the bow. The Japs were shelling *our* ship! Was there *no* safe place on or off Iwo Jima? The third one hit the yardarm. Luck was with everyone on board, as none of the falling debris or shell fragments hit us.

The clank of anchor chains was the next thing I heard. The *Doyen* was under way *on the double*. The area was "hot" and the destroyer steamed off at full speed ahead. In fifteen minutes we were out of range. I suspected the shells came from a Japanese artillery unit near an area marked "Kitana Point" on artillery maps; the point was located near the eastern tip of the island, to which the enemy had been pushed.

With Tremulis and me safe aboard the steaming *Doyen*, we learned that our new ship had been in on a lot of action in the South Pacific. From its low APA number, I knew it had been built before the war started. It was a real classy APA, with tile showers and a top-notch ship's store selling ice cream and pogey bait.

SWAP MEET

I hoped the Marine Corps would forgive me. I sold my folding-stock carbine for twenty dollars to a souvenir-hungry sailor. Tremulis sold his for twenty-five. I guessed Greeks were better traders than Okies.

We had been completely out of cash, since money had no value on Iwo. With a million bucks you couldn't have bought your way off that hellhole island. We spent the money from the sale of our weapons at the ship's store for items like shaving gear, soap, towels, cigarettes, ice cream, and pogey bait.

Shopping at the *Doyen*'s store made it seem like we were in a civilized place again. I tried to draw some Marine clothing so I would look like one again, but the ship didn't stock regular-issue outfits for Marines, so I was stuck with cast-off Navy blues.

The trip from Iwo to Saipan took three days; in Saipan, the *Doyen* delivered us to the 369th Army station hospital. Ambulatory Marines like Tremulis and me disembarked on LCVPs. The 369th hospital was three miles from the beach.

What I saw on the island amazed me. The 2nd and 4th Marine Divisions had fought a heroic battle to capture Saipan and nearby Tinian more than a year earlier. In that brief time, Seabees had worked their brand of construction magic on the Pacific island, now a base from which our B-29 bombers could pound Japan. The 369th Army hospital consisted of row after row of wooden military buildings fifty feet long and thirty feet wide. It was situated on a high plateau overlooking the main airfield from which we could see the bombers take off and land.

SHELL-SHOCKED

Tremulis and I felt completely out of place. We were among seriously wounded Marines and I almost felt guilty that I wasn't wounded physically. Our wounds were to our minds and there were no bandages that could be applied to them. There were no drugs we could take that would erase the images of war that filled our heads. Mother Nature, with assistance from modern medicine, could heal the flesh. But the mind is different. You can never forget the pain you suffered in a place like Iwo Jima and the scars will always be there. Tremulis and I had been labeled "SSCF" or "Shell Shocked—Combat Fatigue."

This label had a negative connotation; I supposed this was the result of the general misunderstanding about this type of condition. It did not denote a lack of courage or the resolve to fight; it was a condition caused by the inability to continue past physical or mental exhaustion. Most Marines who suffered combat fatigue were the ones who had survived to fight another day . . . and another day after day. The lucky ones got the million-dollar wound on the first day and lived to recover. They didn't go back into the siege time and time again, as Tremulis and I had done, each day to see the decimation of young lives, the deaths of buddies who were closer than brothers, boys whose parents' hopes would be dashed by a message from the Navy saying, "We regret to inform you . . ."

Most people never have to witness the killing of someone they are close to, a loved one who is shot, or decapitated, watch a brother whose face is filled by the look of deep shock that precedes death. They never feel the helplessness of watching the life bleed out of a mortal being. Those who know war know of what I speak. I decided on Saipan that I would never apologize for my actions on Iwo Jima or for falling prey to combat fatigue—I gave it my all.

Our trip to Saipan and a few days' rest had restored both our morale and our physical condition. In the following days, Tremulis and I explored the island, visiting the B-29 airfields. We became friends with the crews and were invited on board to inspect America's "number one airplane." Dubbed the "Silver-Winged Devils" by the Japanese, they were gorgeous ships. Our Air Corps friends felt that the Marines were A-OK, and we decided this attitude was due to the new air base the Marines had just "bought" called Iwo Jima. Now, in the event of an in-flight emergency on the long round-trip from Saipan to Tokyo, pilots could stop off at Iwo. Many thousands of them would do just that—saving countless lives in the process. Suddenly some of all those sacrifices we witnessed on Iwo began to make sense. And our thoughts went to our buddies who were still making those sacrifices—Sergeant Windle and anyone left from Baker Company. Windle was too tough not to still be in the fight.

At the end of our second week on Saipan, a sergeant medic handed us our walking papers, saying, "You have sponged off the Army long enough. If you hang around Saipan any longer, you'll have to join a *real* fighting force—the U.S. Army." He also made some disparaging remarks about "seagoing bellhops," which we let slide only because of our appreciation of the hospitality we had received from the personnel at the 369th.

CHAPTER TWENTY-SEVEN

March 5–26, 1945
Same Battle, Different Ends

"Keep your damn heads down! Snipers are having a field day. Stay spread out so mortar shells won't get you! With luck we'll make it to the end of the battle!"

Tremulis and I shipped out from Saipan on March 21, 1945, bound for Pearl Harbor. During that weeklong ocean voyage, the battle for Iwo came to a bloody conclusion, although we had no idea of this. But in the weeks, months, and years afterward, from talking to other lucky survivors of Baker Company, I was able to piece together a version of what transpired on the battlefield after I had left my unit.

IWO'S FINAL DAYS

On the night of March 5, D+14, after Tremulis and I left Baker Company, Sergeant Windle was alone and brooding. What hung heaviest on his mind was the depletion of his machine-gun platoon. Sending the two of us to the rear was the right decision, because we had become basket cases and could get ourselves or others killed, but Windle was left with two fewer veterans.

Of the platoon's original fifty-eight-man roster, remaining were: Ralph Jeffers, John "Le Nose" Luman, James Memory Martin, Billy Joe "Babyface" Cawthorn, Charles "Pops" Whitcomb, Gunnar Johnson, Chester Truszkowski, Joe Perry, and Robert Feld. Sergeant Windle was one of two NCOs left. Windle knew there was plenty of deadly fighting ahead for the platoon. Total effective strength was reduced, the few surviving veterans were exhausted, and his replacements were greener than their new dungarees.

On D+15 and D+16, all three divisions pushed forward in a renewed attack along the line with unprecedented fire support. Major Tumbleston, the 1st Battalion XO, said it best: "If this fire doesn't blow the Japs to hell, nothing will."

Telegram, March 7, D+16
From: Lt. General T. Kuribayashi, Commander, Iwo
    Jima
To: Major Y. Horie, Commander, Detached HQ, Chichi
    Jima

Although the attacks of the enemy against our Northern Districts are continuing day and night, our troops are still fighting bravely and holding their positions thoroughly.

Divisional radio station was fighting under the siege of many enemy troops from the 8th, but, finally, today at 1130 . . . the enemy . . . destroyed the radio-telegraph. 200 or 300 American infantrymen with several tanks attacked "Tenzan" all day. The enemy's bombardment came from a battleship or cruiser . . . and 11 destroyers. Aircraft [attacks] are very severe, especially the bombs and machine guns fired at Divisional Headquarters by 30 fight-

ers and bombers. These attacks . . . are so fierce
that I cannot express . . . their impact, nor write
it here.

Before American forces landed on Iwo Jima there
were many trees around my headquarters, but, now
there is not even a blade of grass remaining. The
surface of the earth has changed completely and we
can see numerous holes from bombardments.

At Tamanayama, the Second Mixed Brigade Headquarters became dangerous and they might go out
for a "Banzai!" charge on the midnight of the 8th
because we cannot contact them after that.

At daybreak, with Baker Company in reserve, Captain O'Herron
called a meeting of NCOs at a temporary CP behind a small vertical
ledge. There was only one Baker Company officer left of those who had
landed on D-Day, Second Lieutenant Arthur Thrower, the mortar-
platoon leader. He assumed the administration and logistic functions
and was, in effect, acting as company XO. The rifle and weapons platoons were in the hands of veteran NCOs like Windle, whom O'Herron
would use to lead the company during the coming days.

At this juncture, our G-2 (Marine-speak for "regimental intelligence gathering") estimated that 3,500 Japanese were left. Although
desperate and short of food and water, the enemy was still well supplied with arms and ammo and *very* determined to resist to the death.

On D+17, Baker Company came out of reserve and joined the
fighting. We soon lost one of our platoon's heroes, Private Ralph Jeffers, of Paducah, Kentucky. Jeffers was the Camp Tarawa replacement
who'd set his gun on a precarious ledge on D+13, inflicting so much
damage on the enemy that they turned an antiaircraft gun on him—
without effect. Jeffers's young, unfinished life was snuffed out by
Japanese machine-gun fire on the eighteenth day of the battle for Iwo
Jima; he died with the Silver Star waiting to be awarded to him, its

citation "signed for the President" by James V. Forrestal, secretary of the Navy.

A MARINE CORPS FOR ANOTHER FIVE HUNDRED YEARS

Forrestal actually visited Iwo Jima earlier in the campaign along with General Holland "Howling Mad" Smith. After viewing the landings from a command ship, Forrestal went to the beach with Smith, and while the two men were standing together on Iwo's black sand, the secretary said, "Holland, this means a Marine Corps for another five hundred years." With tears in his eyes, the general nodded his appreciation.

By now, the Japanese must have realized this as well. There was no stopping the Corps. Trapped and desperate, men, like cornered animals, fight the hardest. The Japanese had a saying, "Death is lighter than a feather, duty heavier than a mountain." The circumstances on Iwo seemed bent on proving their motto correct!

```
Telegram March 8, 1945 (D +17)
From: Lt. General T. Kuribayashi, Commander, Iwo
   Jima
To: Major Y. Horie, Commander, Detached HQ, Chichi
   Jima.


Today from 0630, the enemy is attacking Northern
District. His bombardment from mortars and war-
ships [is] very strong. Several troops of the enemy
are advancing towards Naval Headquarters Hill and
Tyouruboku. All surviving fighting units have sus-
tained heavy losses, but their fighting spirits are
running high and they are giving great damages to
the enemy.
```

Troops at Tamanayama and Northern District are
still holding their positions . . . and continued
giving damage to the enemy.

I am very sorry I have let the enemy occupy one
part of . . . Japanese territory, but I am taking
comfort in giving heavy damage to the enemy.

DURYEA'S DOWN!

On March 9, D+18, our 1st Battalion renewed its offensive. At 1:30 p.m., our battalion CO, Lieutenant Colonel Duryea, and the 2nd Battalion CO, Major Tony Antonelli, met to confer on the progress of the fight. Colonel Duryea called for his runner. Rushing forward to answer his summons, the man detonated a mine and was instantly obliterated. A huge shrapnel fragment severed Colonel Duryea's arm at the elbow and another tore into his knee.

Major Antonelli was stunned by the blast and suffered a ruptured eardrum and embedded particles in his eyes. Duryea was immediately evacuated on a stretcher but was shot in the leg by a sniper as he was carried to safety.

Major "Tough Tony" Antonelli was promptly treated but returned to assume command of his battalion. During the day, he remained at the front and at nightfall he was in a field hospital, receiving further treatment. This routine continued for several days until Colonel Thomas Wornham, regimental commander of the 27th Marines, requested Antonelli's evacuation before his wounds became infected.

On March 10, D+19, the 1st Battalion continued attacking. Baker Company experienced extra-hard fighting, which resulted in eight KIAs (Marine-speak for "killed in action") and thirteen WIAs (Marine-speak for "wounded in action"). The northern sector of Iwo was proving to be a tough nut to crack.

BLOODY GORGE

On March 11, D+20, as the battlefield shrank in size the enemy relied on their expert snipers to slow our advance. The terrain in "Bloody Gorge" at the northern end of Iwo afforded excellent cover for their one-man assault forces.

Sergeant Jay D. Laycock, of Hamilton, Ohio, passed the Word to his men in the 3rd Platoon, saying, "Keep your heads down or a damned Jap will blow it off." Laycock had assumed leadership of the 3rd Platoon, and during the twelve days he had commanded, he had witnessed the steady erosion of his command and had lost two replacement officers.

Then a Japanese mortar shell became Laycock's undoing. A "close one" exploded, sending white-hot fragments ripping into him. Sergeant Laycock was treated at a field hospital and air-evacuated to Guam, with a ticket off Iwo—while he was still breathing! He would later be awarded the Bronze Star for courageous action on March 5, when he rescued his platoon from an untenable position during a full-scale Japanese attack.

Sergeant Laycock's warning to keep our heads down was a valid and timely one on Iwo Jima, anywhere troops were moving. Danger lurked at every twist and turn of the landscape. Jap snipers hiding in concealed positions waited hours for an unsuspecting target. This deadly combination cost Baker Company three good men: Private Herbert Leroy King, Pfc. Kenneth A. Liljergren, and Pfc. Kenneth J. Olson. This unlucky trio fell victim to snipers no one ever saw.

ON-THE-JOB TRAINING

James Memory Martin of Rapid City, South Dakota, our last-minute replacement at Camp Tarawa, had little time to train with us before shipping out for Iwo. However, the Corps and Japs made up for this shortcoming.

I'm not sure if the term *on-the-job training* had, at this point, entered the vernacular, but if it had, Martin would have been one of the first to undergo it. Landing with Corporal Guy Brookshire's squad on D-Day, Jim was thrust into the thick of battle.

Starting on his first day of combat, Martin was the fifth ammo carrier. On D-Day, he was rapidly promoted from fifth ammo carrier to first because of the high casualty rate in his squad.

The appalling decimation of squads like Brookshire's was common in Baker Company personnel rosters. Brookshire (Baker Company's resident banker) himself was wounded on day one and evacuated.

As the front lines crept and slogged forward, Private Martin continued his on-the-job training as a machine gunner, and even celebrated his nineteenth birthday on Iwo Jima—with a candy bar from his K rations.

At 8:15 a.m. on D+20, twelve massed battalions of artillery fired for twelve minutes to kick off the assault. To cover the advance, Martin and a private named Thomas Keith set up their machine gun on a ridgeline to protect advancing riflemen.

When Marine artillery ceased their barrage, the enemy knew immediately that an extensive attack was under way. Trying to blunt the assault with a counterbarrage of giant 90mm and small knee mortars, the Japanese got the range right.

Martin's gun was in their line of fire, and with rounds falling close to it, his position became untenable.

Martin and Keith were ordered to fall back. While making their way past cliffs that appeared to offer protection, Martin turned to speak to another Marine. In what seemed like a blinding flash, he saw a mortar round land next to the man.

Martin thought to himself, *Boy! That guy got it for sure!* His next recollection was of something hitting him in the right shoulder hard—

like a pile driver. He staggered. Putting his hand on his shoulder, he saw it was covered with blood.

Sinking into deep shock, Martin couldn't remember the code word for "corpsman." Hazily he tried to recall. "Tullula? . . . Tallulah?"

Several members of his squad rushed to help him, and from them he learned that there was a nasty hole in his right hip. Eager hands removed his "782 gear" (Marine-speak for canvas web belts, etc.) and carried him to an overhang, providing protection from falling mortar shells.

A corpsman placed compresses on his wounds and used a syrette to give him a full injection of morphine. Next, the medic calmly made out a casualty slip indicating that Martin had received the drug, attached it to his jacket, and turned him over to waiting stretcher bearers.

As he was carried away, Martin attempted to pick up his helmet, but couldn't hang on to it. "Good-bye . . . good luck! Keep your heads down," he whispered to his buddies, offering a weak farewell wave. At a field hospital where he lay exhausted and numb, a corpsman gently removed live hand grenades from his jacket pocket. Probing his wound, a doctor said, "The fragments are too deep and embedded in the bone to remove here."

Martin said, "Doctor, if you get them out, will you save them for me?"

The Doc said, "You are lucky as hell. A few centimeters higher and the fragments would have torn your kidney."

Lying in the field hospital, Martin realized his fighting on Iwo Jima was over. At 4 p.m., he was taken to Motoyama Number One for loading on a transport plane headed for Guam.

WIPE 'EM OUT

The morning of March 12, D+21, Captain O'Herron spoke to Baker's platoon leaders, telling them the enemy was compressed into a series of narrow ravines and gorges in the northern part of the island. It was this hellish rock pile that was sardonically nicknamed "Bloody Gorge." Regimental intelligence estimated that one thousand organized Japs remained there. Their "guesstimate" was off by a factor of *300 percent.*

Thousands of Japanese survivors were dug in and supplied with weapons and ammunition. Water supplies were low—but not their fighting spirit. True to their Bushido code, each soldier resolved to fight to the death.

Captain O'Herron said, "Because of the terrain and capabilities of the enemy to remain safe in their caves, close to and adjacent to our lines, artillery fire will be limited to 37mm and 75mm support."

"Tank backup will be plentiful," he promised. O'Herron also asked his platoon leaders to make good use of the company 60mm mortars if any enemy soldiers were caught in the open.

Windle assembled his machine-gun platoon and gave them the scoop on the plan of action. Repeating his earlier warnings, he said, "Keep your damn heads down! Snipers are having a field day. Stay spread out so mortar shells won't get you! With luck we'll make it to the end of the battle!"

At exactly 8 a.m., the attack started. It was the *third* straight day that 1st Battalion was on the offensive. Enemy fortifications that had stopped the previous day's attack were the prime objectives.

THE LAST REDOUBT

Terrain in this part of Iwo was especially rocky, with crazy ravines and strange outcroppings. The topography in front of the squads would dictate the best avenue for attack. Our Japanese opponents were hidden in deep caves. Enemy machine guns covered the ravine's approaches. Open areas were swept by deadly fire, so the day's tactic was to advance behind tanks, bulldozers, and tank dozers. Sherman tanks with flamethrowers were particularly deadly—and effective.

Infantry followed behind the tanks and contact was maintained by radio. Japanese positions in this part of Iwo were taken at bayonet point and with grenades and flamethrowers.

Smoke from explosives in one cave entrance escaped from numerous apertures surrounding it, indicating air shafts and other exits. It was part of a *big* underground complex.

At 9:15 a.m., shortly after the attack was under way, Windle was walking behind a leading Sherman with assault squads deployed to his rear and flanks. He was talking to the "buttoned-down" tank commander through an extension phone. Windle thought the day was going well. His men had taken some of the tough positions that had previously stopped Baker Company's advance. His Marines and others had destroyed pillboxes, cleared caves, and overrun nasty spider traps. Flamethrower Shermans were the key to their successful drive.

When a Baker Company BAR man noticed a Jap emerging from a spider trap to Windle's right, he let go a long burst from his automatic rifle. The rounds that this Marine poured into the Japanese spider man and his trap set off ammunition that had been stored there. This caused an explosion that got the good Sergeant Windle in his right leg, and he went down to one knee and then rolled over, grasping his leg in pain.

Doc Marsh rushed to his side and told Windle, "You are going to be okay," as he injected him with morphine. Windle's luck had just run out and the machine-gun platoon had lost their leader. B Company's best Marine was now out of action. Before he would allow himself to be evacuated, Windle insisted that his souvenir Japanese book, which had a bullet hole in it—put there by Windle when he killed its former Japanese owner—be placed on the stretcher with him. No way would he leave Iwo without his prize of war; he had paid a lot for it. Then he fell unconscious as stretcher bearers carried him southward, toward the beach and the rear areas. There, medical care had greatly improved by this point and the 5th Marine Division had its own hospital ashore. It now took less than twenty minutes to make the trip from the front lines to the rear areas, where a Marine would be under expert care and treatment.

Captain O'Herron and his troops ended the day on top of an enemy-occupied fortification. When they had used C4 to blow it shut, eight Japanese ran out screaming and were chopped down. The day's effort cost Baker Company two killed and eight wounded—and had eked out a measly hundred bloody yards. When the attack ended and Baker Company secured for the night, the terrain was so bad it left the company vulnerable to attack through a ravine in the left sector of the lines. To cover this avenue of attack, acting sergeant Pops Whitcomb singlehandedly moved his machine gun forward of the front lines. The ledge he set his machine gun on was so small only one man could occupy it and he was exposed to enemy small-arms fire and mortars.

Whitcomb was ordered to move to a more protected position, but volunteered to stay where he was. During the night, his skillful operation of his weapon prevented the Japanese from forming for a Banzai charge in the ravine—but the battery in Whitcomb's lucky charm finally ran down. During his valorous defense, enemy counterfire inflicted multiple grazing wounds on his body. Whitcomb was evacuated to the rear, where he was treated. His Iwo-earned combat experience, courage, and cool determination had been put to good use in the last days of the battle.

```
Telegram, undated but most likely March 12, D+21
From: Lt. General T. Kuribayashi, Commander, Iwo
   Jima
To: Major Y. Horie, Commander, Detached HQ, Chichi
   Jima
```

Surviving strength of Northern District (Army-Navy) are now 1,500. On the 9th, we inflicted 798 men and one tank as losses to the enemy.

On the 11th, one M4 tank stopped on the rugged ground of the Northern District and one man was trying to get out through the canopy. Just at that time, Superior Private Gondo sniped him, threw a hand grenade into the tank, and burnt it.

Since yesterday . . . we could not contact the commander of the Tamanayama District.

From early this morning, the enemy began to concentrate their shooting from warships, firing of mortars and heavy artillery and bombing by aircraft on the northern district.

As dusk settled over the battleground, Gunnar Johnson (my fellow Okie) and his gun crew were completing night defense preparations. While Johnson was trying to take a piss, the enemy let go with a mortar barrage (their most effective weapon in the gorge). One round found Johnson's position and Baker Company lost five of its best machine gunners, all wounded in one shattering explosion. Johnson, Joe Perry, Robert Feld, and the names of the two recent replacements were added to the long list of our company's wounded for D+21. It had been a terrible day for Baker Company.

WINDLE'S FATE

The next day, March 13 (D+22), found Sergeant Windle regaining consciousness in a military hospital on the island of Guam. He had been air-evacuated the seven hundred air miles from Iwo to Guam, where we had top-notch medical facilities to expedite treatment. Windle had received the million-dollar wound and was off Iwo for good!

Air evacuation proved to be a vital factor in saving many lives on Iwo Jima.

Sergeant Windle was told a large fragment had broken his femur and the following day he would undergo an operation. Checking his X-rays before surgery, a surgeon found that what had looked like a broken femur was actually a metal nail neatly wrapped around his thighbone!

Army medics had to surgically remove Windle's combat shoes and wash his feet with warm water and boric acid to remove his rotted socks—they were almost a part of his flesh! The attending physician had never seen such a severe case of athlete's foot and worried that infection would set in.

How could a doctor on Guam imagine men fighting on Iwo Jima not being able to change socks or wash their feet for weeks? Only someone who had fought on the island and knew how devoted Sergeant Raymond Windle was to the Corps and his men could appreciate the dedication and valor that had led to the deteriorated condition of his socks and feet.

The simple fact was there was no place to get clean socks in the front lines of Iwo Jima, so Windle must have thought, *Why wash dirty ones?* After treatment and some recuperation on Guam, he would be transferred to Naval Hospital Number 10 at Pearl Harbor.

LAST MEN STANDING

Superstition or not, March 13 was a lucky day for Baker Company— we didn't lose anyone. But this didn't change the fact that of the original seventeen men in the second section of the machine-gun platoon, only one remained in combat, Pfc. Billy Joe Cawthorn, our "baby-faced Marine." The second section was now composed of replacements, and at this point not many of *them* were left. Some gun crews had to be combined in order to have an operational weapon.

```
Telegram, Specific date unknown, most likely D+22
From: Lt. General T. Kuribayashi, Commander, Iwo
    Jima
To: Major Y. Horie, Commander, Detached HQ, Chichi
    Jima


By captured documents we found out our enemy is the
3rd, 4th, and 5th Marine Divisions and the 5th is
now in the Northern District.
    On the 12th we inflicted the following casualties
on the enemy in the Northern District. Shot down
one aircraft and killed about 200 men.
```

"SECURED" BUT STILL DEADLY

On March 14, D+23, our 1st Battalion continued attacking as in days prior, with flame-throwing tanks acting as a spearhead, spraying a firestorm of napalm and lead as they blasted a path toward the sea. It was on this day that Major William Tumbelston was severely wounded and evacuated. He was the *third* commander of 1st Battalion—which seemed to prove that leading the "1st" on Iwo was injurious to an officer's health!

Replacing Tumbleston was Major William Kennedy, who had landed as the operations officer for the 3rd Battalion and was now given a new assignment, as our battalion's *fourth* commander.

In the early afternoon, Baker Company lost one of its best leaders, Platoon Sergeant John Leary, who was wounded—another veteran gone. The only good news for the exhausted platoon was that Pops Whitcomb had returned and was ready to take over a machine gun! Billy Joe Cawthorn was glad to see him. Now the original second-section roster was up to *two* men again.

Even as men were falling left and right, on this day, Fleet Admiral

Chester M. Nimitz declared Iwo Jima "secured" and ordered a message read to the troops (in Iwo's rear areas) to proclaim the fact. Unfortunately, Marines at the front didn't get the Word and no one told the Japs. According to Nimitz, the battle for Iwo had now entered the mop-up stage. Meanwhile, at the front, the grinding battle wore on and the 5th Division took 145 casualties. None of its weary members knew they still faced *ten more days* of the deadliest combat ever fought by the United States Marine Corps.

A BUDDY FALLS

One of those casualties was Pfc. Edward Joseph Tucker, my friend who had a foreboding of his death. He once told me that he wouldn't survive Iwo Jima. I told him, "Bullshit, Tucker! You are wrong!" Tucker, Lloyd Hurd, and I had pulled some liberty together in Hawaii. I guess we were simpatico. From Detroit, Michigan, Tucker was a former paratrooper and a gunner in Corporal Brookshire's squad. While I liked nearly everyone in the machine-gun platoon, Tucker was something special.

I left the island thinking that Tucker was killed on the beach on D-Day, but I was mistaken. He had been wounded on D-Day by shrapnel in his left leg. This only put him out of action for six days before he returned to Baker Company. I did not know he was back—things had been so chaotic. The company was out of corporals, so Tucker took over the duties of the squad leader in his section.

Six days was not enough time for his wound to heal and he was in continual pain, with the wound still draining. The truth is, his wound was a million dollar wound, bad enough to get you off Iwo Jima and so bad that no one would ever expect to or send you back to the front.

The truth is that Tucker volunteered to come back, even after the medical doctors told him not to. Tucker had given me fatherly advice once: "Never, ever volunteer for anything in the Marine Corps," and here he had violated his own advice. But Tucker had the safety and welfare of his squad foremost on his mind.

This was to cost him his life. Through the hellish assault on Hill 362A, and day-in and day-out phases of the "siege," Tucker was in the thick of it, against the entrenched enemy. The loss of friends and comrades had awakened a real animosity in him and the other Marines against our unforeseen enemies. This fight was now more than a fight—it was a vendetta. We wanted revenge. We vowed to kill ten for one. We had learned to hate our enemies. Men who are mad are hard to stop.

Sadly, the Japanese did stop Tucker on March 14, 1945. His love for helping his men cost him his life. The citation for his Silver Star recorded his last deeds:

> For conspicuous gallantry and intrepidity as a squad leader, serving a platoon of Company B, First Battalion, Twenty-Seventh Marines, Fifth Marine Division, in action against enemy Japanese forces on Iwo Jima, Volcano Islands, 14th March 1945. Heedless of his own painful wounds and refusing evacuation in order to remain with his men in continuance of an assault against the bitterly defending Japanese, Private First Class Tucker unhesitating braved a deadly hail of hostile rifle and machine gun fire to rescue a wounded Marine lying in an exposed position. Although mortally wounded while administering first aid to his stricken comrade, Private First Class Tucker, by his unselfish courage and devotion to duty, had strengthened the morale and fighting spirit of his entire company, thereby reflecting great credit upon himself and the United States Naval Service.

The eloquence of this citation for the Silver Star says it all about Edward Tucker. His death certificate read "GSW [gunshot wound],

Heart." Tucker's premonition of death was accurate. The one thing he couldn't predict was that he'd die a hero.

Meanwhile, trapped in an ever-tightening snare, the Japanese responded with the courage of men who knew they were doomed.

```
Telegram, date unknown, most likely D+23
From: Lt. General T. Kurihayashi, Commander, Iwo
   Jima
To: Major Y. Horie, Commander, Detached HQ, Chichi
   Jima
```

```
The attack on the Northern District this morning
became much more severe than before and at about
noon the enemy approached with 10 tanks and broke
through our left front line and approached to
within 200 meters east of the Divisional Headquar-
ters.
```

NEAR, YET SO FAR

After twenty-five days in combat, Pfc. David Gaston, of Reidville, South Carolina, was thanking his lucky stars. It was March 15 (D+24), and he was still on deck. An original member of the third section, machine-gun platoon, Gaston could see the end of the island. It was near—*yet so far.*

There was no telling how many bullets had missed him by a hairsbreadth or land mines he had *almost* stepped on, or shell fragments he had dodged. Was he living a charmed life? Not exactly.

The enemy rummaged around and at last found some steel with his name on it. During the mop-up phase of the final campaign, Gaston took command of his squad as acting corporal. While scouting ahead, he stepped in a clearing surrounded by the jagged rocks that composed the Bloody Gorge landscape.

At that moment a Japanese knee-mortar man leaped from a cave and fired three rounds toward him. One of the incoming shells had "Gaston" written all over it. Gaston staggered from the impact and fell toward a large rock, hoping to prop himself against it for support. Struggling against waves of shock in the fading light, he was almost mistaken for an enemy soldier by a Marine who was about to shoot him when his squad members ran to his side. A corpsman administered emergency aid and Gaston was evacuated on a small, tracked vehicle called a Weasel to a field hospital. After initial treatment for his wounds, Gaston was flown to a naval hospital on Guam for additional treatment. With Gaston out of action, there were only ten of Baker Company's original machine-gun platoon left.

Would *anyone* make it to the end?

On their end, the Japs did not face such ponderous questions. Their commander, Lieutenant General Tadamichi Kuribayashi, made his intentions clear. That day, a radio broadcast from Tokyo featured "The Song of Iwo Jima" to the defenders of Iwo Jima, a song composed for the fighting men before the American forces landed. Kuribayashi sent a thankful reply by telegram, to his men and all of Japan: "I am determined to go out and make 'Banzai' charges against the enemy at midnight of the 17th. Now, I say good-bye to all senior officers and friends . . . everlastingly." He included the titles of three farewell songs in the telegram. With the days whittling down toward his deadline for a final Banzai charge, he notified his superiors of his remaining manpower.

Telegram, March 16 (D+25)
From: Lt. General T. Kuribayashi, Commander, Iwo
    Jima
To: Telegram to Chichi Jima for Transmission to
    Tokyo

```
Our surviving strength is now as follows:
   Northern Districts 500. Southern Districts 300.
```

Kuribayashi seemed set to fulfill his promise to his men and the people of Japan. In the early morning of March 17, at 2:00 a.m., he addressed his troops by telegram:

```
Telegram, March 17 (D+26)
From: Lt. General T. Kuribayashi
To: The garrison of Iwo Jima


To All Surviving Officers and Men: The battle sit-
uation has come down to the last moment. I want my
surviving officers and men to go out and attack the
enemy tonight. Each troop is to go out simultane-
ously at midnight and attack the enemy until the
last. You have all devoted yourselves to his Maj-
esty, the Emperor. Don't think of yourself. I am
always at the head of you all. Lt. General T. Kuri-
bayashi
```

Meanwhile, on the island of Chichi Jima, a garrison commanded by Major Y. Horie operated the "detached headquarters of Iwo Jima," sending and relaying messages for the besieged defenders of Iwo. Horie later wrote in his memoirs: "From the morning of the 17th we were unable to communicate with him [Lieutenant General Kuribayashi] . . . so, we thought that the 17th of March was his death day. He was promoted to "General" on the 17th. But we were greatly surprised when we received his telegram on the 21st, in the morning. We knew from his telegram that he and his men (Army and Navy), all together 400 men, went out on the midnight of the 17th and hid themselves in a cave 150 meters northwest from his old headquarters."

TERRIBLE TERRAIN

Since Kuribayashi's promised Banzai charge failed to materialize, on March 18 (D+27), our Marines had to go back to the ugly chore of rooting out the enemy. A final Banzai charge almost sounded appealing compared with this gut-wrenching duty. On D+27, the 1st Battalion fought as a unit for the last time. But they made the deepest penetration yet of the northern island. It is nearly impossible to describe with words the terrain where the final battle for Iwo Jima took place. Jagged rock valleys with ragged sandstone outcroppings, crevices, deep gullies, gorges—all disarranged as if blown in by evil winds.

The Japs had chosen the devil's own rock pile for the final defense of Iwo Jima. Utilizing the rough terrain to augment their advantage, they had "planted" their fields of fire to inflict maximum casualties on the Marines who entered this "Valley of Death."

Colonel Don Robertson was commanding our sister battalion, the 3rd Battalion, and he remembered: "The Japs were on the sides of the valley when we attacked. They had no way out and we pushed them toward the ocean. Division command gave me operational control of the tank battalions, which I used to lead our attack. All tanks moved slowly up the valley covered by our troops while firing their napalm on the Japs trapped on the sides of the valley.

"It didn't take many days to kill all of those remaining as we kept steady fire and pressure on them. As a flamethrower tank ran out of fuel, it would depart the valley to refuel and then return to fight with a full fuel load."

Later reports indicated that up to ten thousand gallons of napalm were consumed each day during the last push to snuff out all Japanese oppositions.

By evening, the 1st Battalion's bleeding remnants and her sister battalions were withdrawn from combat and sent to the rear echelons. After a month of hell, the handful of Baker Company Marines still standing could almost smell the hot chow of the troopships waiting offshore to take them back to Camp Tarawa.

Other books and publications on Iwo Jima have reported that our 27th Marine Regiment was so decimated that it was disbanded. Decimated—*yes!* Disbanded—*no!*

```
Telegram, March 19 (D+28)
From: Lt. General T. Kuribayashi
To: Chichi Jima for Transmission to Tokyo


The enemy besieged us on the 18th and 19th approach-
ing us by firing and using flamethrowers on their
tanks. Especially they are trying to approach the
entrance to our cave with explosives.
```

Bloody Gorge, the Japs' last pocket of resistance, was not fully subdued until March 23 (D+32), when units of the 28th Marines had the dubious honors of conquering it. Still, the fight for Iwo was not yet over, as Kuribayashi's string of telegrams revealed . . .

```
Telegram, March 21 (D+30)
From: General T. Kuribayashi, Commander, Iwo Jima
To: Major Y. Horie, Commander Detached HQ, Chichi
    Jima


20th and 21st, my officers and men are still fight-
ing. The enemy front lines [are] 200 to 300 meters
from us and they are attacking . . . with direct
tank firing. They advised us to surrender by a loud
speaker, but we only laughed at this childish trick.
We have not eaten or had drink for five days. But,
our fighting spirits are still running high. We are
going to fight bravely till the end.
```

Telegram, March 21, (D+31)

From: General T. Kuribayashi, Commander, Iwo Jima

To: Major Y. Horie, Commander Detached HQ, Chichi
    Jima

Naval Headquarters came to our cave on the 16th
and are fighting with us . . . Officers and men
are continuing to fight. Supply arrived from Japan
by aircraft. I pay my respects to the two brave
aviators who supplied weapons (hand grenades and
flame projectors) to Iwo Jima by aircraft . . . It
is indeed difficult to express how the hearts of
the fighting youth of Iwo Jima who could still
stand rejoiced when they saw these brave fliers!

On March 23, (D+32), Major Horie, received the following message from a radio operator on Iwo Jima: "All officers and men at Chichi Jima, good-bye from Iwo."

This was the last message sent from Iwo Jima. Major Horie continued trying to communicate with Iwo Jima for three days after that, but to no avail. As the sounds of explosions slowed to a trickle in the Bloody Gorge and the campaign wound down to its inevitable conclusion, most of the 5th Marine Division, including the shattered remains of the 27th Marines, had already departed Iwo or were in the process of loading onto ships bound for Hawaii.

THE LAST STAND

At dark on March 25 (D+34), scattered groups of Japanese survivors began gathering at a preassigned assembly area near the western beaches. Many of these stragglers were officers or NCOs and most carried ceremonial swords for their final mission to kill Americans before dying "honorably," for their leader, Kuribayashi, and for all of Japan.

This event would not be a typically futile Banzai charge, but a cunning, organized final assault in large numbers against the Marines. Fueled with hatred and frustration by their failure to stop the conquest of Iwo Jima, the Japanese were determined that D+35 would be the day of their last glorious stand.

THE FIRST WAVE

Although Baker Company of the 5th Pioneer Battalion had come in on the fifth wave of the Iwo landings, tonight they would fight in the first wave. Pioneers were Marine Seabees, specializing in getting supplies to the front, shore-party work, and doing tasks that required jacks-of-all-trades. Most were multiple-skilled individuals and were talented in mechanical arts. Pioneers were handy with explosives and could be called on to blow up a tenacious fortification or fix a general's toilet.

Because they were Marines, Pioneers were skilled combat fighters, and on Iwo they were often called upon to support frontline troops. On Iwo, their battalion suffered 30 percent casualties. While their battalion's casualties were not as severe as the 90-plus percentage racked up by assault units, the survivors of the 2nd Battalion Pioneers, like Private Menard A. Brouillette, from Alexandria, Louisiana, were deeply relieved the fighting was over so they could leave the island of death.

The next morning, at daylight, they were scheduled to complete loading out for home. For the first time since D-Day, Brouillette and his fellow Pioneers looked forward to a full night of restful sack time. Neither they nor anyone else heard the Japs coming.

Stealthily, at 5 a.m. in the predawn hours of March 26 (D+35), the remnants of Kuribayashi's forces approached a group of tents belonging to the Army Air Force's 21st Fighter Group. The tents were located in the center of the island, along Airfield Two, and the enemy crept upon them from three directions. The Air Corps pilots and crewmen, soldiers, and medics were inside this "secure area," sound asleep, when hundreds of shrieking Japs struck suddenly and savagely out of the darkness.

Fanatical Jap attackers leaped out of underground holes and appeared to come from everywhere, slashing a bloody pathway through tents and overrunning a medical unit filled with helpless patients. Unarmed Marines and soldiers were cut down in bed or as they stumbled out of tents to meet the Jap charge of death. Men were killed wholesale in a fury of flashing swords, gunfire, grenades, and bayonet thrusts. Stunned and shocked, the weaponless Americans could offer little effective resistance.

Nearby, members of the 2nd Pioneer Battalion were yanked and shaken from their racks by frantic officers and ordered into formations. Groggily snatching weapons, the men rushed to meet the attack head-on.

Private Brouillette had the presence of mind to grab a .30-caliber machine gun and boxes of belted ammo before moving with his unit toward the sound of battle. He could clearly see the flash of explosives and hear the wild, screaming melee in Charlie Company's Pioneer bivouac area. Brouillette's group of Pioneers was the first organized unit to fight to stop the surprise Jap assault.

When Brouillette's group arrived in Charlie Company's area, Captain Henry Martin of Charlie Company led them in a counterattack. Martin personally shot four enemy soldiers and destroyed a number of hastily established Japanese Nambu machine-gun positions as his men killed the gunners. While leading an assault into the center of the enemy forces, just like in the movies, Martin was killed by a grenade. He would become the last 5th Division Marine to win the Medal of Honor—in this case, for his leadership during the last organized resistance on Iwo Jima.

As dawn arose, a grim count of bodies revealed 262 dead Japanese scattered across the landscape after ninety minutes of savage fighting.

Eighteen had been captured, most wounded seriously. Burial parties counted 44 dead American airmen and 88 others wounded. The 2nd Pioneer Battalion had 9 men dead and 31 wounded. A large proportion of the dead Japanese were officers, and it was immediately rumored that General Kuribayashi was among them.

THE LAST MYSTERY

General Kuribayashi's body was not found after the last Japanese assault; nor was it ever recovered, although the Americans searched for it. No one living today, including the general's family, actually knows what happened in his last hours. Toro Kuribayashi, son of the general, wrote the following to the author:

As for Dad's last hours, I believe the true facts are: From sunset of March 25, 1945, to the dawn of March 26, surviving Imperial Japanese Forces launched their last all-out attack with my father at the top [in the lead]. After midnight on the top of the west precipice, the Japanese forces were obliged to stand still [take cover] under the onslaught of showering [falling] shells.

Under such circumstances he [Kuribayashi] had his sword in his left hand and ordered the chief-of-staff officer, Colonel Takaishi, who was beside him, "Send snipers to shoot." Sergeant Oyama testified that he heard the order. Sergeant Oyama, who was seriously wounded in the last combat with my father, fell unconscious, and was hospitalized by the U.S. After having served [sic] as a POW, he came back and testified his dreadful account of the night to me.

My father believed it a shame to have his body discovered by his enemy, even after death, so he had previously asked two soldiers to come along with him, one in front and the other behind, with a shovel in hand. In case of his death, he had wanted them to bury his body then and there.

It seems my father and the soldiers who were killed by shells were buried at the foot of a tall tree in Chidori Village along the beach near Osaka Mountain. Afterward General [Holland] Smith spent a whole day looking for his body to pay respects accordingly and to perform a burial, but in vain.

I pray from the bottom of my heart for those who sacrificed their precious lives for their nations. May their supreme souls rest in peace.

The last Banzai-like charge was a final and violent statement on behalf of the Japanese defenders and their dedicated general Kuribayashi, who had devoted every ounce of his strength to prevent the Marines' conquest of Iwo Jima.

The battle for Iwo Jima was finally over. Private Menard Brouillette and his fellow 2nd Battalion Pioneers didn't look back with any regrets when their ship finally left anchor for Hawaii, where the division's lucky survivors were headed. As for Baker Company, we had 268 Marines when we landed on the black sand beaches of that godforsaken island of Iwo Jima. Only 38 walked off at the battle's end.

CHAPTER TWENTY-EIGHT

Catch-22

We raised our glasses in a salute to one another. Tremulis leaned over and in a stage whisper told the man, "We just got back from Iwo Jima." The banker type was impressed.

During the weeklong voyage from Saipan to Pearl Harbor, Tremulis and I spent a lot of time discussing the liberty we would pull once we hit civilization again, at Pearl. On March 28, 1945, we arrived at Navy Hospital Number 10, Aeia Heights.

The Word was that the Navy was not granting Iwo returnees liberty until they had been medically cleared. Tremulis and I didn't like this, but what could we do? Liberty wouldn't have done us any good, anyway. We didn't have any money. Our payroll records were with the 5th Division. Since we had no records and no money, the Navy advanced us five dollars each for health and comfort, but we could only draw these funds every two weeks. After buying cigarettes and toilet articles, there was no money left for shore leave. We spent the days recuperating and waiting for orders. We didn't know if we were to be reassigned or sent back to the 5th Division. The 5th Division was still scattered all over the Pacific. Some were in Naval and Army hospitals and the remainder were in widely dispersed and intermingled groups. There was no more Company B by this point. There was no more 27th Marines; the 27th had been so shot up that it was now part of a composite battalion. I don't believe the 5th Division could have put a full regiment together.

At Aeia Heights, both Tremulis and I had to undergo physical and psychiatric evaluation. The physical part we passed all right. It was the psychiatric phase that we were having trouble with. Navy psychiatrists thought I was off my rocker. I told one, "I'm all right mentally and physically and I want to rejoin my old outfit, B Company, First Battalion, Twenty-seventh Marines, Fifth Division."

It was like Joseph Heller's postwar book *Catch-22,* about World War II life in the Army Air Corps. The term *catch-22* described the situation I was trapped in. I wanted to go back and the Navy doctor thought I was wacko for wanting to. So, I received *more evaluations.*

I looked at one of my papers on his desk when the doc was gone. It had a notation: "suspected psychic anxiety." How could I have this? I didn't even know what it meant. I couldn't even spell it! When you're eighteen, what do you know? My doctor, a full Navy commander, had diplomas on the walls certifying that *he* was okay. Personally, though, I thought *he* was a little wacky himself when he asked me questions like "How did you feel after the concussion? Were you sick to your stomach? Did you have headaches? How severe? Do you still have them? Do you still have ringing in your ears?" I felt like I was going to be the subject of a "white paper" on the effects of concussion and combat fatigue on Marines. Tremulis told me that he was experiencing the same treatment with his Navy sawbones.

WE MEET AGAIN!

At Aeia Heights Hospital we ran into none other than Pfc. George Van Conkelberg! He was recovering well from having been shot through the back on Hill 362A while operating his machine gun with Steve Evanson. He told me that my best pal, Steve, hadn't made it. He had died that night after being gut-shot and was buried in the 4th Division Cemetery on Iwo Jima. I wasn't surprised. I had felt it all along and had mourned Steve every day since I'd last seen him. And now I heard it from someone else: Steve was dead.

To change the subject, Van asked how things had been for us on Iwo Jima after he left. He told us that he was scheduled to return to the battalion at Camp Tarawa as soon as he healed completely. As we parted company, Van humorously quipped to me, "One thing about being in a hospital: There's plenty of time to play cards."

SENTENCED TO STATESIDE

A few days later, in early April, my doctor said he was sending me stateside to a hospital that was better equipped to treat my condition. Well, that news didn't make me mad. Now I was being told I *had to go* stateside. If this wacky doc said, "Go stateside," I *would go stateside*! When I told Tremulis, he said, "Guess what? I'm going with you!"

In the mysterious way of the Navy medical bureaucracy, Tremulis and I had received the same orders and were being shipped back to the States on the same boat.

We embarked for San Francisco on April 10, 1945, aboard the magnificent USS *Lurline*. "California, here we come!" I could have sung out loud, but I didn't—Tremulis didn't like my singing.

It would be great to be home again and be able to see my mother, stepfather, brothers, and sisters. That would be all the therapy I would ever need. *Yes sir! California, here I come!*

Prior to the war, the *Lurline* was the queen of the Matson Line, whose fleet of luxury liners serviced the rich tourist trade between the West Coast and Hawaii. Now part of the war effort, it continued the same run, except its passengers were sailors, Marines, and other service personnel.

The *Lurline*'s conversion to wartime service couldn't disguise the fact that under her now-dowdy-looking paint job, she was still a gracious lady. For me, she was "Queen of the Pacific" after all the other tubs I had been on! Though she was still regal in appearance, some liberties had been made to accommodate the *Lurline*'s new class of "steerage passengers." I thought to myself, *This is the first time I ever went steerage—first class!*

The staterooms assigned to us had been designed for two passengers, but the sleeping accommodations now in the space were for ten! Steel bunks were stacked to the ceiling. There was no reason to feel bad about the crowding, though, because the heads (toilets) were deluxe, with marbled showers and floors. The food service, however, had slipped from its former days. The *Lurline* was the first Navy ship I had been on that served only two meals a day. Oranges were passed out at lunch—was this a bonus?

Tremulis and I, not surprisingly, were not asked to join the captain at his table. Nor did we play shuffleboard on the upper decks. The swimming pool was closed, and so was the bar. We could wander around the decks a bit, but due to the ship's status as a troop transport, everything was pretty stark. A highlight of the trip was participating in an abandon-ship drill! I wondered if "they" knew something we didn't.

There were the usual card games—everyone was trying to find something to do. With no tour director to organize things, though, shipboard life was dull. There wasn't any use in writing letters; we would be home before we could mail them! But no matter how fast the ship went, it was never fast enough. The joy and anticipation of going home made every minute seem like waiting for Christmas morning.

Tremulis and I did discuss his future in the flower business. When I asked him why he wanted to do this, he answered with complete logic: "Listen, Tatum. When the war is over, there's going to be a lot of weddings! There's always Mother's Day! Then there's the other biggies, like Valentine's Day. And there are a lot of funerals around

Chicago. Take it from me, Tatum, flowers are going to be big business."
I always knew Greeks were great thinkers; now I was finding out they
were good businessmen, too!

COMMANDER DOWN

I will always remember April 12, 1945. We were two days out of Pearl
when the ship's public-address system announced, "Franklin Delano
Roosevelt, thirty-second president of the United States, has died of a
stroke!" He was sixty-four.

The war had claimed the free world's leader, our commander in
chief. The passengers and crew were in a state of shock and disbelief.
Roosevelt had always seemed so strong. How could this happen to
America—and to the world?

Tremulis and I felt a strong sense of personal loss. We had both
seen the president at the 5th Division's invasion rehearsal back at
Camp Pendleton. Tremulis put it best, "Tatum, we've lost a great man."

The *Lurline*'s flag was immediately lowered to half-mast.

The radio news bulletins that were broadcast were brief: "President
Roosevelt died of a stroke at his summer home at Warm Springs.
Georgia." Our new president and commander would be former vice
president Harry S. Truman, who had been an artillery captain in
World War I. Truman had first come to Washington as a senator from
Missouri. Could anyone take the great man's place? Would the ship
of state be sailing without a rudder now?

SAN FRANCISCO—THE HOME FRONT

Sailing under the Golden Gate Bridge on April 17, 1945, told me I had
finally made it back to the good old USA. Many times I doubted if I

would ever see our glorious land again. The sun was setting over the fantail as we sailed under the giant span of gray steel.

Mother Nature put on a special light and color show, using the Pacific Ocean and the orange-red sky as her canvas. This was a spectacular welcome! I had an indescribable feeling in my heart knowing that I WAS HOME AT LAST!

We docked in San Francisco and disembarked to waiting Navy buses—our destination, a Navy "holding hospital." We learned that *holding hospital* was another word for *quarantine*.

"What about liberty?" we asked. A corpsman told us, "New Marine arrivals are held for five days before being allowed liberty." Yeah, "held"—like hostages. Navy health experts didn't want "jarheads" (Navy-speak for "Marines") importing any form of pestilence they might have contracted in the Pacific.

Still, I could understand the precautions they were taking. What the Navy didn't understand, though, was that Corporal Angelos Tremulis and I hadn't been in civilian company in *four months*. Our last liberty had been at Pearl in January 1945. We were going stir-crazy! We were disappointed. No—let me say we were highly pissed at the "poor relative" treatment we were receiving at the hands of Navy medics. "It just isn't fair!" I told Tremulis.

"Don't worry, kid, I'll think of something," was Tremulis's reply. I didn't worry—after all, the Greeks were the world's greatest thinkers.

Our daily life in the holding cell was totally unstructured. "We ought to call our folks and let them know we made it back and we survived Iwo and all the Navy's hospitals," Tremulis suggested. The line to use the pay phone was long. There was only one, and five hundred returning Marines were all trying to use it.

Tremulis told me to stand in line and he would go reconnoiter the base. I was so far back in the line I couldn't see the telephone booth. My hometown of Stockton was only eighty miles away. I could have walked home before I would get to use the telephone.

Since there was nothing else to do, I stayed in line. I didn't know why I was doing this. My mother didn't even have a telephone. When I was the fifth guy from the phone, Tremulis appeared with a Navy enlisted man in tow. "Tatum! Give him your place in line," he ordered. He was my senior and I had to obey. I did what he told me.

"What's this all about?" I asked.

"I charged this guy five dollars for your place in line; we're going to need some money when we go on liberty."

"Liberty?" I asked. "Did the Navy change its mind?"

"Hell no, they didn't, but I'll think of something."

That was okay by me. After all, I *still* believed the Greeks were the great thinkers. The next morning, after chow, Tremulis and I went for a walk, skirting the perimeter of the hospital grounds.

STALAG SAN FRANCISCO

The fence surrounding our hospital was made of galvanized chain links with three strands of barbed wire stuck out at a forty-five-degree angle at the top. Navy enlisted men patrolled it night and day. I didn't know if it was to keep people *in* or *out*. The security looked good to me—there was no way out of *this* camp. We were prisoners in our own country!

The afternoon of our second day at the receiving hospital, I was lying on my sack, reading a book to while away the time until the next chow call, when Tremulis came in and said, "Let's go for a walk."

Our walk took us down to the tennis courts, which were for "Officers Only." In one corner, the land sloped off sharply and there was a washout under the fence and a hole, just big enough for a man to slip through. Heavy undergrowth concealed the size of the aperture. It looked to me like a *lot* of people had used this gateway before. Tremulis explained, "This hole is our path to liberty."

That night at about eight o'clock, Tremulis said, "Hang on to this," and handed me the fiver he'd gotten from the sailor. We moseyed down to the tennis courts, pulled back the undergrowth, and slipped our way through to freedom. At last we were free in the land of the free.

We walked about seventy-five yards to the boulevard in front of the hospital. We were dressed in faded Marine green dungarees that had been issued in Hawaii. I was thinking to myself, *We will never get away with this.* We started hitchhiking. The first car that went by was filled with shipyard workers. The second one stopped and the driver asked, "Where are you going?"

"Market Street," Tremulis said with a cunning smile.

The nice driver dropped us off two blocks from Market.

Soon enough, we were walking down the famed Market Street in San Francisco, the best damn liberty town in the States! The time by now was just after nine o'clock and the thoroughfare was teeming with servicemen and women from all branches.

We saw two shore patrolmen half a block away and, having no liberty permission papers, ducked into a street bar loaded with servicemen. I wanted to order a drink, but Tremulis said, "No!"

We left and started walking again. "Where are we going?" I asked.

Corporal Tremulis said, "To the financial district."

"Why there?" I asked.

"Money—that's where the high rollers drink," he said.

We went to a little bar near a bank. After our eyes got accustomed to the dark, we could see that it was a classy place. Indirect lighting beamed on overstuffed chairs with small cocktail tables that had little candles burning in colored glass chimneys.

The place was busy, so we took stools and sat at the bar. The bartender asked, "What'll it be?"

I didn't know what to order—I wasn't old enough to drink legally. I was old enough to fight for my country, but not old enough to drink in it. It was a good thing I didn't have an ID card, because if the bartender had asked, he'd have found out that I was only eighteen years of age. I ordered a Seven and Seven; it was the name of the only drink

I knew. Tremulis ordered a Manhattan and poked me in the ribs to let me know I should pay for the drinks. I took the fiver out. Two drinks came to eighty cents.

Tremulis complained loudly to me, "See what the war has done! It has driven the price of everything right through the roof! I remember when a drink was only two bits."

Tremulis leaned over and told the bartender to give the man next to us a drink. While serving it, the barkeeper told the well-dressed gentleman, "You are drinking with the United States Marine Corps."

We raised our glasses in a salute to one another. Tremulis leaned over and in a stage whisper told the man, "We just got back from Iwo Jima."

The banker type was impressed.

Iwo Jima had been in the headlines. I guessed everyone who could read knew of the bloody battle we fought there. Soon, the banker type introduced us to all present in the bar. Everyone wanted to buy us a drink—and we let them. Tremulis let them know we were in a Navy hospital and this was our first liberty. The bartender kept our glasses full.

My liberty-smart corporal sure knew how to work a bar! I had the distinct feeling he had worked this operation before. Whenever he mentioned the *Yorktown* in other bars, drinks must have started flowing. He had probably worked bars from San Diego to Chicago, his homeport, with this story.

We were having the liberty of our lives. The well-dressed man was soon joined by a good-looking lady and we all moved to the overstuffed chairs and small cocktail tables. At eleven o'clock, the lady asked if we were hungry. Of course we were!

She said, "I know a quaint Italian restaurant—let's all go there."

We took a taxi. It was a short trip; the meter only racked up a buck. The name of the restaurant was Tony's. (Aren't all Italian restaurants in San Francisco named Tony's?)

It was closing time. But the lady must have been a regular customer and an important one. Tony reopened his restaurant when she told him, "These Marines are just back from Iwo Jima!" Tony had a son fighting in Europe.

The spread—make that feast—that Tony put on was a culinary delight. I had veal doré with spaghetti. Tremulis ordered the wine. He seemed to know a lot about it. Were ancient Greeks great drinkers as well as thinkers? Did they invent wine?

Our meal was fit for two kings.

We all used the wine to toast to the Marines, the Army, and Tony's son in Europe. There were so many toasts I got woozy. It was time to go.

HOLLYWOOD MARINES

Leaving the bar almost proved to be our undoing. We walked right into a Navy shore patrol. With no obvious way to avoid them, we stopped. They stopped.

"Why are you out of uniform?" one swab-jockey cop asked.

Corporal Tremulis, without blinking, said, "We aren't *real* Marines. We are actors working on a movie being made in San Francisco." The presence of the well-dressed couple added credibility to the story.

Tremulis's story was so preposterous that the SPs thought it *had* to be true! No service personnel would go on liberty in San Francisco wearing dungarees. Still looking a little dubious, though, they shrugged with slight smiles and walked away.

"How are you getting back to your hospital?" our hosts asked.

I couldn't remember how to get back! Tremulis said, "We're so drunk we don't know where it is."

Lucky for us, the lady knew, and she chauffeured us back in her 1941 Buick with a special gas stamp on the windshield.

At the hospital, we thanked our hosts for their hospitality, the lift, and said our good-byes. That was when our real troubles started.

We were drunk and couldn't find the opening under the fence we had used to escape. Tremulis said, "We'll have to climb over the fence to get back in."

I took off my dungaree jacket and threw it over the barbed wire.

Tremulis gave me a leg up, and as I reached the top, I heard a voice shouting: "*Stop* right where you are!"

Turning, I found myself looking down the barrel of a Reising submachine gun, a nervous sailor with a nervous finger on the trigger.

He told me, "Get down at once. You are under arrest for trying to break into a Naval installation."

This was a serious situation! It's one thing to break into a Naval installation during wartime. It's quite another to be AWOL as well, as Tremulis and I were. We had a general court-martial staring us in the faces!

We had to do something quick to save our butts or we would be so far back in a Navy prison they would have to mail us sunshine.

Corporal Tremulis didn't survive the sinking of the USS *Yorktown* and Iwo Jima by being slow-witted. When we were brought in front of the chief petty officer in charge that night, he went to work at once.

The story he told the petty officer and the SPs would have made anyone cry. He explained how he survived after the *Yorktown* was torpedoed and sunk. That's when he was seagoing. He continued, "Now we are the only two surviving Marines from a *battalion* at Iwo Jima!"

He continued, "We are both shell-shocked and face extended treatment. I have to get to Chicago to see my parents before they die."

I had tears in my eyes when he finished. So did the Navy shore patrolmen.

The petty officer in charge smiled at us and said, "I haven't seen a damn thing. Did anyone see anything tonight?"

The others shook their heads. "No, we didn't see anything," they chorused.

Thank God, our luck was holding.

The ordeal had me as scared as I'd been on Iwo Jima—well, *almost* as scared. But I don't think anyone could have matched the fun we had on our liberty night in San Francisco!

SO LONG, BUDDY!

The next morning, we received our orders. Tremulis was being sent to a Naval hospital in Astoria, Oregon. My orders were to go to Oak Knoll Naval Hospital in San Leandro just seventy miles from my home!

Tremulis walked me to the Navy bus that would take me to Oak Knoll. We shook hands and looked each other in the eye, knowing full well we would probably never meet again. It was like parting with Steve on Iwo Jima—when all I got was a thumbs-up and a glimpse of the sadness in his eyes. But sometimes a look says more than words.

I was right about Tremulis—we never did meet again. But years later, I heard that he did, in fact, join his family's florist business, met a girl, married her, and started his own flower shop. Seems flowers can be a way of life for a warrior, even after what Tremulis had seen. I like the thought of that.

What Became of My Buddies?

Some sixty-six years after the fact is a long time to remember any-thing, but I can't forget the Marines I served with in the big war, World War II. On the fortiethth anniversary of the end of the battle, I vowed to get in touch with my squad mates, if they were still around making roll call. Here's what I've learned had happened to some of those Marines after the war:

C Company Marine corporal Tom Piper, from the same home-town as me, gave me a scare when Van showed up wearing his jacket, which he found in the dead man's pile near the beach. Piper was okay at the time, but later on was badly wounded on Iwo. He survived and left the Corps as a sergeant. He lived a few blocks from me in Stockton until his death a few years back. I attended his services—he was a great Marine and man.

My close friend Private Lloyd Hurd was one of those thirty-eight lucky Baker Company Marines to walk off the island at the battle's end. He returned to Sartell, Minnesota, raised a family, and became successful as a foreman in the paper mill that was the town's main employer. At the fortieth reunion of the 5th Marine Division in 1989, in Phoenix, Arizona, which I attended with great excitement— it was my first—I was to meet Lloyd for the first time in forty-five years.

The hotel where we stayed had booked us rooms just two doors apart. I had instructed the desk to have Mr. Hurd call my room on his arrival. Just as I was finishing shaving, the telephone rang (as it always does when you're in the bathroom). It was Lloyd. I told him that I would come to his room as soon as I finished shaving and got dressed. In less than five minutes, I was knocking on his door. The door opened and my foxhole buddy and I were reunited after all those long years. We shook hands and embraced. I must confess that a tear or two suddenly appeared in the corners of my eyes. Lloyd had to wipe his eyes also. Across the room, I could see a nice-looking lady sitting on the bed. Lloyd introduced me to his wife, Amelda. I had heard so much about her during those long nights in our black sand foxhole. Lloyd and I would stay in touch. In fact, his son, Ron, and I became friends. I remember Lloyd showing me Ron's baby picture on Iwo Jima. A couple of times it seemed he would never see his son again. But he did.

Pfc. Charles "Pops" Whitcomb started as my squad's second ammo carrier and became a gunner before the end. Wounded, Pops returned to combat and was there till the end. The last time I saw him was the day I was sent back to the beach. I searched for him for years and discovered that he was awarded the Bronze Star for his actions one night in defending the company's position. Apparently, Whitcomb decided the Marine Corps was a good billet and stayed in, becoming a first sergeant. If you see him, tell him Tatum is looking for him. Same goes for Pfc. John "Gopher Gus" Henderson—tell him I tried to reach him and still owe him a beer for that grenade prank at Tarawa.

I had no luck finding Pfc. John "Mr. Clean" Luman either. I bet the Ivory Soap company is looking for him, too, in order to offer him a spokesmodel job. I heard that Sergeant Rheal "Biz" Bissonnette, our company's extroverted instructor of all-things-Marine, made it off Iwo, but not before being decorated, twice. I wasn't surprised a bit to hear this; he was a brave Marine. Although I never met him, I heard Captain Edmond O'Herron did well for himself after the war, founding a big drug company. I did meet Corporal Ralph Belt again, whose demolition squad worked with Basilone, Steve, and me to knock out that blockhouse on the beach. We would visit at reunions, and Belt became a good friend; he's going to write some chapters for my next book about Iwo, if I ever finish this one.

Forty years passed before I talked with Pfc. George Van Conkelberg again. I knew that Van had lived in a town in California named Taft. After I managed to reach his mother, she helped me reach him. Van and I had a long talk. He told me he owned a card room and a bar in Taft. And, yes, he still liked to gamble. Many years later, I was coming back from L.A. when I saw the sign for TAFT, CALIFORNIA— 35 MILES, so I turned off the highway to see my old squad mate. I found Van's card room, went in, and asked one of the old men playing cards, "Where can I find George Van Conkelberg?" He said, "You can't. He's dead." I had waited too long to visit. "What did he die from?" I asked. The old man said, "Lung cancer, two packs of Camels a day." This brought back memories of Van's lecturing me about my chain smoking on Iwo Jima.

For forty-three years I thought Corporal William Whaley had been killed on the beach on D-Day. Then, while reading a Marine Corps casualty report prior to the writing of this book, I discovered that the corporal from Tennessee had survived his wounds! I resorted to the old phone directory again and found Corporal Whaley's son Ronald. We had a nice conversation about his father. It seems that Corporal Whaley had lost his life in 1962 in an automobile accident when Ronald was only thirteen and his brother Randal was nine. Ronald helped put me in touch with Corporal Whaley's widow, Arline, who wrote: "(William)'Fred' Whaley and I were sweethearts all through high school. We had fifteen blissful years together before his tragic death in a car wreck on January 16, 1962. He was returning from Ioka, Missouri, lost control of his car and ran off the highway hitting a Church of Christ building. Both church and car burned. I then took on the role of both mother and father to two boys, 9 and 13. Fred was an excellent and handsome husband, a super father, and a devoted son-in-law. One incident on Iwo caused nightmares as long as Fred lived. He was wounded on the first day on the island, February 19, and lay in the volcano ash for 36 hours before someone with a stretcher saw him move and removed his body to the ship that took him to a hospital in Hawaii and later to Oceanside, California. While he lay in the volcano ash seriously wounded, he could hear the screams for help from some men trapped in a burning building. He always regretted he couldn't help rescue them. Fred was discharged in February 1946 . . . he used his GI Bill to get two college degrees from Memphis State University: a B.A. and an M.A. degree. He worked as a teacher, insurance salesman, salesman for National Cash Register selling accounting machines, and was principal of a junior high school and a high school."

The Marine Corps had many heroes, but my favorite is Sergeant Raymond Windle. He was our machine-gun section leader as far back as the early days of Camp Pendleton and at one time led Baker Company after Captain Sohn was wounded until headquarters sent a replacement officer. After being wounded on March 12 (D+20) and evacuated to Guam for treatment, Windle was transferred to a hospital at Pearl Harbor. That was where I lost track of him.

During our reunion in 1989, Lloyd Hurd told me he had seen Windle decades prior. It seems that the sergeant had been in Lloyd's neighborhood of Sartell, Minnesota. He came to see Lloyd at the St. Regis Paper Company, where Lloyd had worked before joining the Marine Corps and again after the war. Lloyd told me that Sergeant Windle, now a civilian, had married a lady from St. Cloud, Minnesota, and just stopped by to say hello. Lloyd said that the sergeant was now in sales. But where Windle resided, Lloyd had no clue.

Then, in November 1990, I picked up an issue of our 5th Division Association's newsletter, *Spearhead News*. While reading the "Welcome Aboard" section, I came across a name that rang a bell: Gunnar O. Johnson of Lawton, Oklahoma. I remembered that our machine-gun platoon of Company B had a Gunnar O. Johnson in it. The long-distance operator gave me his number, I dialed him, and in a few minutes Gunnar and I were talking about the old days in the machine-gun platoon. During the conversation, Windle's name came up, and then I got a real surprise. Gunnar said he used to live in Snyder, Oklahoma, Windle's hometown. He told me that he had been in touch with the sarge over the years and that he lived in a small town in Texas named Valley View. The next surprise was that Gunnar had the sarge's phone number and his address. What a break!

Gunnar O. Johnson and I must have talked for the better part of an hour. It takes time to bridge forty-five years. Gunnar told me that he had recently retired from the U.S. Postal Service and had seen my request for information about Windle in the *Spearhead News* and he had intended to call me and give me Windle's address, but just hadn't gotten around to it. Would his information lead to pay dirt or would this be just another blind alley? I couldn't wait to find out.

I picked up the phone and dialed the number Gunnar had given me. I heard the telephone ringing on the other end, and after the third ring, I thought, *Oh well, there's no one at home.* But on the fourth ring, a lady's voice answered hello. I asked if this was the residence of a Raymond R. Windle. The lady replied that it was and asked who was calling. I told her that I was a former Marine who had served with Sergeant Windle. She said, "All right," and I could hear her call Windle. The next voice I heard was Windle's. "Windle here," he said.

I said, "Is this Sergeant Windle, USMC?"

He replied, "I was a sergeant in the Marines, who is this?"

I said, "This is Pfc. Charles Tatum, reporting in, sir!"

Windle said, "Who did you say?"

I replied that I was Charles William Tatum, who had been in his section of the machine-gun platoon. "Do you remember me?" I asked.

There was a short pause. Then he replied, "Hell, yes, I remember you very well. You were from California. Is that where you are calling from?"

I told him I was calling from my hometown of Stockton. Then he asked how I had found him. I told him that Gunnar Johnson had given me his address and phone number. We got a good laugh that we were both still on deck and awaiting orders from our big Commander in the Sky.

We began asking each other questions: How have you been? What have you been doing? Where did you work? How many children do you have? I asked what happened to him on Iwo Jima after he sent me back. Windle told me about the day he was hit, March 12, 1945. I knew his actions that day had won him the Silver Star medal. Now, that Silver Star was just for one day. The Sergeant Windle I knew should have received at least one citation *per day*, ranging from the Medal of Honor to a letter of commendation, and all of the medals in between. The trouble was, no one was left to do the write-ups for those citations.

It turned out that Windle had made it to gunnery sergeant before he left the Corps. He ended his career with the post office, working on trains that carried the mail.

We were just about to hang up when Windle told me that he and Lenore, his wife, had planned a little trip to Las Vegas. "Why don't you join us?" he asked. I wrote the dates down, booked my ticket, then waited and waited. I knew I was too old for even the least of the sin in Sin City, but I would have gone straight to hell to be with Sergeant Ray Windle. My last, vibrant memory was of seeing him coming through the rocks and crevices on Iwo to rescue me and lead me back to the platoon.

Finally, I found myself with my old hero, amid the lights, roulette balls, and clanging slot machines of Vegas. We spent three days visiting and mostly talking about the Marines we had served with. Meanwhile, Windle's wife hit the jackpot and won five grand. Those were lucky days for us all.

Just as all good things must come to an end, Windle and Lenore returned to Texas and I went back to California. Time passed, until the day I received a letter etched in black, from Lenore. Gunnery Sergeant Raymond Windle had been called to the Baker Company muster in the skies. Seems God must have needed a good platoon leader. But I'd gotten my happy ending when I reunited with my old sergeant in Vegas. I hope life gave him his.

Through Windle and buddies like Hurd, I pieced together what happened to my old nemesis-comrade Gunnery Sergeant Stanley Kavato. Apparently, Kavato died of his wounds on February 20, 1945 (D+1) aboard the USS *Highlands* (APA-199). He is buried in Grave 97, Section F, National Cemetery of the Pacific, also known as the Punch Bowl, on Oahu, Hawaii. I still want to go there to pay my respects. When I looked into what Blackie had done before the war, I was told that he had joined the National Guard. This would explain his gunnery-sergeant rank with only two and a half years in the Corps. Apparently, Kavato had worked as an instructor at the YMCA in Pottstown, Pennsylvania, before the war. I hope someone there remembers him to this day.

The Navy recognized our beloved "Doc," Navy pharmacist's mate third class Curtis Marsh, for his conspicuous gallantry, courage, and medical skills, by awarding him the Silver Star. It should have been the Medal of Honor as far as the Marines of 2nd Platoon, Baker Company, were concerned. Just ask one of the Marines whose life he saved. After Iwo, Marsh served with the 1st Battalion, 27th Marines, in the occupation of Japan and was promoted to pharmacist's mate second class. When the war ended, Doc Marsh separated from the Naval service, hopped a train for Cincinnati, and rejoined his wife, Dorothy, and their son.

Marsh's old job as a tool and die maker waited for him at the

Crosley Corporation and he took it. While he had been fighting the Japanese and tending to the wounds of his Marines, his wife and his dad, George, had continued working at the Crosley Corporation in the same department where he had worked. Doc Marsh retired from the Crosley Corporation after decades of service and enjoyed attending functions of the 5th Marine Division Association. These days, Marsh is doing duty in the sky, probably giving out pills. Doc Marsh and his fellow corpsmen deserve the finest accolade a Marine can give: "He's a Marine!" May their shields of honor shine forever.

As the years passed, I developed a thirst for knowledge about my hero, Gunnery Sergeant John Basilone. I began a ceaseless digging in public and private archives. My first important break came when I met Captain John Butler III, son of my old leader Colonel Butler, commander of our 1st Battalion, 27th Marines, at Iwo Jima. Colonel Butler had been John Basilone's commanding officer and had also been killed during the battle. Captain Butler had met Mary Basilone, sister of my hero, and gave me her phone number. She still lived in the family home at Raritan, New Jersey. I couldn't wait to get her on the phone.

"Getting out of Raritan was the real hook which attracted John to join the Army," Mary Basilone told me. "And John wanted to send home money; there were eleven children to feed." Mary's intimate knowledge corrected many statements I had read and accepted or found confusing in important historical books about Guadalcanal and Iwo. Now I was infused with a mission. I wanted to know the truth about Gunny Basilone. She gave me additional telephone numbers.

Probably the last man to see and talk to Manila John was C Company's commanding officer, Lieutenant John T. Casey. He had trained C Company at Camp Pendleton and led it ashore on Iwo. He knew Basilone as a friend and trusted noncommissioned officer. In an interview he told me, "He was *the* Marine. No doubt about it. A professional soldier in every respect, Basilone had it all: poise, intelligence, and demeanor. Everyone in the First Battalion, Twenty-seventh"—and the entire Marine Corps—"respected John, not just because of his Medal of Honor but because he earned your respect with his professional approach to soldiering. For Basilone, being a Marine wasn't a part-time job. He wasn't in the war for 'the duration'; the Corps was his life."

Lieutenant Casey described Basilone to me as a "reluctant hero" who felt that his celebrity status interfered with his main occupation of being a Marine. He didn't take well to the phonies he had encountered on war bond drives and he suffered fools poorly. Casey's most important new information was that Basilone had lived for twenty minutes after being wounded. Casey, in his advance toward Motoyama One Airfield, came across Basilone where he lay bleeding. "He was still alive when I spoke to him and he knew he was a goner. I couldn't stay with him as the assault was proceeding and I had to lead my company. Several of my men had been killed by the same shell that got Basilone." He paused, then added, "I will never reveal what Basilone said to me as he lay dying."

I located Chief Warrant Officer John A. Daniels. By a strange twist of fate, CWO Daniels was the 5th Division's burial officer who undertook the awesome task of collection and interment of some of the 6,800 of Iwo's heroic dead. One of the sad legion of fallen Marines he cared for was Gunnery Sergeant "Manila John" Basilone. Now in his eighties, CWO Daniels remembers D-Day on Iwo Jima and events that transpired on its black sands with pride and reverence. "At about 1200 hours, Major Amedao Rea, the executive officer of the 2nd Battalion, 26th Marines, reported to the battalion command post [on the front lines] and said to me, 'Gunnery Sergeant Basilone is laying [sic] dead on the end of the first airstrip.' "

The CWO found Basilone at the south end of Motoyama One, where he had died of massive wounds, and immediately recognized his close friend. Ignoring intense mortar and shell fire, Daniels tenderly rescued Basilone's remains and those of other C Company Marines killed in the same blast. By late D-Day afternoon, Daniels and his men had collected ninety dead Marines. He would later create the cemetery for the 5th Marine Division. The furious battle ranging across Iwo and confusion on the beaches prevented him from burying anyone until D+2 (two days after Basilone's death). CWO Daniels noted to me, "John Basilone suffered fatal injuries from a mortar explosion or large shell fire." This assessment was confirmed by the official casualty report that stated tersely, "GSW."

Amid solemn and impressive military ceremonies, on April 20, 1948, the earthly remains of Gunnery Sergeant "Manila John" Basilone were laid to rest. The service was attended by the Salvatore Basilone family at Arlington National Cemetery, seemingly a fitting close to the hero's brief life.

The memory of John Basilone grew dim in the half century since his violent death on Iwo and the posthumous award of the Navy Cross. But in Basilone's hometown of Raritan, New Jersey, his friends never forgot. Across the street from the original Basilone family home at 113 First Avenue stands a heroic-size statue of a bare-chested Basilone, a .30-caliber machine gun cradled in his powerful arms. Every September, Raritan hosts a "John Basilone Day" parade. Fewer and fewer of Basilone's old comrades stand in formation each year at this event, their ranks sliced thin by the passage of time, but other veterans gather in remembrance of the gunny on this occasion. At Bridgewater Raritan High School, football teams compete on Basilone Field. New Jersey commemorated Manila John with the eighty-foot Basilone Memorial Bridge on the New Jersey Turnpike. The U.S. Marine Corps recalled their hero by naming a major thoroughfare at Camp Pendleton, California, and a busy street at its Quantico, Virginia, base after him. The Navy honored their shipmate Basilone when they launched the USS *Basilone* destroyer in December 1945. Commissioned to serve in the fleet in February 5, 1950, it was decommissioned and sunk off the coast of St. Augustine, Florida, after nearly twenty-nine years of service— retired at virtually the same age that its namesake was when he died.

Today, John Basilone's mortal remains lie in Section 12, Grave 384—a plot personally selected by his father, Salvatore, while a guest of President Harry S. Truman at the White House after John's tragic death. As I later learned, the legend is true: John's widow, Sergeant Lena Basilone, never remarried. Until her death in 1999, she remained the epitome of the devotion and the tragic stature that so many Americans displayed during World War II.

From the Marine casualty reports, I learned that Pfc. Clifford Blaine Evanson, "Steve," was buried in the National Cemetery of the Pacific, Section M, Grave 311—a hero's grave. After he was wounded, he was carried back from the front lines to the doctors at the 5th Marine Field Hospital, who provided the best medical treatment possible but could not save him.

Steve hailed from Opportunity, Washington, and was only about three months older than I was. Steve and I were better than friends, we were boon companions. We were always on somebody's bad list. It wasn't that we did anything wrong (of course not), but when you're only eighteen, you just have a lot of energy. We were always involved in some type of practical joke.

While training at Camp Tarawa, Steve and I went on liberty once, to Hilo, a bum liberty town with its lack of females. Despite this, we still had a high old time, hanging out at the USO club, taking in a motion-picture show, and walking all of the streets. That's where we accidentally knocked down the Chinaman's Coca-Cola sign and had to pay him restitution.

For decades after the war, I felt guilty that I didn't contact Steve's parents and tell them firsthand what a great Marine their son had been and of the valor he showed on Iwo Jima. What would they think if they knew that he had helped Gunnery Sergeant Basilone knock out a blockhouse on the beach of Iwo Jima? Mentally, I just couldn't reopen those pages from my past, until 1988.

I felt that someone in Opportunity, Washington, should know this, so I put the Bell Telephone Company to work. At first I had no luck. The long-distance operator told me "there are no Evansons in Opportunity." So I widened my search to nearby Spokane. The operator reported that Spokane had six Evansons listed, but she was only allowed to give me two numbers. I picked two names. I called the first, but it belonged to a family new to the area. The next I called was a "J. A. Evanson."

A friendly voice answered. I found I was talking with Jenness Evanson, who remembered that her uncle had a son named Cliff Evanson who had died young and had a brother and sister. She knew his brother, Ben, lived in the Portland area. I called Ben and, boy, was he surprised to be getting a call after forty-three years about his brother. We had a nice conversation. He revealed that Steve grew up on a farm and wasn't crazy about farming life. He begged—no, pestered his parents until they consented to let him enlist in the Marines. Plus, he told a fib about his age: Steve was only sixteen when he joined the Marines, which means he was only seventeen when we invaded Iwo Jima. And I thought I was young at eighteen.

Ben and I talked for most of an hour. I discovered that he still mourned Steve, as did I. Before we ended our conversation, he had to mention that he was surprised that his brother went by the name Steve because his real nickname was "Sonny." Through my tears, this gave me a laugh. It all made sense. Steve would have never survived in the Marines as "Sonny." The troops would've made mincemeat out of anyone with a "sissy" nickname like that! I told Ben that I planned someday to write a book in tribute to his brother and the other heroes I watched fight, bleed, and die. I guess if you're reading this, then I did it. Better late than never.

ROSTER OF RECURRING CHARACTERS, IN ORDER OF APPEARANCE:

Pfc. Charles "Chuck" Tatum—wounded, combat fatigue
Lieutenant Colonel John Butler (1st Battalion CO)—killed in action
Captain Benjamin "Big Ben" Sohn (B-Co, CO)—wounded in action

Captain James "Jimmy" Mayenschein (B-Co, XO)—killed in action

Second Lieutenant John A. Dreger (platoon CO)—died of wounds

Gunnery Sergeant Stanley "Blackie" Kavato (platoon XO)—died of wounds

Gunnery Sergeant John Basilone (MG instructor, C-Co NCO)—killed in action

Pfc. George Van Conkelberg (squad mate, cardsharp)—wounded in action

Sergeant Raymond Windle (MG section leader)—wounded in action

Sergeant Rheal "Biz" Bissonnette (MG instructor)—one of Baker's thirty-eight to walk off Iwo

Corporal Tom Piper (hometown C-Co Marine)—wounded in action

Corporal Angelos "The Greek" Tremulis (leader, 1st Squad)—wounded, combat fatigue

Pfc. Bruno "Spike" Mierczwa (platoon "physical specimen")—killed in action

Pfc. Loyal Leman (Spike's sidekick)—killed in action

Pfc. Billy Joe Cawthorn (baby-faced Marine)—one of Baker's thirty-eight to walk off Iwo

Pfc. John "Gopher Gus" Henderson (victim of grenade prank at Tarawa)—wounded in action

Corporal William Whaley (squad leader)—wounded in action

Pfc. Clifford "Steve" Evanson (squad mate, best buddy)—killed in action

Pfc. Carl "Tex" Thompson (squad mate, Clark Gable look-alike)—killed in action

Pfc. Charles "Pops" Whitcomb (squad mate, never liked me)—one of Baker's thirty-eight to walk off Iwo

Pfc. John Luman (platoon's Mr. Clean)—one of Baker's thirty-eight to walk off Iwo

Pfc. Edward J. Tucker (death premonition)—killed in action

Pfc. Theron W. Oriel (seldom showered, helped prank Kavato's target)—wounded in action

Sergeant George Lutchkus (MG section leader, Guadalcanal hero)—wounded in action

Corporal Guy Brookshire—(3rd Squad leader, resident banker)—wounded in action

Corporal Frank Pospical (L.A. liberty buddy)—killed in action

Private Lloyd Hurd (squad mate, married man)—one of Baker's thirty-eight to walk off Iwo

Pfc. Lavor Jenkins (squad mate, Tarawa replacement from Wyoming)—killed in action

Private Thomas Jeffries (squad mate, Tarawa replacement from Colorado)—wounded in action

Private Lawrence "Cookie Hound" Alvino (rifleman, 1st Platoon)—wounded in action

Private James Memory Martin (Tarawa replacement, from South Dakota)—wounded in action

Corporal Ralph Belt (1st Battalion demolition assault team)—walked off Iwo

Corporal George Chelf—(3rd Squad leader after Brookshire, great penmanship)—killed in action

Private Ralph Jeffers (Tarawa replacement, posthumous Silver Star)—killed in action

Pharmacist's Mate Third Class "Doc" Curtis Marsh—one of Baker's thirty-eight to walk off Iwo

Sergeant Jay Laycock (3rd Platoon NCO)—wounded in action

Lieutenant Colonel Justin Gates Duryea (battalion CO after Butler)—wounded in action

Pfc. Gunnar Johnson (platoon mate, fellow Okie)—wounded in action

Captain Edmond O'Herron (B-Co replacement CO)—one of Baker's thirty-eight to walk off Iwo

From *Red Blood* to *The Pacific*

After arriving back in the States, I was assigned to the Oak Knoll Naval Hospital located in Hayward, California—about sixty-five miles from my hometown of Stockton.

I say I was "assigned," but I guess what I should say is "admitted" or "committed," I'm not sure which. While I was pleased to be back in the States, I didn't like what was happening to me medically. The ward I was in wasn't for the physically wounded; the Marines interned with me were in what we called the "psycho" ward. There we underwent "psychiatric evaluation," as the Navy doctor explained to me.

"I'm in perfect physical condition, I feel perfectly normal," I told the wacky doc. "I'm ready to go back to duty, somewhere." I told him I would like seagoing duty or to pursue my strong mechanical interests—I would take the Marine Air Corps, if they would let me. It all fell on deaf ears.

The Navy doc began talking about my being discharged from the Marine Corps. I pleaded with him, "No way! I am more than okay, I just want duty somewhere." I figured that there were plenty of jobs for an Iwo Jima survivor in the Marine Corps. The harder I tried to convince the docs that I was mentally okay, the more convinced they were that I was off my rocker for wanting to stay in the Marines.

I saw my dream of becoming an officer in the United States Marine Corps going down the drain. I had never told anyone this before, but my dream was to become a Marine officer. I intended to make the Marines my career and was aware that there were programs where qualified Marines with combat experience could be sent to officers' training school.

I got the bad news on June 14, 1945. The orders read: "Pfc. Charles William Tatum, USMCR is to proceed to the Mare Island Naval Yard for a discharge under honorable conditions."

That was it. I was officially discharged in July 1945. I suppose I should have been happy. After all, there were a million guys in the armed services who would have swapped places with me in a minute and never shed a tear. But to me it felt like my own family had kicked me out of the house. I knew that I was too old to cry, so my feelings turned to anger.

This isn't fair, I thought. But wars never are. The Marine Corps was part of my plans for the future. My complaint about the turn my life had taken was softened by the realization that a lot of people's plans for the future had been interrupted by the war. I thought of all the Marines that were never coming home for their futures. Besides, there was a big old world out there for those with the courage to hit it head-on. *Hop on the merry-go-round and grab for the brass ring!* I thought.

In August 1945, the United States zapped Japan with the two big mushroom clouds that dissolved the Japanese desire to continue the war. Victory in Japan day, or VJ Day, was a red-letter day for celebration in Stockton for anyone wearing a Marine's uniform, me included . . . but just for that day.

So, with plan number one, the Corps as a career, now out of the way, it was time bring on plan number two. This consisted of Charles William Tatum, civilian, becoming a race-car driver. My third greatest idol was a famous racing driver by the name of Wilbur Shaw, the Indianapolis winner (my number one idol was Gunnery Sergeant John Basilone, and my second idol was Sergeant Raymond Windle, my old section leader). As a very young boy, I had read *Popular Mechanics* and discovered a picture of Wilbur Shaw and his Maserati racing car. I spent hours studying that photo of this sleek and complex vehicle. I dreamed of being the driver of this kind of racing car someday, or at least becoming a mechanic for Wilbur Shaw. So what if the Marines didn't want me? I would devote my life to becoming a race-car driver! I didn't have the foggiest idea of how this was to be accomplished.

My $210 mustering-out pay didn't last long. I spent half of it for a diamond engagement ring that I gave to a longtime friend and great girl. Our marriage upset my plans to become a racing-car driver, so I worked as a fireman at a local Army supply depot for a few years.

Then I received a letter from the Marine Corps informing me that I was to receive the Bronze Star and Purple Heart medals. I went to San Francisco in 1946 to receive these honors during a full dress formation. This was a proud moment in my life. My new wife and my dear mother were in the audience. My mother was very proud of her son.

I was still dreaming of becoming a racing driver when the arrival of my first child, Nanci, almost derailed my dream completely. The salary the government pays firemen was just barely enough to buy a car and a washing machine, and pay for food, doctor bills, etc. I couldn't complain because I did have a good job. What the heck, I was living the American Dream. We bought our dream house under the GI Bill's loan provisions. Then our second child, Pam, was born.

Life was really great, except for one thing. The marriage didn't take. We had messed up a good friendship by getting married. The divorce decree said "irreconcilable differences." Some say it was my ambition to become a racing driver that split us up. There is more to this story, but why bore readers with personal troubles? The divorce went off without a hitch, except one small thing: It nearly broke my heart and almost drove me out of my mind!

To recover, I hung around a lot of racing garages, changed a lot of tires, painted other drivers' racing cars, towed other people's racing cars a million miles, and repaired cars when other drivers broke their toys; I paid and paid my dues, but still had no ride in a sleek racing car. It was the "what came first, the chicken or the egg" deal. Without a reputation as a known racing driver, you can't get a ride in someone's racing car, and when no one will allow you to drive their racing car, how in the heck do you become a full-fledged, experienced racing-car driver?

My mechanical expertise improved as time went by and I gained a local reputation as a good race-car builder, but that didn't satisfy my dream. The solution was to build my own car, but a serious lack of funds kept this plan on the back burner until I met Eddie Hudson. Eddie and I shared the same dream in a manner that dovetailed: He wanted to own a racing car and I wanted to drive one. This allowed both of us to share in the same dream. I agreed to build the car, and for building it, I would get a shot at driving it. Now I will confess that I built up my reputation as a race-car driver by telling a little white lie. I told Ed that I had driven in the Los Angeles area. I failed to tell him I was only on the highways and not on the racing tracks when I did so. I think Eddie really knew the truth, though.

Good luck will overtake you if you don't give up. The third race I entered, I won the main event! This launched a racing career that spanned the early fifties. My fame was confined to the Northern California area, although I spent one season racing out of the Chicago-area racetracks at Soldier Field, Blue Island, and Rockford. I also raced some tracks in Milwaukee and some in the state of Indiana.

The vehicle that gained me nationwide recognition as a race-car designer was named the "Tatum Special." I also did stunts for racing movies and became an actor with a local theater group. I became an inventor, too. I invented the "Traction Master," an auto safety device that enjoyed a small measure of success. The Ford Motor Company used my device on the early Shelby Mustangs.

About then, I got married for the second time, to my wife, Evelyn. This time it took better than the first one: We've made it for thirty-nine laps so far! Evelyn blessed me with two children: Chuck Jr. and Rhonda. The sudden and stark realization that three people were depending on me required that I approach my life with a new serious-ness. I had my thirtieth birthday, too, which helped to improve my seriousness. I needed to get a real job and hang on to it, no more quitting every summer to follow the auto-racing circuits.

To make ends meet for the next thirty-two years, I managed and owned automobile dealerships, on and off, in the Stockton, California, area. My racing background proved to be an asset when I became an automobile salesman. What local fame I had garnered helped me to sell cars to some of my old fans. I also have a lot of relatives in the Stock-ton area who helped me launch my new career. About this time, Eve-lyn and I were blessed with two more children, Blake and Tracy.

Now, everyone knows that car dealers make the best TV com-mercials, never corny and always with high production values. Okay, well, most aren't that way, but mine aspired to greatness. I became the pitchman for my dealerships, appeared in car commercials, and wrote the scripts for them. In doing so, I discovered a new, up-to-then-latent talent: writing. But I never knew it would lead to *Red Blood, Black Sand*.

MANY YEARS LATER

In early 1995, as the fiftieth anniversary of the end of World War II approached, all I saw on TV and read about were programs and events to commemorate the war's end. But all were based on, or around, D-Day in France and the defeat of Germany. I asked myself, *Where is the story about the Pacific war? What about the battles of Iwo Jima, Guadalcanal, and Peleliu? Will everyone just forget these battles?*

I was disturbed, so I called the big news outfits like NBC, CBS, and ABC to see what their plans were about Iwo Jima. I asked one of the producers who would take my call, "What about Iwo Jima?"

"Where is that?" she replied.

I told her it was the biggest battle the Marine Corps fought in World War II.

"When was it?" she asked.

I told her, "Nineteen forty-five."

"Oh, no wonder I haven't heard of that," she said. "I wasn't born until 1955."

Good grief. I realized I had a duty to fulfill, the duty of a survivor. So I wrote this book.

IN APRIL 2004, MY LIFE CHANGED

The voice on the other end of the phone introduced himself as "Bruce McKenna." He said that he was writing a miniseries about the war in the Pacific that hopefully would be bought by HBO. The working title was *The Pacific.*

Bruce said he liked my book because it carried the story of Iwo Jima beyond the death of John Basilone on the beach and through the full thirty-six days of intense fighting. He said he would like to do a filmed interview with me about my book and my knowledge of Gunny Basilone and the Iwo Jima battle itself. I accepted his invitation.

The production company spared no expense in transporting me to Hollywood. I got the works, a limousine to Sacramento from my house in Stockton and from the airport to the hotel. There, I received a call from Bruce and set a date for dinner. The meeting was very exciting for me and resulted in this book being optioned as one of the three primary sources for Bruce's script. I sold my writing to Hollywood!

Over the next few years, I worked closely with Bruce on this exciting project. Along the way, I was told that the production company had hired an actor to play me in the miniseries, which had been purchased by HBO and titled, officially, *The Pacific*. The actor was from Australia and had red hair. I never told anyone that I had had coal-black hair, not that it mattered. The movie was on its way to becoming a major hit miniseries. A month later I received an e-mail from a young man named Ben Esler. His e-mail stated that he had been hired to play me in the miniseries. He also stated that he would like to come to California and meet me. My message to Ben was "Come to California!" I wanted to meet him. He did, and we hit it off.

Another friend, a local teen, Dustin Spence, wanted to play me, or any Marine for that matter, in *The Pacific*. To this end, he arranged for a visa and paid his way to Australia, where the production crew had assembled. I played matchmaker. I sent Ben and Dustin each other's e-mails and suggested that they might like to meet. They exchanged messages and agreed to get together. The meeting was fortuitous for both. They became friends and Dustin was invited to live at Ben's parents' home while in Australia.

Dustin did get employed as a historical consultant and was on deck when HBO started to film the Iwo beach footage. In a twist of fate, they needed more actors. So they picked Dustin, who appears in Episode 8. While they were filming, Dwight Braswell, the young man who was hired to play Steve Evanson, met with Dustin and they, too, became friends. Dwight did a great job of playing Steve Evanson. After a long, long wait, I received an invitation to the Hollywood premiere of *The Pacific*, on February 24, 2010. The "big parade" had begun.

THE BIG PARADE

At long last, *The Pacific* was not a dream but a ten-part miniseries that was set to debut on HBO in early March 2010. The premiere itself was to be held at the famous Grauman's Chinese Theatre in Hollywood.

My invitation to the premiere included tickets for myself, my wife Evelyn, our son Blake, our daughter Tracy, and my daughter Nanci from my first marriage. We had rooms booked for us at the famed Hollywood Roosevelt Hotel, a beautiful old hotel with all the glamour of early Hollywood. It was a gala occasion and we were ready to celebrate.

At the premiere, I spent most of my time with Ben Esler, the Australian actor who played me. And, I was surrounded by a flock of the best-looking women in Hollywood, all there for the premiere: my wife, my daughters, and my great granddaughters, Rachael and Natasha. Further gracing the scene were Natalie Simpson, Ben's Australian girlfriend, and Audrey Phillips, a real life southern belle and the granddaughter of Sid Phillips, my fellow Marine and a prominent character in the series.

On the night of the premiere, we gathered in the lobby of the Roosevelt Hotel, and when the time came, we walked across the street to Grauman's Theatre, where we were met by the HBO publicity guides who escorted us down the red carpet. On both sides of the runway, camera lights were flashing a mile a minute, nearly blinding us. Ben and I were the leaders of the walk. The guides led us to the most important Hollywood reporters and columnists, whose questions we answered at each stop. It was a lot of fun to be so important. We were then directed to our family's seating area—there was a big sign saying *Tatum Family*—and we were surrounded by other war-veteran guests, including Sid Phillips and R. V. Burgin with their respective families, and the widows of Eugene Sledge and Robert Leckie, Jeanne Sledge and Vera Leckie.

Every big shot in Hollywood was present. Tom Hanks, Gary Goetzman, Steven Spielberg, and my friend Bruce McKenna, the head scriptwriter. Hanks, Goetzman, and Spielberg devoted four years of their time to develop *The Pacific,* and Home Box Office (HBO) provided the capital to finance the production, a total of around $150 million by last count.

Soon the lights dimmed and the beautiful film score of *The Pacific* began to play. It was a thrilling moment as the audience sat spellbound by the unfolding story. The first episode was called "Guadalcanal," the first battle after Pearl Harbor that the Marines fought and won. After this forty-minute episode, Tom Hanks, Steven Spielberg, and Gary Goetzman came onstage to congratulate the actors, writers, directors, veterans, and the entire filming crew for their extraordinary accomplishments. During the accolades, Tom Hanks asked us three veterans to stand as the audience applauded.

After the premiere, there was a special party to which 1,500 people had been invited. HBO pulled out all the stops. The 1930s interior of the Roosevelt Hotel was transformed into a replica of life in the 1940s, complete with a canteen; a dance floor; club-style dining; red, white, and blue furnishings; and vintage posters from wartime. The food was delicious and the bar open; lots of people were having a great time. My family and I had our own table. During the course of the evening, we were visited by Tom Hanks, who, upon seeing me, remarked, "You look like a jazz player. And, my God, you look fifty-five years old! You'll make so much money that you will be pestered by people wanting your advice. Women will seek you out and you will be courted by the media. How does that sound, Chuck?" It sounded fine by me. Hanks and I posed for pictures. He is quite a wonderful person.

The bands played on until the wee hours of the morning, and up until the last moment, we enjoyed the festivities. But even old Marines can get tired of partying, and I eventually decided to call it a night. Before I did, though, a thought crossed my mind: *I wish Steve could see this.* But I'm sure from some bar up in the heavens, he was drinking with us.

Semper Fi.

Portraying Chuck Tatum in *The Pacific*
by Ben Esler

When I learned that Steven Spielberg and Tom Hanks would be film-ing their follow-up to the critically acclaimed *Band of Brothers* in my native Australia, I immediately resolved to be part of it. For actors working in my hometown of Melbourne, opportunities are scarce. The local film industry is small and hard to break into, television production is largely confined to low-budget soaps, and the theater doesn't pay.

Suddenly two of the cinematic heroes of my youth (Spielberg executive-produced *Back to the Future*, which made me want to be an actor, and Hanks's *Splash* was the first movie my family ever owned on VHS—we wore it out from overuse) were bringing the Hollywood production line to my doorstep.

The series, to be called *The Pacific,* would tell the story of a group of Marines at war with the Japanese in World War II. Like many oth-ers, I had been deeply impressed by *Band of Brothers*. The story of the men of Easy Company was the most well-developed and personal account of war I had ever seen put on-screen, and I still believe it to be one of the finest television series ever produced. To be a part of something like that would be to fulfill an actor's dream. I knew an opportunity like this would not come a second time.

Looking back on the experience of making *The Pacific*, I can happily say that it lived up to my hopes. I am a part of something that I know I will be proud of for the rest of my life. What I did not anticipate was that of all the personal rewards I would reap as a result of my participation in this series, potentially the most satisfying would be the relationship I would form with the man I was to play—a war hero from Stockton, California, named Chuck.

The process of auditioning had lasted several months. I now found myself at Fox Studios in Sydney, at the request of the producers and about to read for the role of Sidney Phillips. The production had paid the price of my airfare from Melbourne, so I assumed they were serious, but it hadn't started out that way. Initially, they had refused to see me at all.

Sensing that my big opportunity was slipping through my fingers, I had taken matters into my own hands. To my good fortune, a friend of mine had already auditioned for the part of Robert Leckie, and I was able to talk him into giving me his audition scenes. I immediately began preparing to put something on tape, knowing that this would be my only chance. However, I suspected that the casting directors would likely be receiving thousands of similar submissions. It would be no time for subtlety. With the support of a few friends, I produced the least subtle audition tape I possibly could, complete with professional lighting, authentic World War II costumes and props, and a set built from cardboard boxes.

I sent off the tape, crossed my fingers, and waited by the phone, but I received no word. Impatient, I called the casting directors personally to ask them if they had received it. They told me politely that they had, but that they were, as I suspected, inundated with unsolicited auditions from hopefuls such as myself. In other words, "Don't get your hopes up." The next day I called again and received a similar response. For a while this became routine, until finally, after so many calls that I wonder why they put up with me, they relented and agreed to watch my tape.

I was terrified. If they didn't like it, this was the end of the line. However, a few hours later, I received a call from my agent. I had been invited to audition in person.

It would be over a month before that first audition would materialize, which was both a blessing and a curse. The wait was difficult, but it gave me a lot of time to prepare. Coincidentally, I had already scheduled a trip to Japan with my mother and youngest sister, and it was there that I did the bulk of that preparation. As I was touring the temples, gardens, and war memorials of Tokyo and Kyoto, thoughts of the Pacific war rarely left my mind.

I returned to Melbourne, where I auditioned for the casting department. It went well and I was invited back, this time to meet with producers Tony To and Bruce McKenna, as well as casting directors Meg Liberman and Christine King. I was nervous at first, but the atmosphere in the room was friendly and the people welcoming. It's rare that I can remember much of what happens in any of my auditions, but of this one occasion I do remember that I enjoyed myself. I had admired both Tony and Bruce's contributions to *Band of Brothers* (Tony directed one of the episodes, "The Last Patrol," and Bruce wrote another, "Bastogne"), and it meant something that they treated me well.

Now I was to meet with them again, this time in Sydney. I had arrived at the studios with plenty of time to spare. I paced in the waiting room, nervously running through my lines and glancing at myself in the mirror. My girlfriend's dad had loaned me some dog tags for my big day. They had once belonged to his own father, who had in turn received them from a buddy who was a sergeant major in the 2nd/9th Australian Armoured Regiment in New Guinea and Borneo. I wore them around my neck, glancing down at them from time to time.

The casting assistant handed me a copy of Eugene Sledge's *With the Old Breed,* and I thumbed through it, passing the time and contemplating its contents. At one point Bruce McKenna passed me on his way to get a cup of coffee.

"That's a good story, that one," he said. "You'll like it."

I was finally called inside, and we did the scenes a handful of times. After every run-through there would be a long pause as the producers weighed their options and I listened to the sound of my own heart beating in my chest. A few minutes later, Christine emerged with some new pages. Written in marker at the top of the first page was the name "Chuck Tatum." My flight home was promptly canceled, and I was asked to spend the next short while preparing the new scenes.

"Chuck is an easygoing California kid," Bruce explained to me. "After the war he went back to Northern California and built racing cars. He's very likable."

The audition scene, which was ultimately omitted from the series, occurs after the death of the heroic John Basilone. As word of John's demise spreads through the Marines at Iwo Jima, they start to panic. Stepping up to the plate in the absence of his hero, Chuck begins giving orders.

We ran through the scene a first time, but something was missing.

Bruce stepped in to help, explaining to me, "Chuck's not used to telling people what to do. He's a private. Not a leader. He's as scared as everybody else. But with John gone, he knows that someone has to take responsibility."

I felt that I understood. Chuck wasn't a hero by birthright. He was a hero by choice. Having seen enough of Basilone in action, he knew how a hero was supposed to act.

I performed the scene again. Tony smiled. "Get on a plane," he said. "We'll see you soon."

It was another nail-biting month before I heard the official word.

When it finally came, I was overjoyed. My parents and sisters took me out for a celebratory dinner. Exhausted, I fell asleep in the restaurant.

———

Chuck does not appear until Episode 8 of the series, so I had plenty of time to kill before I was needed on set. I knew that in time the production would provide me with research materials and would likely connect me with Chuck, but impatient as always, I decided to begin my preparation in advance. With a little poking around online, I was able to track down Chuck's e-mail address, and I nervously wrote him a letter of introduction. I told him who I was and how lucky I felt to have been chosen to tell his story. I said that I hoped he would be proud of the result and expressed my admiration for his generation's wartime contribution. Then I sat, chewing my nails. Chuck replied within a few hours, warmly congratulating me on receiving the part and promising his help with anything I needed.

In the following months, Chuck and I would talk on the phone often. He sent me a copy of his book, which I read and enjoyed. Eventually we made plans to meet in person. I had flown to Los Angeles, and from there I drove north toward Stockton. Arriving at the address I had been given, I was greeted warmly at the door. Chuck is in his eighties, but he looked to be about sixty-five, and when he shook my hand, his grip was strong and firm. He introduced me to his wife, Evelyn, and soon we were all on the couch in their living room talking as friends.

Happily, I found Chuck to be exactly as Bruce had described. I had met veterans before who still seemed hardened by their experiences, even to this day, as though whatever lightness of spirit they once possessed had been left behind on the battlefield, but Chuck was notably different. Unflappably good-natured and at ease, he has a youthful twinkle in his eye and a jovial sense of humor that is always on show. Perhaps, I had thought, I would have to work backward, learning what I could from an old man of his former self, through vague recollections and probing analysis. But none of that would be necessary. After spending time with him that afternoon (and on many occasions since), it was easy to imagine what he must have been like as a young Marine, and I could see there would be no need to look into the distant past to discover the boy I had been asked to portray: The boy was right in front of me.

We talked for hours. Chuck is quite willing to speak openly about his experiences at war, and does so with candor and narrative flair. He told me of his reaction to Pearl Harbor and of joining the Marine Corps at age seventeen, after his mother gave in to his repeated requests. He told me about his time at Camp Pendleton and his first encounter with the legendary John Basilone, the hero of Guadalcanal. He told me about Steve Evanson, his best friend, and of characters like Tremulis and others with whom he served. Chuck is a gifted storyteller, and his recollections were crisp and evocative. The years that have passed since the Second World War have not diminished his memories of the period, or the depth of his emotion upon their recollection. When he spoke about landing on the beach at Iwo Jima, he invoked the shrill sounds of the Japanese mortars and his fear at the unrelenting chaos erupting around him. When he recalled watching as his hero, Basilone, was felled by a mortar, his words resonated with the memory of a young man awakening to a new understanding of both the extent of his predicament and the weight of his responsibility. Finally, he spoke about the loss of his best friend, Steve. When he did so, it was with grief etched anew upon his face.

I stayed till sundown, and Chuck showed me a family slide show of his life after the war. I watched his children grow up and saw the race cars he would spend much of his career working on, having escaped the horrors of Iwo Jima. I learned about his time in Hollywood working in the movie business.

Thanking Chuck and Evelyn, I left Stockton reflecting on my good fortune. I would soon be sharing some of these very same stories with the world.

———

The Melbourne set for *The Pacific* was enormous, like nothing I had ever seen. In an area of the You Yangs Regional Park, about a forty-minute drive from downtown Melbourne, the production team had replicated some of the most brutal battlefields of the Pacific theater of World War II (and a number of other locations) in elaborate detail. Were someone to take a five-minute drive around the compound, he could observe the massive Peleliu airfield to his left, followed shortly after by the Peleliu hills (which would later be converted to resemble a portion of Okinawa). A short ways up the road was a small section of Pavuvu, and then the enormous set for Camp Pendleton, California, composed of obstacle courses, tents, and military barracks. Finally, rounding the bend toward the crew unit base, the black sands, terraces, and airfield of Iwo Jima would appear down the hill.

It was here that I would spend the majority of my time working on the series. The climax of Episode 8 is an epic ten-minute battle sequence, which follows John Basilone, Chuck Tatum, and Steve Evanson as they make their way from the beach at Iwo Jima toward the airfield, and it would take weeks to shoot. We shot the episode in reverse, starting with this sequence and then moving on to the training sequences at Camp Pendleton. Before either of those things could happen, however, I would need to be trained to act like a real Marine.

Dale Dye's Warriors, Inc., is legendary in the film industry, having trained actors and advised directors on virtually every major military-themed Hollywood movie of the last two decades. When I arrived on set, much of the cast had already participated in Warriors, Inc.'s signature boot camp, intended to acquaint them with some small measure of what the boys in the Pacific had gone through. Released into the jungles of Far North Queensland, they had been deprived of food and sleep for days on end, under constant assault from people portraying Japanese troops. Perhaps luckily for me, Chuck's story line ends only a few hours into the assault on Iwo Jima, and my job was therefore to depict not a battle-scarred veteran but a wide-eyed recruit. As such, I was spared all those hardships. All the same, Captain Dye's reputation for pushing actors to their physical and emotional limits in the name of authenticity had preceded him, and so while I was excited to be working with him and his team, I would be lying if I said I wasn't the slightest bit apprehensive as well.

If the intention was to make me feel "green," it worked. Dwight Braswell (who played Steve) and I arrived on set and were immediately thrown into weapons training. The two of us had met a few days earlier when they cut off all our hair, and bonded quickly over a shared sense of having been thrown in at the deep end. For the duration of our training and well into the shoot, we were referred to only by our characters' names (and, on occasion, by others I won't repeat in print) and were expected to behave in a fashion becoming of a Marine at all times. Above all, we had to master our weapon, and were constantly reminded of our responsibility to the real men we were portraying and the veterans who would be watching the series. Sometimes it was difficult, and I was made to eat dirt more than once, but it was also great fun. Dwight has a great sense of humor, and we came to rely on each other to lighten the mood when things occasionally got tough. By the time we were introduced to Jon Seda (who played Basilone), the two of us were already good friends. Unlike us, Jon had already been shooting for months. He wielded the machine gun like a pro and things we were only just learning seemed like second nature to him. While we were goofing off and making each other laugh, he remained quiet, professional, and authoritative, guiding and supporting us through the entire process. I imagine the dynamic between the three of us in those early days must have paralleled what it was like for Chuck and Steve upon meeting their hero at Pendleton.

As for the shoot itself, every day on set was a privilege. I was living my dream, but I was also going to school, surrounded by the best in the business at all levels of production. In particular, I was fortunate to work with two terrific and respected directors in David Nutter, who directed the Iwo Jima sequence, and Jeremy Podeswa, with whom we shot the scenes set in California. The two could not be more different in their approach, but both are among the best at what they do, and to work with them in succession was a fabulous opportunity to listen and to learn.

By the time we shot our final scene, I didn't want to leave, and I remember drawing out my good-byes with the crew so as to prolong the experience by just a few more minutes.

———

Two years later I attended the premiere for *The Pacific* at Grauman's Chinese Theatre in Los Angeles and was honored to walk the red carpet with Chuck by my side. Chuck handled the press with his typical humor (Reporter: "What have you been able to share with this young man?" Chuck: "Pizza"), but there is one moment in particular that stands out in my mind as special.

Chuck and I had just completed an interview for *Entertainment Tonight* on the subject of his Bronze Star, when a familiar face emerged on the carpet. It was Dwight, and he was being led over to us by Jon Seda. It was an important moment for the four of us, and as the two men were introduced for the first time, Chuck's expression became solemn. As we listened attentively, he began to speak about the events that transpired at Hill 362A, where Steve was mortally wounded and where Chuck fired his machine gun from the hip in retaliation, decimating the cave full of Japanese responsible.

As anyone who has ever walked the red carpet will tell you, it is a crowded and chaotic affair, the most important rule of which is to keep things moving. In spite of this, for a few minutes, as Chuck recounted his story of heroism and loss, reliving every moment, the red carpet at the Chinese Theatre ground to a halt. Nobody asked us to move. Nobody interrupted. Everybody waited. Even the

Hollywood PR machine knew to pay the moment and the man the proper respect.

A few months later, Episode 8 aired for the first time on HBO, and the very next day I again made the drive from L.A. to Stockton to see Chuck. Chuck's children had organized a screening of the episode at the local cinema and I was lucky enough to score an invite. To be surrounded by Chuck's family and friends, some of whom served with him on Iwo Jima, made it a perfect night and a perfect ending to what had been an almost three-year journey.

———

Chuck Tatum's memoir is of inestimable historical value and will be of benefit to those who read it for decades to come. As John Basilone's story was ending on the airfield at Iwo Jima, Chuck's story of courage, sacrifice, and the bond shared between friends was only just beginning. While so much of what we portrayed in *The Pacific* reflects everything that young men stand to lose in times of war, *Red Blood, Black Sand* shows us what it is possible for them to retain. The boy who pestered his mother to join the Marines is still with us, and we are better for it.

Chuck: For your heroism, your service to your country, and for your personal friendship, I will always be grateful.

Semper Fi Semper,
Your friend,
BEN

INDEX

Page numbers followed by "n" indicate notes.